MW00513186

1979 TAMPA BAY BUCCANEERS

McKAY'S MEN

THE STORY OF **WORST TO FIRST**

Brendon,
Congratulations on your
engagement, Go BUCS!
Best of luck to you
and Brittany.

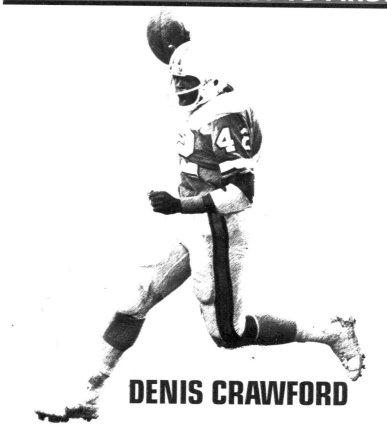

1979 TAMPA BAY BUCCANEERS
McKAY'S MEN
THE STORY OF WORST TO FIRST

DENIS CRAWFORD

Furious Who Publishing
Boardman, OH 44512

Author
    Denis Crawford

Publisher
    Furious Who Publishing

Cover Design, Interior Design and Typesetting
    Desktop Miracles, Inc.
    Stowe, Vermont

Additional copies of this book may be ordered online at:
    www.furiouswhopublishing.com

Or you may write the publishers at:
    Furious Who Publishing
    1356 Redtail Hawk Drive
    Boardman, OH 44512

ISBN-10:   0-9791125-0-8
ISBN-13: 978-0-9791125-0-8
LCCN: 2006931636

To my wife Amy.

Table of Contents

Acknowledgements

A book like this requires so many more people than just the author to create that it seems almost laughable to thank them in only a page or so of manuscript. I hope those named in the following lines will realize just how much their contributions meant to me.

First I would like to say thank you to my family for all of their support. My wife Amy had to sacrifice late nights, weekends and vacations for me to have the time to complete this book and I owe her a debt of gratitude that I could never hope to pay back. My sister Denise and her husband John along with their sons John Jr. and William were my unpaid proofreaders almost from Day One and my parents spurred my interest in words almost from birth by having a house that was continually filled with books.

I also wish to say thank you to Frank and Karen Nabozny and their staff at Seaside Publishing for the wonderful job they did in editing the book. This is the first book I have ever written and Frank was more than patient with my continual barrage of questions and naiveté. Barry Kerrigan and his staff did a masterful job of laying out the book, and I appreciate all that they did.

The book just wouldn't be the same without the photographs and I must thank Ron Kolwak of the Tampa Tribune for allowing me to use the resources of his photo archive. Julia O'Neal and Roxanne Kosarzycki of the Tampa Bay Buccaneers were also very patient with my constant phone calls to make sure I used the photos properly. Because of these two ladies I am as big a fan of the Bucs legal staff as I am the team on the field.

Thanks should also go to Doug Williams, Lee Roy Selmon, Rich McKay and Natalia Bell Jacke for allowing me to use photos of either themselves or their loved ones in this book. Mr. Williams and Mr. Selmon along with Richard Wood, Bill Kollar, Hubert Mizell, Rick Odioso and Jack Harris also went out of their way to give me time for personal interviews that helped greatly in the creation of this book.

First person accounts were not always possible so the bulk of anecdotes and quotes in this book were found with the assistance of Paul Stewart and Chad Reese. Paul runs Bucpower.com, quite possibly the most detailed accounting of the history of the franchise to be found anywhere in the world. Paul has also been gracious enough to have me write for his site, a task I have found unceasingly rewarding. I think in Paul I have found the one man with more of a passion for this team's history than mine.

Chad Reese showed me how to use the archives at the Professional Football Hall of Fame in Canton, Ohio. It was there that I found press releases, game programs, inter-office documents and the like that helped me to go behind the scenes of the 1979 Buccaneers.

Finally, thanks to all of my co-workers at Seven Seventeen Credit Union in Warren, Ohio. As I said, this is my first book and my job at the credit union helped to keep me afloat while writing. While many in Warren are probably sick to death of the 1979 Buccaneers by now, they went out of their way to help cover for me when I needed to do an interview or came to work a little less than fresh following a long night of writing. I appreciate it my friends.

So as you can see the book you are about to read may have my name on the cover, but it is the culmination of a lot of teamwork. Just like the championship won by the 1979 Tampa Bay Buccaneers. Enjoy.

A Long Flight Home

A somber mood permeated the visiting team's locker room. A few moments earlier the Tampa Bay Buccaneers had limped off the field after an atrocious loss. With a playoff berth theirs for the taking, the Buccaneers had been blown out by the San Francisco 49ers at Candlestick Park. Worse than the 23-7 loss itself was the feeling that the magic was quickly running out on the season.

The Buccaneers had once been the talk of the NFL. The laughing-stock of the league for so long, the Bucs had set the sporting world on its collective ear by racing out to a 5-0 record. Just a few weeks earlier they had clinched the first winning record in franchise history in a demolition of the New York Giants. That victory had navigated the Buccaneers into uncharted waters: playoff contention. Those waters had become quite violent in the last three weeks as November turned to December and Buccaneer players found themselves unsure of how to move forward.

Quarterback Doug Williams was the most conspicuous of those play-ers searching for calmer waters. Williams, in only his second year in the league, had suffered through a brutal game against the 49ers. Williams completed less than fifty percent of his passes and threw five intercep-tions against San Francisco. Those thefts helped the 49ers, which had enjoyed only one victory in 14 games all year, to a commanding victory over a supposed playoff contender. To add to his woes, Williams had been pulled from the game and replaced by back-up Mike Rae. It was the second game in a row that Williams had been benched and some suspected he would not play again in 1979.

Calling all the interceptions "my fault," Williams took the blame for the loss. "I had a bad day."

When asked how he would prepare for the season finale, if he was still the starter, Williams answered, "The only thing I know to do is to concentrate and hope things go my way again. I feel we can win and go to the playoffs. But all games are tough. Getting one victory is tough."

No one needed to tell the veteran players on the team how difficult winning one game could be. Two years before the Buccaneers had won the first game in franchise history, snapping a record 26 game losing streak in the process. In an amazingly short period of time the Bucs had improved to the point where they were in a position to clinch a playoff berth. One win was all they needed.

Linebacker David Lewis, stunned and angered by the outcome on the field, told *Tampa Tribune* columnist Tom McEwen that unlike the 1977 team, this group of Buccaneers seemed to be scared of doing what it took to win that one game.

"There is some choking going on," Lewis said. "Here we are ready to become division champs and we lose 23-7. That's not championship football. I don't care how it sits with everybody. Three weeks straight, there's got to be some choking going on. I'm a team leader and I'll tell it like it is."

"We have come too far to let this happen."

Looking back on the atmosphere of the locker room in Candlestick Park many years later, defensive end Lee Roy Selmon agreed with Lewis' assessment but in a much more diplomatic style.

"I think we were experiencing things we had never experienced as a team," Selmon said. "We had never been in a situation before as a team where the outcome of a game meant so much. In a way I think we tensed up, but it certainly wasn't a lack of focus."

Selmon continued, "You win, you get the division championship, you are in the playoffs, you get the bye week. We thought to ourselves 'Wow!'"

The possibility of a playoff berth only heightened expectations among the players said Selmon. Unfortunately, the Bucs were mired in a string of bad luck at the time when they needed a victory the most. "I think it was just something where as hard as we tried the Good Lord said this day just isn't the one. We got out there and played our hardest and ended up on the short end of the games."

John McKay walked into a maelstrom of a locker room. The offense of the Buccaneers had turned the ball over eleven times in just the last two games. The defense had allowed a 1-13 team to move the ball effortlessly up and down the field The special teams had been mediocre at best, a vast improvement over the past two weeks in which they had suffered multiple blocked kicks.

The Buccaneers hired McKay in 1975 to be the first coach in franchise history. McKay's resume as a college coach was legendary. At Southern Cal, McKay's teams had won some version of a national championship four times in his sixteen years in Los Angeles. McKay's keen eye for football talent had brought two Heisman Trophy winners and numerous All-Americans to the USC program. McKay was expected to bring that same personnel ability and on-field success to the expansion Buccaneers.

McKay had built his team almost in defiance of conventional wisdom. Trading for players very few had heard of, putting a quarterback from a small school in charge of an NFL offense and not once, but twice refusing to draft the reigning Heisman Trophy winner, McKay's fingerprints were all over every aspect of the Buccaneer roster.

But now McKay's personnel were struggling at the worst possible time.

The one struggling most was McKay's quarterback. Doug Williams had played superbly earlier in the season to put the team in contention, but had struggled mightily over the past two weeks under mounting playoff pressure. McKay knew he could turn to back-up Mike Rae, who in 1976 had won some critical games for the Oakland Raiders Super Bowl champions when Ken Stabler had been injured.

On the surface switching to a proven veteran was the logical choice, but the decision was much more complicated than that for McKay. Doug Williams was the future of the franchise and needed to be on the field to learn and improve. A benching at this time of the year could seriously undermine all of the progress Williams and the offense had made in 1979. After three straight losing seasons, McKay faced a choice that no coach would envy. Replace the team's young starting quarterback with a veteran and risk shattering Williams' confidence or go with the youngster in the most important game in franchise history and risk the entire season.

In addition to the quarterback issue, McKay also needed to confront the fact that a poor San Francisco team had exploited his defensive unit. McKay's 3-4 defensive alignments required smaller, quicker players to execute the system properly. Critics had often stated that smaller players tired quickly and could be pushed around in the war of attrition that was professional football. San Francisco had done just that on this day against the Buccaneers. McKay faced a week of looking at film to see if what had occurred was a fluke or a sign that his defensive schemes just couldn't work. If the former, McKay could make adjustments over the coming days as most coaches do. If the latter, McKay would be faced with the unpleasant possibility that the critics were right, his defense just could not work in the NFL.

The Buccaneers had also hired McKay as their first coach for his public relations abilities. Quick with a joke or an anecdote, McKay's press conferences were always high in entertainment value. When the team struggled through a winless first season, McKay's post-game comments were always eagerly anticipated by a local press contingent that had been forced to witness one uninspired game after another. Legend has it that after one particularly brutal loss McKay was asked what he felt about the execution of his offense. With a timing that Jack Benny would have admired, McKay thought for a moment and then evenly replied, "I'm all for it."

McKay's ability to keep his chin up and fire off one-liners like a Catskills comic endeared him to his team and most members of the local press. This affection bought McKay the needed time to build a team in the way he thought best, slowly and with an eye always on a future playoff push. It had not been easy, especially during the 26 game losing streak, but McKay had finally achieved in 1979 what he thought would be the best team in the NFC Central Division. With the team losing three in a row and in danger of missing the playoffs, McKay would have to return to his 1976-1977 form.

After talking to his players for a few moments, McKay came out to the assembled media and answered questions. Most answers were straightforward. McKay stated that he did not know who would start at quarterback the next week. McKay quipped that it might not matter who started because, "We have had ten interceptions in two weeks. We have two choices and one might be to never throw the ball again."

McKay also stated that he did not know why the game had gone so badly, he would need to look at the film. To close the session McKay hinted that the Bucs were not dead yet, but that they would really need to give their best effort the following week. His closing comments would go down in history as the quintessential McKayism.

"What we needed today was Knute Rockne and he wasn't available. We will attempt to come back next Sunday in Tampa Stadium, in front of our own crowd.

"We have now proven that we can't play on the road or in front of our own crowd, so we would like to have a neutral site."

With the press conference over McKay headed back to the locker room to be with his team and prepare for a long flight home. After all the showers had been taken and all the equipment packed, the Buccaneers rode to the airport and boarded the team charter. The flight from San Francisco to Tampa would take roughly six hours.

For the players it would be six hours to think about all that had gone wrong at Candlestick Park. Six hours to think of the passes that had been intercepted. Six hours to think of the tackles that had been missed. Six hours to think of the untimely penalties. Six hours to think of the blown assignments. They would be a very long six hours.

For head coach John McKay, seated in his customary spot in the back of the plane, those six hours would be spent pondering what needed to be done to win the season finale against the Kansas City Chiefs. McKay's list included:

- Should he start Williams or Rae at quarterback?
- If he started Williams, should he build a game plan that wouldn't put the pressure of victory on the young quarterbacks shoulders?
- Did the defense need to be adjusted slightly, or did it need a massive re-working to prevent the disaster in San Francisco from re-occurring?
- Could he count on the special teams if the game came down to a field goal?

These questions could easily fill the six-hour flight time. As he sat there pondering the answers to these questions it is also quite possible that McKay thought about all that he had done to bring the Buccaneers to this point. The men who filled the seats on the plane in front of him were his men. They had all been hand picked by McKay to bring winning football to Tampa Bay.

A good deal of the players had been brought to Tampa against the better judgment of so-called experts. Ricky Bell, Jimmie Giles, Wally Chambers, Richard Wood and Randy Crowder were all acquisitions that for one reason or another raised eyebrows. An offensive line of mismatched parts included a college-trained guard at center and a converted defensive lineman at right tackle. Steve Wilson and Charley Hannah, the players in question, joined with a rookie and two discarded veterans on a line charged with protecting Williams. The defense was composed of individuals such as Mark Cotney, Mike Washington, Bill Kollar and Jeris White, men who had been thought of as expendable by their old teams. These were some of the men expected by McKay to win football games.

With nine wins on the season so far, they had accomplished that mission. History was beckoning to them however. A tenth win on the season would make the Buccaneers the first team to accomplish such a feat so early in their existence. That many of these men had also been a part of a team that had lost 26 games in a row made this chance all the more remarkable.

All they needed was just one more win.

CHAPTER 2

0-26 and Beyond

I t was amazing that the early Tampa Bay Buccaneers were even capable of being competitive in a handful of games during their inaugural season. The National Football League had awarded franchises to Tampa Bay and Seattle to begin play in 1976. The process the NFL instituted for stocking the roster severely hamstrung the Bucs chances for early success.

With unfettered free agency only a gleam in the eyes of the NFL Players Association, there were only two ways for the Buccaneers to acquire football talent, the allocation draft and the collegiate draft.

The allocation draft mandated that each of the established 26 teams expose a portion of their roster to the Buccaneers and Seahawks. None of the established teams could lose more than 3 players, so the Buccaneers and Seahawks competed with each other to find the best men available among a group the rest of the league felt was expendable.

McKay had insisted upon being hired that he was going to build the Bucs with an eye on the future and not sacrifice the development of the franchise to merely win a couple of games the first year. "We don't want any 34-year-old running backs," McKay said tipping his allocation draft strategy.

True to his word, McKay did not select a 34-year-old running back. Instead McKay focused on defense bringing in players such as Council Rudolph, Dave Pear, Pat Toomay, Larry Ball and Mark Cotney.

In addition to defense, McKay also brought in many players with ties to Southern Cal. It was McKay's hope that having players who he knew and who knew him would significantly cut down on the learning curve. Ex-Trojans Jimmy Gunn, Manfred Moore, Rod McNeill, Danny Reece and Jimmy Sims joined the squad as did McKay's own son, JK McKay. The younger McKay had been a solid receiver at USC and while many decried the signing as nepotism, the older McKay would be counting on the youngster to bolster his receiving corps.

In addition to the allocation draft, McKay executed a trade with the New York Jets to bring in yet another USC alum, linebacker Richard Wood.

The allocation draft was meant to provide the Buccaneers with veteran talent. The second phase of player procurement, the collegiate draft would provide John McKay with the youth around which he would build Tampa Bay's football future.

McKay's strategy of drafting defense continued in the collegiate draft as he selected University of Oklahoma defensive end Lee Roy Selmon with the first draft choice in Buccaneer history. McKay raised some eyebrows in the second round when he drafted Lee Roy's older brother Dewey, also an Oklahoma defensive lineman. It was the first time in NFL history that two brothers had been selected in back to back rounds by the same team in the same draft.

The rest of McKay's selections included running backs Jimmy Dubose and George Ragsdale, defensive back Mike Washington and offensive lineman Steve Wilson.

The conclusion of the two drafts did not end McKay's quest for talent. One of the players McKay brought in through a trade was quarterback Steve Spurrier. McKay planned to have the former Heisman Trophy winner from the University of Florida start until he could find a younger man to take over the job on a permanent basis. McKay wouldn't find his man until 1978 but it definitely wasn't for a lack of trying. In fact McKay would look at over 140 different players during his first season in Tampa. With the team's headquarters, One Buccaneer Place, located on property adjacent to Tampa International Airport, the joke was that many a player tried out for the Bucs and was sent home without ever leaving sight of the terminal they had arrived at.

McKay opened training camp in July of 1976 with a collection of cast-offs and inexperienced rookies. NFL Films was on hand to capture the birth of a franchise and they recorded McKay's first address to the team. The theme of the address was to layout McKay's expectations for the upcoming campaign. Those in attendance got their first look at how unorthodox the legend from USC could be.

"It bothers me that they (the national media) have picked us to be the worst team in football," McKay told his new charges. "Because what they are doing is challenging your physical and your mental capacity and my ability to coach you. Now, this hurts me. Second worst team, I could stand it. But not the worst team."

McKay told the team he did not expect playoffs in1976, but instead he set Tampa Bay's goal as equaling the records of the most recent expansion teams, but he did so in his own distinctive style. "We've broken down the expansion teams and they've averaged winning 2.7 games their first year, which to me is rather difficult. I figured out the 2, but the .7 has got me wondering what the hell is going on."

McKay's player laughed good-naturedly at the quip. Little did McKay or anyone else suspect that seventeen months would pass before the team achieved their first victory. During that time many would begin to doubt that McKay knew what the hell was going on.

Tampa Bay's first regular season game against the Houston Oilers was a total disaster. The team only managed 108 yard of total offense, barely more than the 80 yards on penalties that they lost. The 20-0 final score was hardly indicative of how badly they had played. When asked after the game about the performance of the offense McKay replied, "What offense?"

Things only would get worse as the season went on.

The home opener the following week saw the Buccaneers shut out again, 23-0 by the San Diego Chargers. Tampa Bay finally scored in their 14-9 loss to Buffalo, the third straight loss of the season. The three Dave Green field goals had kept the Bucs competitive in a game for the first time but that competiveness was missing the next week when the Bucs fell 42-17 to Baltimore. The loss to the Colts did contain another franchise first as Danny Reece returned a fumble for the initial touchdown of Buccaneer existence. The ball should have been bronzed, because the next week the Bucs suffered another shutout, 21-0, at the hands of the Cincinnati Bengals.

With their record at 0-5 the Buccaneers were desperate for a victory and felt their best chance had arrived with the arrival of the Seattle Seahawks at Tampa Stadium in the "Expansion Bowl." Ironically, the Seahawks were also 0-5 and viewed their match-up with the Buccaneers as their best chance for victory. The stakes of the game were high: the winner would be able to celebrate the fact that they were the better of the expansion teams, the loser would be left with the sinking feeling that not only were they the worst team, but might possibly be forced to endure a winless season.

With that kind of pressure on their shoulders, neither team played particularly well, but Seattle played slightly less lousy and pulled out a 13-10 victory. Tampa Bay and Seattle matched each other almost bumble for bumble. Both teams combined for 35 penalties, fumbled often, misfired on pass after pass and generally set the game of professional football back about seventy years. The Seahawks were able to view the contest as a thing of beauty thanks to a last second block of Dave Green's potential game tying field goal. Football fans were probably thankful for the block because it spared the nation the sight of a game such as this going into overtime.

The Bucs on the other hand saw the game as perhaps their one best chance for victory going by the boards. So ugly was the Buccaneer's performance that even the first touchdown pass in team history, their first touchdown ever at Tampa Stadium, was in error. On a botched run at the goal line, tailback Louis Carter threw the ball to a surprised Morris Owens. The alert wide receiver snared the pass for a one-yard touchdown reception that cut the Seahawks lead to 13-10 in the third quarter. That was unfortunately the lone offensive highlight of the day for Tampa Bay.

The next week saw the high water mark of the season for the Buccaneers. Playing host to cross-state rival Miami, the Buccaneers hung tough against the Dolphins. Matching their much more talented neighbors touchdown for touchdown, the Buccaneers found themselves tied 20-20 with moments left. The chance to achieve their first victory at the expense of another Florida team proved too great for Tampa Bay. The Buccaneers defense couldn't stop Bob Griese when it counted most and the future Hall of Fame quarterback drove the Dolphins into field goal range. Miami kicker Garo Yepremian booted a 29-yard field goal with 55 seconds left to put the Dolphins ahead 23-20. Steve Spurrier, who had been playing flawlessly throughout the game, threw his only interception on the next drive to seal Tampa Bay's fate.

The tough loss to Miami seemed to suck the life right out of the team. The Buccaneers lost their next seven games, all of them by large margins, some of them laughably so. Included in the streak were losses to the Denver Broncos (48-13), New York Jets (34-0), Oakland Raiders (49-16), Pittsburgh Steelers (42-0) and New England Patriots (31-14).

When it was all said and done the 1976 Buccaneers had finished with a record of 0-14. This was the first time in the modern era that a professional football team had lost every single game. The 1960 Dallas Cowboys had also gone winless, but they had least managed a 31-31 tie against the New York Giants.

Coach McKay had said the first year team might not be competitive, but even he had to be surprised at how bad a season the Bucs endured. They had scored only 125 points while giving up 412. That translated to an average final score of 30-9. After the season-ending loss to New England McKay told the press, "I'll probably take a little time off and go hide somewhere. We will be back. Maybe not this century, but we will be back and we will be a better football team."

When the 1977 season rolled around, many could be forgiven for not believing in McKay's powers of prognostication.

Tampa Bay fans expected better results in 1977 but in four straight losses to open the season the Buccaneers offense failed to score a touchdown. Incredulous fans and media members began to turn their wrath towards the most visible face associated with the franchise, John McKay.

Fans brought banners and shirts to Tampa Stadium emblazoned with logos such as "Throw McKay in the Bay" and "Go For 0, McKay Must Go." Local and national sportswriters openly questioned whether the system McKay had used so well at USC could work in the NFL. Dave Klein of Pro Football Weekly stated bluntly that there seemed to be "a wastebasket full of things wrong with the offense." Klein's words were a direct assault on McKay's I formation and were representative of the disdain with which it was viewed.

Even Hollywood joined in piling on the woeful team. As the losing streak grew Johnny Carson started to incorporate game tapes of the Buccaneers into his monologue on the Tonight Show. In the film Semi-Tough, the character played by Robert Preston, a conniving, do anything to win football team owner, threatens to send Burt Reynolds to Tampa Bay as punishment for his wayward behavior.

To his credit McKay was able to keep his composure and not allow himself to become distracted from building his team. Every man has limits to patience, and after a solid year of taking verbal abuse McKay finally snapped following a 10-0 loss to the Washington Redskins.

After the game Redskin defensive lineman Bill Brundige criticized the Bucs offensive system and questioned McKay's ability to compete in the NFL. "Sooner or later," Brundige told the press, "McKay has got to learn that his old Southern Cal offense won't work in this league. He's not playing Stanford now. Running from that I formation on third and ten makes no sense."

When he was informed of Brundige's comments McKay fired back. "Anybody in his right mind who says the I formation won't work is an idiot. What formation was Washington in out there when they scored their first touchdown? What the hell does Brundige know about football? A dumb-ass tackle down on all fours probably doesn't know the offensive set and probably doesn't care."

After responding to Brundige, McKay turned his attention to the Steve Rudman's of the media. "Criticism doesn't bother me, because I'm critical myself. The thing that bothers me is the silly-ass comments that are made. Let me tell you people something, and I want you to listen to me. None of you know anything about football." With that the press conference ended.

Though he was frustrated enough to fire back at his critics, McKay never turned his sarcastic wit on his team. Despite the losing streak McKay saw that his team was improving, even if it was imperceptible to the outside world. While he was taking fire from all sides, McKay kept his young players protected and worked tirelessly to make sure they kept focused on becoming better players.

Looking back on McKay's efforts in 1976 and 1977, Lee Roy Selmon remembered his coach fondly. "He was very witty and had a lot of funny stories to tell," Selmon said. "McKay had a great sense of humor. I think that evolved through his career. It appeared he wouldn't let the stress from coaching overtake the fun part of it, he still found humor in it."

"He took pressure off the team," Selmon continued. "He did a fabulous job of building our team and taking a lot of the pressure off of winning and losing. He did not make that the focal point that was determining week to week where we were as a ball club. His focus as he shared it with us was that he was looking for this team to improve from week to week. His evaluation of us as a team was 'Did we perform better this week than last week?' When he positioned it that way even though we were losing games we were still encouraged to try and get a little bit better. That philosophy and psychology reduced our disappointment."

The Bucs lost their 26th straight game, 10-0 to the Chicago Bears, on December 4, 1977. It was a typically dismal offensive performance as Tampa Bay managed just 21 yards passing. Fans who had been sarcastically chanting, "Go For 0" were just two more losses away from seeing that wish fulfilled.

Then the team that held the record for the longest losing streak in NFL history did something completely unexpected, they started a winning streak.

On December 11th in the Louisiana Superdome the Buccaneers faced the New Orleans Saints for what many believed would be loss number 27. Tampa Bay players showed up in a sour mood, and not merely because they had yet to taste victory. They were angered over comments from the New Orleans quarterback.

Archie Manning had told reporters he felt a great deal of pressure in playing the Bucs because he didn't want to be on the first team to lose to Tampa Bay. "It would be a disgrace to lose to the Bucs," Manning was quoted as saying.

Tired of being the punch line of a national joke, the Buccaneers took out 26 weeks worth of frustration on the shocked Saints. Throughout the first half Manning and the Saints were battered, pressured and beaten by a relentless Tampa Bay defense. The Saints did not earn a first down until six minutes were left in the first half. Lee Roy Selmon in particular acted as a one man wrecking crew. The second year defensive lineman recorded three of Tampa Bay's five sacks.

Lost in the mire of losing 26 straight games, was the fact that McKay's personnel decisions on defense had paid off. The defense, while still young and inexperienced, was growing more and more dominant. Against the Saints they showed off just how dominant they could be by outscoring the Saints offense. Three turnovers were returned for touchdowns as Tampa Bay cruised to a stunningly easy 33-14 victory.

The post-game locker room was the scene of a celebration akin to a Super Bowl champion. The players embraced, threw each other into the showers and happily talked to every reporter who came their way. Many of the players thanked Archie Manning for giving them a little extra motivation. Linebacker David Lewis told Hubert Mizell of the *St. Petersburg Times*, "Hey man, those are nasty words. It's a case of respect. When a man says that, it's like somebody talking bad about your momma. When you don't give a man respect, then you are messing with a man as a man and not just as a football player. I was after his ass."

The flight home became a non-stop airborne party. WFLA locker room reporter Jack Harris recalled seeing players and coaches dancing in the aisle, drinking beer and liquor and generally carrying on as though they had been freed from prison. "The pilot came on the intercom and said that everyone needed to take their seats so we could land. He repeated it several times but no one listened, they just continued to dance in the aisles. The plane landed anyway and it is the only time I have ever been on a plane that landed with all of the passengers still standing and dancing."

From his customary seat in the back of the plane, John McKay smoked a victory cigar and drank some celebratory ale and happily watched his players celebrate their first victory.

The party continued on the ground as thousands of fans greeted the team at Tampa International Airport. While many fans had grown weary of the losing, they had stayed loyal filling up Tampa Stadium to watch dreary game after dreary game. But on this day all was forgiven and players and fans alike partied on the tarmac and in the parking lot of One Buccaneer Place.

The good times continued the following Sunday at Tampa Stadium in the season finale against the St. Louis Cardinals. To help celebrate the first win in franchise history the team eschewed the customary player-by-player introduction before the game. Instead the entire team took to the field en masse and waved to the fans. It was a simple gesture that turned Tampa Stadium on its collective ear.

The volume level never lowered as the Bucs pasted the Cardinals 17-7 to secure their second victory in a row. Many fans rushed the field to tear down the goalposts while those who remained in the stands gave the team a standing ovation. The players in turn saluted the spectators. This group of people, players and fans alike, had been through a lot over the previous two seasons, but at this time they belonged to each other as they never had before.

In the post game locker room John McKay smoked his second victory cigar in as many weeks and directed his comments to the fans. "We were most appreciative of the fact that we could win at home for the fans," McKay said. "They never got to see us win before. But I guess a lot of people can say that."

With a record of 2-12 the Buccaneers still finished with the worst record in the NFL, but at least they had stopped their horrendous losing streak. McKay was encouraged by the improvement of his defense. Lee Roy Selmon in particular seemed to be maturing into a dominant presence. Mixing a speed that was unusual in a man his size with his natural power, Selmon collected 110 tackles and 13 sacks. Selmon's brother Dewey, now playing linebacker, surpassed Lee Roy's tackle total by recording 167. With the Selmon boys leading the way, the Buccaneer defense could be counted on to keep the team close until the offense could catch up.

Fixing the offense would be McKay's priority in 1978 and he would execute a controversial trade in the off-season to do just that.

Tampa Bay elected not to draft first in 1978, trading the top overall pick to Houston for the Oilers seventeenth choice and tight end Jimmie Giles. The move raised the eyebrows of some because many draft experts had figured Tampa Bay would gladly select Texas Heisman Trophy winner Earl Campbell. Instead the Oilers picked the Texas native. Tampa Bay chose little known quarterback Doug Williams of Grambling.

Williams had been a small college sensation; an AP All-American who set an NCAA record with 93 career touchdown passes. Overshadowing his resume was the fact that Williams became the first African-American quarterback to be drafted in the first round by a National Football League franchise.

Looking back at his selection, Williams feels that he didn't really make history because many other African-American quarterbacks had been drafted in the first round, but he was the first to be drafted specifically to play the position. "I think to be drafted number one and *given the opportunity to play quarterback is more correct,*" Williams said. "There were guys like Marline Briscoe who came before me but weren't given the same opportunity. I was fortunate at a later date to get the chance mainly because of a guy like John McKay to whom race did not matter."

At the time of Williams' selection black quarterbacks were not highly regarded by the decision makers of the league. Many of the old guard NFL establishment still believed that blacks lacked the intellectual and leadership qualities required of a quarterback. During the first half of the 1978 season Williams would dispel those notions by doing what no other Buccaneer quarterback had done, lead the team.

Williams debut in the season opener was a nightmare as his second pass attempt was intercepted and returned for a touchdown in a 19-13 loss to the New York Giants. Williams didn't waver after the setback and two weeks later he led the Buccaneers to their greatest victory yet, a 16-10 victory over perennial NFC power Minnesota. The win over the Vikings was followed by a 14-9 victory over the Atlanta Falcons that evened the team's record at 2-2.

McKay's goal of improving the offense seemed to be paying off. The defense had shown in 1977 that it was capable of being dominant at times. With an offense that could hold its own, McKay's Bucs had become a formidable opponent. As Williams told reporters after a victory, "We are no longer the little boys on the block who people can come along and slap on the head."

Tampa Bay split their next four games and after eight weeks found themselves in playoff contention with a record of 4-4. Things quickly fell apart though when Williams suffered a broken jaw in an excruciatingly close loss to the Los Angeles Rams. Without Williams the team's offense fell apart. The lack of production on offense put a greater strain on the defense as the season wore on. Lee Roy Selmon suffered a knee injury and missed the final three games of the season. Without Lee Roy, the defense wasn't nearly as stout as they had been. The Bucs would win only one of their final eight games and finished last in the division again with a 5-11 record.

While the final record was disappointing, McKay was heartened by the improvement that had been shown. Accolades rather than invective were shown to the team after the season ended. Defensive lineman Dave Pear became the first Buccaneer named to the Pro Bowl. Pear's fellow lineman Lee Roy Selmon also was honored. Lee Roy was named to the Associated Press All-Pro Team, another first in Tampa Bay history.

While Pear and Selmon received honors, John McKay continued to have his ability as a professional coach questioned. Rather than quieting critics, the 4-4 start had only raised their expectations. When injuries to Williams, Selmon and other key contributors crippled the team, skeptics used the second half slide as proof that McKay's systems could not succeed in the NFL. The critics seemed to have statistics on their side as McKay's three-year record of 7-37 was far from sterling.

McKay was undaunted in the face of such criticism. Over the course of three years he had painstakingly put together a roster of player he felt were tailor-fit to both his offensive and defensive systems. As 1978 became 1979 McKay changed only one thing, his expectations.

McKay met with players and coaches during the off-season and informed them that he expected the Buccaneers to contend for the NFC Central Division championship. McKay's words were enthusiastically received by his charges.

One especially excited player was Lee Roy Selmon. "At the end of the 1978 season I felt there was a whole different level of confidence about the team as we finished up the year. There was an anticipation and excitement about 1979. We felt we had a team that had enough talent to get it done," Selmon said. "The whole team was like, 'We feel real good about '79 and can't wait to get started.'"

A major motivating factor entering 1979 was the job status of their head coach. While owner Hugh Culverhouse had given McKay a vote of confidence, Buc players knew that a fourth straight losing season might put McKay's job in jeopardy. For three years McKay had provided cover from the fans and the press by being outspoken and accessible during all of the trying times. In the course of those three years many of McKay's players had started to blossom, especially on defense. Players such as Lee Roy and Dewey Selmon, safety Mark Cotney, defensive backs Curtis Jordan and Mike Washington, and linebacker Richard Wood would need to repay their coach by having their finest season. Cotney spoke for the attitude of the defensive platoon when he told the press, "This is a no-excuses year. We've had time to produce. I believe we will, we have to."

As the 1979 training camp approached McKay hoped that the players he had selected would prove him right and validate the systems he had been defending since he got to Tampa.

The System Pays Off

*T*wo characteristics marked John McKay's tenure at the University of Southern California, his on-field success and his off-field comments.

The on-field success enjoyed by McKay's Trojans was extraordinary. In his sixteen years on campus, McKay's team won 127 games, nine Pac-8 championships and four national titles. McKay also coached Mike Garrett and O.J. Simpson to Heisman Trophies in the 1960s.

Success in the Los Angeles media market made McKay a national figure. With the Trojans competing for a national championship annually, reporters of all stripes from across the country came to Los Angeles to see the coach at work. What they discovered at practice was that McKay did not conform to the stereotypical prototype of a coach.

In contrast to the militaristic approach of contemporaries such as Paul "Bear" Bryant and Ara Parseghian, McKay oversaw practice from afar, choosing to let his assistant coaches do all of the teaching as he strolled from drill to drill making mental notes. The form the practice took was also unusual in that McKay did not favor full contact, opting instead for run-throughs. To McKay, the practice field was a classroom and not a combat zone.

In his autobiography, "McKay: A Coach's Story," McKay listed many of his core beliefs in regards to teaching the game of football.

- "You have to realize that not all your players are as interested in football as you are. Don't get so involved that you forget to let them play."
- "You have to handle your players as individuals, not as a group."
- "We're not trying to make Marines, we're trying to make football players."

The predominant aspect of McKay's coaching style that would make him famous was his use of humor. The coach didn't believe in using fear and intimidation to get his message across, he felt it was counterproductive. McKay would yell and scream as any coach would, but he would always follow it up with a one-on-one teaching moment and a friendly jibe. McKay believed that a good-natured quip had to accompany a brutally honest assessment because it kept the players spirits up. To McKay, spirit and morale were very important.

In his autobiography McKay wrote, "Without a sense of humor, football can be unbearable for players and coaches.

"I realized we're going to lose and we're going to make mistakes, and if I can't laugh about it sometimes I'll just drive myself out of my mind. As for the players, there are times when everything is going wrong, so I'll say something funny to break the tension. I have to show them it's not the end of the world."

The media that followed McKay on game day dutifully recorded some of the coach's best comments in regards to alleviating the tension his team felt:

- After a 51-0 loss to Notre Dame McKay tried to put the loss in perspective by telling his players, "Do you realize 700 million Chinese don't realize the game was played?"
- During practice the week after the 51-0 loss McKay told his players that he had just received several letters from China wondering what the hell had gone wrong against the Irish. That quip broke up the team in gales of laughter.
- When one of his running backs tripped and fell without being touched by an opponent, McKay exclaimed for all on the bench to hear, "My God, they shot him!"
- Trailing Notre Dame 24-7, McKay told his team at halftime,

"Fellas, if we don't score some points in the second half we're probably going to lose." The line got the players laughing, but more importantly it got them playing better. USC stormed out in the second half and beat the Irish 55-24.

Mike Garrett claimed that McKay's style absolutely endeared him to Trojan players. "When we lost or he didn't like the way we practiced, he was tougher than hell on us. But just when we thought he was getting unbearable, he'd crack a joke and that would draw us closer to him."

The one drawback to McKay's use of humor was the fact that it quickly overshadowed the coach's reputation as an innovator. As a young assistant at the University of Oregon in the early 1950s McKay became known as a free and radical thinker when it came to offensive strategy. While McKay did not invent the no-huddle offense and rollout pass, he was one of the first to make them a regular part of a gameplan.

McKay's boss at Oregon, Len Casanova, was sometime caught off guard by his mad scientist assistant and would have to reel him back in. "I've never known a man with more ideas on football attack than McKay," Casanova was quoted as saying. "Some of the stuff he suggested was too far out for us at Oregon. We had to reject some of his plays because we would have needed motorcycles to make them work."

McKay's signature offensive innovation was developed over his tenure at USC. McKay pioneered a fundamental change to the I formation that made his Trojan teams one of the most formidable offensive units in college football. The I formation is an alignment where the quarterback, fullback and tailback all line up one behind the other. The twist to the I formation that McKay added was to have the tailback stand up with his hands on his knees so that he would have an unobstructed view of the defense. This allowed the running back to read the defense in the same manner as the quarterback.

In the past a running back had to run to a pre-determined spot based on what the coach called from the sideline. Reading the defense meant that the running back had the *freedom to change direction from where the coach guessed would be the best route up field to where the running back actually saw the best route.*

For years football had been a battle of wits between coaches on opposite sides of the field, but now McKay was arming his players on the field with decision-making powers. While the thought of ceding strategic decisions to players may have scared some coaches, McKay embraced the idea. McKay believed game day was for the players anyway, his time came Monday through Friday. According to McKay he and his assistants would teach the players the best holes to run through based on what the defense would show, but on game day it would be the player's responsibility to choose wisely.

This ownership of responsibilities also brought the players closer together. "The greatest motivating factor is fear," McKay wrote. "Not fear of the coaches, but the fear of letting down your teammates."

The I formation revolutionized the running game in college football in the sixties and made USC, the home of Mike Garrett, O.J. Simpson, Ricky Bell, Anthony Davis and other great backs, Tailback U.

McKay's contribution to offensive football was noteworthy because of the flash of players such as Simpson and Garrett. McKay's philosophy about the defensive side of the ball was what made USC the power it was.

There is an old cliché that offense sells tickets and defense wins championships, and McKay believed it was the faster defense that won the most. McKay desired speed and brain more than brawn in a defender because he believed these traits led to creating more turnovers. "I've always said, let me have the ball five times on your side of the 50 yard line, and I'll probably beat you by a wide margin," McKay wrote. "The team that plays on the shortest field will win. There are more ways to score on defense."

The formation McKay felt made the best use of speed and agility was the 3-4. Like the I formation, the 3-4 was not McKay's invention, but he did add his own stamp to it. The 3-4 employed three defensive linemen as the first line of defense, backed up by four linebackers and four defensive backs. This defensive formation requires a key ingredient or two from each line of defense. The defensive line required unselfishness, for the job of a 3-4 lineman is to occupy as many blockers as possible in lieu of making a tackle. By tying up blockers the defensive lineman creates gaps in the offensive line. This is not a particularly sexy assignment, but an important one.

The linebackers are the beneficiaries of these gaps. The job of a line-backer in a 3-4 is to run from sideline to sideline finding and running through the gaps in pursuit of the ball carrier. "Shooting the gap," as this is known is only one responsibility. The second is to drop into pass cover-age to assist the secondary when necessary. For this reason linebackers in the 3-4 must not only be strong tacklers, but also be light on their feet and able to match a receiver or tight end stride for stride on a pass pattern.

The final line of defense is the secondary. The secondary consists of two cornerbacks, whose job is to cover the outside receivers, and two safeties to patrol the middle of the field. A member of the secondary in the 3-4 must be able to run with receivers over great stretches and also must be willing to come close to the line of scrimmage to assist on stop-ping the running game.

All personnel in McKay's version of the 3-4 needed to have one thing in common: speed. Rather than push an offense around, the defenders of the 3-4 wanted to get to a spot on the field faster than the offense could. This was how turnovers would be created. On a running play, if the defen-sive lineman successfully tied up blockers and allowed a clear gap for the linebacker to shoot through, the collision with the running back could be so violent as to jar the ball loose. On a passing play, if the linebackers shot the gap on a blitz, the quarterback would be forced to throw the ball before he wanted to, increasing the likelihood of an interception.

This fast-paced, ball-hawking defensive philosophy combined with an efficient running game had paced the Trojans to four national titles. McKay had hoped to generate the same results in the NFL with his innovations.

When McKay unveiled his strategies on the NFL in 1976 they were met with dismissal. The comments made by Washington's Bill Brundige in 1977 had been echoed constantly. The defenses of the National Foot-ball League were too fast for the I formation the conventional wisdom went. It didn't matter what the running back saw at the snap of the ball because the defenders could change direction just as quickly as the ball carrier did. What had gained seven to eight yards a pop at USC would be lucky to gain one to two in the NFL.

On defense, many stated that using undersized defenders was ludi-crous; they would wilt under the constant pounding from men who outweighed them by 20 to 30 pounds. Factor in the oppressive heat and humidity of Florida and one could see that McKay was crazy to run such a defense against professionals.

From 1976 to 1978 it had appeared that the critics were right as the Buccaneers struggled mightily. The offense could barely get out of its own way and the defense, which had gotten off to a fast start in 1978, had broken down physically as the season wore on.

The results of the 1979 pre-season didn't do anything to quiet the critics in the least. While the defense played well in losses to Washington and Miami, the offense was only able to score one touchdown in each game. The defense continued to play well the next week, but the 14-7 victory over New Orleans was notable for a third straight poor showing by the offense.

The offense came somewhat untracked in the pre-season finale, a 24-13 victory against Cincinnati, but failed to show any level of consistency. A 2-2 record in the pre-season at one time would have been cause for a ticker tape parade through downtown Tampa, but after three years of poor football it only added to the sense that 1979 would be another losing campaign.

The feeling wasn't limited to Tampa. Magazines and publications from across the country picked the Buccaneers to finish dead last in the NFC Central Division for the fourth straight year.

It was with some surprise than that Coach McKay told the assembled reporters in the locker of Riverfront Stadium following the win over the Bengals that he expected big things for Tampa Bay in 1979. "How far have we come since 1976? A long way, in every facet, by a wide margin. We had a very successful pre-season."

This comment left many in attendance scratching their heads in disbelief. Exactly what did McKay see in this group that the rest of the nation was missing?

In a just seven days everyone would find out.

The opponent in the opener at Tampa Stadium was the Detroit Lions, a team many picked to win the NFC Central Division. The Lions had just missed out on the playoffs in 1978 and looked to take the next step in 1979.

Detroit was a charter member of the NFC Central, along with Green Bay, Chicago and Minnesota. The division had started play in

1970 following the merger of the NFL and AFL. Nicknamed the "Black and Blue Division" for its members rough style of play, the NFC Central had garnered a cult following of fans that liked the physical nature of the games.

While it made little geographic sense for Tampa Bay to be in a division with these snow-belt teams, it was a marriage of political expediency. The owners of these four teams wanted a chance to play at least one game a year at a warm weather site and felt Tampa would be an inviting climate. With many Midwest retirees settled in the Tampa Bay area, the NFL believed these transplants would gladly spend some money on watching their hometown teams play in Tampa.

Having Tampa in the NFC Central may have made the original four members happy, but it didn't make life easy for the Buccaneers. With their divisional rivals in the upper Midwest, Tampa Bay had four long flights a year just to play their divisional games. The fact that Green Bay, Chicago, Minnesota and Detroit would travel to play in almost perfect weather while Tampa Bay would travel to play in mud, snow, sleet, ice and worse made the Buccaneers insertion into the NFC Central advantageous to everyone but them. The 1978 season was Tampa Bay's first in the division and they limped through to a 2-6 record. Prognosticators foresaw a similar fate in 1979.

For the second year in a row the Buccaneers started their season one day before the rest of the National Football League. Due to the oppressive heat and humidity September brought to the Tampa Bay area, Buccaneer owner Hugh Culverhouse petitioned the NFL for a scheduling break in 1978. Claiming that the weather could put the health of fans and players at risk, Culverhouse proposed that any Buccaneer home games in September be played in the evening or late afternoon. Culverhouse's claims were not without justification. During training camp in 1979, St. Louis Cardinal player J.V. Cain collapsed during a workout and was pronounced dead with heat stroke a mitigating factor.

The NFL agreed to Culverhouse's request and in 1978 Tampa Bay's first two home games were played on Saturday night. Likewise in 1979, the Buccaneers would play Detroit in the season opener on Saturday night. The rest of the Bucs September schedule would be on the road except for a Week Four match-up with the Los Angeles Rams at Tampa

Stadium. The game against L.A. would begin at 4 pm after the worst heat of the day had a chance to give way to the cooling evening trade winds.

Given the combination of a fan friendly starting time and the excitement of opening day, a record crowd of 68,225 was on hand to see if the Bucs could compete with the cream of the NFC Central.

To the delight of the large crowd it became apparent early that the cream of the division was wearing orange jerseys. A stifling defensive effort showed that when run properly, the 3-4 defense was a turnover generating machine. On the Lions' first possession running back Dexter Bussey fumbled and linebacker David Lewis recovered. While Tampa Bay was unable to move the ball, they were in range for a field goal and kicker Neil O'Donoghue delivered a 31-yarder to put the Bucs up 3-0 early.

Later in the first quarter another Detroit running back, this time Horace King, fumbled when hit hard by defensive lineman Wally Chambers. Lee Roy Selmon scooped up the loose ball and promptly fell down. Selmon alertly popped back up before being touched and ran into teammate Jeris White. Shrugging off the unintentional hit of his teammate, Selmon deftly kept his balance and rumbled 29 yards to the end zone. The touchdown gave Tampa Bay a 10-0 led and threw the fans into near delirium.

With the defense staking the Bucs to a double-digit lead, McKay saw for the first time in his tenure the offensive system he cherished so much dominate a game. Running almost exclusively from the I formation, Ricky Bell and rookie tailback Jerry Eckwood gutted the Lions defense for big gain after big gain.

Eckwood set the pace with a 46-yard run in the first quarter and Bell contributed solid runs of his own, including a seven-yard touchdown. Tampa Bay's success at running the ball allowed McKay to unleash Doug William's arm strength on play action passes. One of those passes proved devastating for the Lions.

With the Bucs leading 17-7 in the second quarter Williams faked a hand-off and dropped back to pass. The play-fake had so transfixed the Lions that they failed to see tight end Jimmie Giles crossing the middle. Williams hit Giles in stride with a pass and the big tight end showed his unusual speed in out-sprinting the Lions for a 66-yard touchdown. The score made it 24-7 Tampa Bay at halftime and pretty much ended the competitive aspect of the game.

Giles' combination of speed and size were the reason McKay felt comfortable trading away the first pick of the 1978 draft to the Oilers for the tight end and the choice that would become Doug Williams. The knock on Giles coming out of Houston was that he was talented but raw. At Alcorn State Giles had focused more on baseball than football, only playing on the gridiron for two seasons. When Giles came to Houston he was considered a project, one that the Oilers were happily willing to forego in exchange for the first pick in the draft. This one touchdown pass showed that the two players the Bucs received in exchange for the right to pick Earl Campbell were capable of big things.

In the second half the Bucs offense continued to execute McKay's system flawlessly. Running with power and speed, Ricky Bell and Jerry Eckwood helped Tampa Bay control the ball for the majority of the final thirty minutes. It was a pass rather than a run that became the signature play of the opener.

On the first play of the fourth quarter at the Lions two-yard line, Williams rolled out to throw a pass and lost his footing, landing squarely on the seat of his pants. Not content to take a sack, Williams threw the ball *while seated on the ground* in the direction of back-up tight end Jim Obradovich. The ball not only cleared the line of scrimmage but hit Obradovich in perfect stride for a touchdown. The pass, while not a thing of beauty, showed off just how strong Williams' arm could be.

Commenting on the pass recently, Williams stated that the throw wasn't anything unusual; he was just doing his job. "I rolled to my left and my feet came out from under me and I hit (Obradovich) in the corner," said Williams, nonchalantly analyzing the pass. "I fell flat, but nobody touched me and I had to do something with the football."

"That throw wasn't about my arm being strong enough as much as it was instinct. It was just something that happened. Athletes are not supposed to think 'I can do this or I can do that.' I think a lot of things just happen naturally and that happened to be one of those cases."

The impressive pass capped a game-deciding 18-play, 73-yard drive that took more than eight minutes off the clock. While it could be argued that the Bucs were operating by the seat of their pants, the offense had scored three touchdowns and the defense dominated an opponent using McKay's systems.

The defense was bolstered by the return of a healthy Lee Roy Selmon. His injured knee had healed over the off-season but Selmon and others were nervous how the joint would respond to live action. The touchdown sprint early in the game convinced Selmon that he was more than ready. "That game and that play was a big confidence booster for me," Selmon said. "For me it was significant because it was the first regular season game I played in since having my knee operated on. You always wonder in the back of your mind, 'Is it going to hold up?' That game made me 100% confident my knee was going to hold up."

In the locker room after the game Selmon and his teammates laughed about how clumsy his run to the end zone had looked. Selmon told reporters, "I felt like a big old Mack truck. I couldn't decide whether to fall on it or pick it up so I tried to pick it up."

On colliding with Jeris White, Selmon said, "Jeris? Well, I guess he was excited for me, looking to block someone. I got past him and then I saw a guy coming after me out of the corner of my eye. I saw he was going low after my legs so I raised them up. Hey, I don't have running back ability. I just thought about going forward. It was something else."

Down the way from Selmon, teammate Wally Chambers using a mocking Howard Cosell tone, hollered, "Lee Roy Selmon, fullback, Tampa Bay Buccaneers."

McKay happily reiterated to reporters after the game that what they had just witnessed would be the rule and not the exception of 1979. But he was also quick to point out that no one should print playoff tickets just yet.

"We are an improved team but we certainly are not awe inspiring at this time," McKay opened. "We have a good defense and an offense that can score some points."

"I think that it's a good thing we won the opener. It helps team confidence anytime you win, especially when you prepare for something as long as you prepare for the opener. But it's a long year and we still have to play fifteen more regular season games. All this really means is that we won't go 0-16."

As the weeks progressed some began to wonder if the Bucs would lose a game at all.

CHAPTER 4

Comeback and Redemption

The opening day victory over the Lions was greeted enthusiastically in the Tampa Bay papers but was little noted elsewhere in the nation. The Bucs-Lions match-up was the sole game played on Saturday night but it was not nationally televised. Although ESPN's Sportscenter was scant weeks away from making its debut, there were no national sports highlight shows so only viewers in the Detroit and Tampa Bay markets saw the action unfold.

Reporters in both Detroit and Tampa Bay gave credit to the Buccaneers for playing well but were wary of reading too much into the victory. The Lions had played the entire game without starting quarterback Gary Danielson, who had injured his knee in Detroit's pre-season finale. The fact that the Lions had been forced to play an inexperienced back-up was a major factor in the game and made it difficult to ascertain just how good the Buccaneers were.

During the week leading up to the Bucs next game against Baltimore, John McKay acceded the point that Detroit was at a disadvantage but scoffed at the notion that the Bucs should apologize for their victory.

"I realize the loss of Danielson had to hurt Detroit's offense, but I really don't have too much sympathy for them. We didn't receive any cards and flowers when Doug Williams was injured the week before we played the Lions both times last year (both Tampa Bay losses).

"We did get ten points on fumbles, but the Lions have a good defense and we scored three touchdowns against them. Two were on sustained marches and one on the long pass from Doug Williams to Jimmie Giles. Our offense both controlled the ball and made the big play against Detroit and that pleased me.

"I believe we can compete for our division championship this season. We'll know more after we play Baltimore."

Over the past three years McKay had become the face of the organization, bravely standing up and answering for losses and providing cover for his players. In 1979 it appeared that McKay would have to defend his players abilities and trumpet their accomplishments to a doubting public.

For the second week in a row the Buccaneers were to face a team with an unsettled quarterback situation. Baltimore's Bert Jones, who had led the Colts to three straight AFC East championships in the mid-70s, was out with an assortment of injuries. His replacement was veteran Greg Landry. Still viable though was the stout Baltimore defense known as the "Sack Pack" for their ability to pressure quarterbacks. It would be a very talented team that the Buccaneers would play.

The site of the game was Baltimore's Memorial Stadium. The facility had seen many of the NFL's greatest games in the team's almost thirty year history. From the Colt's title teams of the late 50s to the AFC East power of the 70s the Depression-era relic had been home to great football. It was in this stadium that the Buccaneers would serve notice that much about them had changed.

Over the first fifteen minutes of play however it appeared that very little had changed. The Colts defense harassed the Buccaneer offense into committing two turnovers in just their first eight offensive plays. With Greg Landry looking like the second coming of Johnny Unitas, the Colts cashed in on three Tampa Bay turnovers and took a 17-0 lead into the second quarter. Viewers back in Tampa could have been forgiven for wondering if the previous week's game against Detroit had been a mirage. Were the Buccaneers destined to remain the clown princes of the NFL?

McKay hadn't panicked during the 26-game losing streak and he refused to panic now. Still utilizing the I formation, McKay's offense successfully engineered a 66-yard drive that resulted in a Ricky Bell touchdown from one yard out. The drive had to please McKay for two reasons. First his team had not given up on the contest and second, his young quarterback was using his running backs as receiving threats.

Lost in the way the I formation had revolutionized running was the impact it had on passing. McKay believed strongly in setting up the pass with the run. When a defensive team became pre-occupied with stopping the run, McKay believed they became susceptible to the long pass. McKay preferred the long ball but also wanted Williams to throw to backs more often when something didn't develop down the field. Thought of as "safety-valves" for a quarterback, a running back as a receiver could be an effective weapon.

When Williams came to the Buccaneers he struggled with this aspect of passing. There was no doubt he had a cannon for an arm, capable of high-arching rainbows down the field. The question was whether he could develop the touch to throw shorter passes to his backs. He had answered the question in the affirmative on this drive as he completed screen passes of more than 20 yards to Johnny Davis and Ricky Bell respectively. Neither pass traveled more than ten yards but had the same impact as a twenty-yard throw.

McKay's enthusiasm was tempered somewhat when Neil O'Donoghue's extra point was blocked, making the score 17-6 but Williams was maturing before his eyes.

The next Buc offensive possession saw more of the same, with some strong running by Ricky Bell mixed in. The drive ended on a nine-yard touchdown pass from Williams to wide-out Isaac Hagins. The PAT was good the second time around and the Bucs went into the locker room in much better shape than might have been expected after one quarter of play.

There was very little offensive action in the third quarter as both defenses blitzed and battered the offenses. At the start of the fourth quarter the Bucs struck a serious blow to the Colts on a very controversial call. Bucs defensive back Mike Washington intercepted a Landry pass and raced down the right sideline toward the end zone. Before Washington crossed the goal line it appeared the ball was knocked loose by Landry as he attempted a tackle. The ball flew away from Washington and rolled out of the back of the end zone for an apparent touchback.

The official at the goal line signaled touchdown instead, starting a cascade of boos from the Memorial Stadium stands. Colts coach Ted

Marchibroda angrily lobbied for a touchback but it was too late for the call had already been made. While it was good news for Tampa Bay, CBS-TV replays clearly showed Washington fumbling before he crossed the goal line, but replay was not an officiating tool at the time. The controversy was unfortunate for it overshadowed the fact that the Buccaneers had successfully come back from a large deficit to take a 20-17 lead in the fourth quarter.

The next time the Bucs took possession of the ball McKay allowed Williams to unleash a long pass. After an entire game of throwing short, Williams gladly heaved a pass over the middle that was caught by a streaking Gordon Jones for a 37-yard touchdown.

For the second time on the day though, a blocked extra point tempered a touchdown celebration. The Bucs now led 26-17, but Tampa Bay was about to learn a valuable lesson in why extra points should never be taken for granted.

The Colts defense, which had forced four turnovers in the first half, caused a fifth when linebacker Sanders Shiver intercepted a Williams pass. On the very next play, Landry used one of McKay's favorite plays to burn the Bucs. A short screen pass to Brian Deroo turned into a 67-yard touchdown when the receiver broke a tackle attempt by safety Curtis Jordan. It was the first time since the opening quarter that the Buccaneers defense had been beaten for any yardage and it came at one of the worst possible moments of the game. The touchdown energized the Baltimore fans and clearly shifted momentum in the Colts favor. Fortunately, Lee Roy Selmon was able to blunt some of the momentum when he blocked Toni Linhardt's PAT attempt to keep the score 26-23 with five minutes to play.

Baltimore got the ball back after a feeble Bucs possession and easily moved the ball into field goal range. With 1:26 to play Linhardt connected on a 37-yard attempt to tie the game at 26 apiece. The Bucs were unable to move the ball before the end of regulation, forcing the game into overtime.

This was the first time in history that the Buccaneers would play an overtime period, and they did not shrink from the pressure. Tampa Bay lost the overtime coin toss and was forced to kick off. O'Donoghue boomed his kick into the end zone, causing the Colts to start from the twenty yard line.

The Buccaneer defense wasted little time in atoning for losing the lead. On the third play of overtime nose tackle Randy Crowder jarred the ball loose form Landry on a hard sack. Fellow lineman Bill Kollar recovered the ball on the Baltimore 14-yard line.

Looking back on the play a quarter of a century later, Bill Kollar couldn't remember the exact details of the fumble. Rather Kollar stated the play was just the manifestation of John McKay's defensive philosophy. "(The coaches) always preached hustling to the ball until the play was blown dead," Kollar said. "That was one thing we really worked on and really prided ourselves on. We had a swarming defense. When you are hustling to the ball, it sometimes works out that you have a good chance to get the ball." Thanks to Kollar's adherence to that philosophy, the Bucs were in a great position to win the game.

McKay, not wanting to risk yet another turnover, sent his kicking team onto the field. Shaking off the two extra points that were blocked, O'Donoghue connected on the 31-yard attempt and the Bucs found themselves winners of a game in which they had once been in danger of losing big. The 29-26 victory put the Bucs record at 2-0 and meant they would still be atop the NFC Central Division.

While the players celebrated the largest comeback in team history, McKay held court with the press. According to McKay the win over Baltimore showcased how much the team he had put together three years ago had grown. "In the past I think panic would have stepped in," McKay admitted. "Some of the players would have started wondering what they were going to serve for dinner on the team plane. But this team doesn't have quit in them."

When asked why he went for the field goal right away instead of trying some offensive plays McKay was charmingly blunt. "We kicked the field goal on first down in overtime because fumbles and interceptions are in our playbook. Because it worked I'm intelligent and a hero, but if it had been blocked and returned for a touchdown ... ." McKay let the press figure out what they would have thought had the kick failed.

Commenting on the blocked extra points that almost cost the team the game McKay defended his kicker in his own inimitable fashion. "Neil's extra points got up pretty quickly. Baltimore just blocked them.

There's another kicker in the league who is having a terrible time getting his kicks up. He's hurt several centers. They've been hospitalized to remove the ball."

For the second game in a row the Buccaneers defense had been dominant. The 26 points Baltimore scored belied the fact that the Colts could not consistently move the ball. The Colts ran an astounding 82 offensive plays but only managed 206 total yards, an average of only 2.5 yard per play. Helping that average were ten sacks on the day by the defense.

The performance of the defense was slowly vindicating John McKay's 3-4 alignment. The man who had turned in the biggest play of overtime was vindicating McKay's belief in giving men a second chance. Randy Crowder's sack and forced fumble paled in comparison to what he had been through just two short years before.

Crowder was a stalwart defender for Joe Paterno's Penn State Nittany Lions and was drafted by the Miami Dolphins in 1974. He made a huge impact in Miami, recording more than 100 tackles in both 1975 and 1976. Before the 1977 season Crowder's ascendant career was derailed by a horrible decision.

A stewardess friend of Crowder convinced him to take a shot at dealing narcotics. Believing his celebrity status and her connections to the airlines made securing and transporting drugs rather effortless, Crowder agreed to the deal. With the assistance of teammate Don Reese, Crowder secured a pound of cocaine.

Unfortunately for Crowder and Reese their entry into the world of narcotics distribution ended abruptly. Their very first customer turned out to be a police informant who had been following the stewardess for quite some time. The two football players were arrested for possession and intent to distribute more than $200,000 worth of cocaine.

The arrest and trial of Crowder became a sensation in the National Football League. The defensive tackle faced thirty-five years in prison if found guilty. If he was somehow acquitted, Crowder faced the prospect of being barred from the NFL. In fact Miami Dolphins owner Joe Robbie had already suspended him from the team and stated unequivocally that it would take "virtually a case of mistaken identity before I want him (Crowder) around the Miami Dolphins again."

The trial was long on outrage but short on theatrics as Crowder followed the advice of his lawyer, former Dolphins linebacker Nick Buoniconti, and pled guilty to charges of felony drug trafficking. The advice Buoniconti offered was solid. Crowder and Don Reese were both sentenced to one year with no time off for good behavior.

The Miami community was shocked by the sentences. Editorial boards blasted the judge for giving preferential treatment to Crowder due to his celebrity status. Police officers and prosecutors argued vehemently that persons of lesser status had gone to jail for years for possessing mere grams of cocaine while Crowder would do one year for a pound.

The judge in the case, Joseph Durant, defended his decision thusly, "In front of me were two men who had never been in trouble before. A first offender, especially in non-violent crimes, has to get another shot. Otherwise, you are making sure he'll always be a criminal. To me it's a tough sentence. Jail is no picnic. Do you realize what it is like behind bars?"

On August 14, 1977 Randy Crowder found out what life in prison was like when he was incarcerated in the Dade County Stockade. Over the next 365 days Crowder thought of the poor decision that had led him to this place. He had grown up the son of a Pennsylvania coal-miner and had used football as a means to a college degree and a better way of life, but now he was a convict.

As his sentence wound down Crowder sat for an interview with *Pro Football Monthly's* Bob Rubin. In the interview Crowder claimed that anyone who thought he had gotten off easy should try to live in prison for a year. "I know there are people who say I have a piece of cake with this sentence. But they've never had this experience. They don't know what kind of cake this is. This is the most bitter piece of cake I've ever tasted."

Crowder just hoped that when he was released, someone in the NFL would be willing to give him a second chance.

John McKay listened to what Randy Crowder had to say about prison changing him for the better and took Crowder at his word. Upon Crowder's release from prison in 1978 McKay traded a third-round choice to Miami for the rights to Crowder. Even though Crowder had been provided with access to workout equipment during his stay in prison, he was far from being in football shape.

Many were shocked that McKay would bring in a convicted drug trafficker to play for the club, but the coach saw in Crowder a man who had already been through one of the worst experiences a man can go through and was better for it. Perhaps that level of maturity was just the influence his callow team needed to break away from the stigma of 0-26. Crowder's 1978 production was sporadic, two sacks and sixteen tackles in spot duty. He showed McKay enough for the coach to trade away Dave Pear to the Oakland Raiders. This move angered some who felt that Pear, the Bucs first Pro Bowl invitee in history, was a star on the rise. As his play against Baltimore had shown, Crowder was more than living up to McKay's expectations.

Said McKay, "Randy's done what we've asked of him and we're proud he's on our team." McKay's faith had helped Crowder to put some dark days behind him and the rejuvenated defensive tackle hoped to do the same for McKay's football team.

The opponents for the third game, the Green Bay Packers, were one of the original members of the National Football League. Since their inception in 1920 the Packers had enjoyed much success, winning league titles in the '20s, '30s and '40s. In the 1960s the Packers became as much a part of the American sports landscape as the New York Yankees and Boston Celtics, winning five league championships and the first two Super Bowls under legendary head coach Vince Lombardi. In the 1970s the Packers had fallen on hard times and had been mediocre at best. By hiring Lombardi's quarterback Bart Starr as head coach, the Packers hoped to rekindle the magic and attitude that had brought so much success the decade before.

On this sun-splashed Sunday at Lambeau Field, Starr would be just one of many members of Lombardi's championship teams in town for the game. When the schedules had come out during the off-season, Packer management had felt that the third Sunday of the season would be the ideal time to hold a homecoming event. One reason was that the late summer weather would be beautiful in Green Bay. Second, with the Buccaneers as the opponent the Packers would be almost certain to enjoy an easy victory to entertain the Packer alums that had returned to Wisconsin. As kick-off approached Packer fans and former Packer greats, no doubt buoyed by a weekend of good food, good drink and hearty reminisces of yesterday, sat down for what they expected would be an easy coast to victory. They got what they came for except the wrong team coasted to victory.

In the first quarter it looked as though the Bucs were inclined to play the polite guest as they blew a golden scoring opportunity. Linebacker David Lewis sacked Packers' quarterback David Whitehurst, forcing a fumble that was recovered by Lee Roy Selmon at Green Bay's seventeen-yard line. The Bucs offense couldn't move the ball and Neil O'Donoghue compounded the problem by missing a 32-yard field goal. It would be the beginning of a long day for the tall Irishman.

Encouraged by the Bucs gaffe, the Packers drove the ball 60 yards in 15 plays, chewing up over six minutes. They finally stalled and settled for Chester Marcol's 38-yard field goal. At the end of the first quarter the Packers led 3-0, and the alums were quite pleased.

In the second quarter the Bucs defense and running game started to slowly take over. On a run attempt, Packer tailback Terdell Middleton fumbled the ball, which was quickly pounced on by linebacker Richard Wood. "Batman," as Wood was known by his teammates, brought the ball to the Packers 40 yard line. On the Bucs very first play following the turnover, Jerry Eckwood followed backfield mate Ricky Bell to the outside. Bell made a key block, turning Eckwood loose down the sideline for a 40-yard touchdown gallop. The touchdown by Eckwood not only stunned the Lambeau crowd, it set a team record as the longest run from scrimmage ever by a Tampa Bay Buccaneer. The PAT was good, and just like that the Packer alum saw their team down 7-3.

The teams exchanged punts for the rest of the half, but a tone was being set. Where the Bucs were able to make positive yardage on their drives, keeping the field position battle in their favor, the Packers offense was quickly forced to punt the ball by the stingy Bucs defense. If former Packer linemen Jerry Kramer, Fuzzy Thurston and Forrest Gregg were in attendance, they might have been experiencing déjà vu. The Bucs were running Lombardi's old staple, the power sweep to near perfection. In the second half the Bucs would show the old Packers that they had indeed mastered the play.

On the opening drive of the second half Doug Williams engineered the type of drive that up until now Coach McKay had only dreamed of. Utilizing all receivers and showing patience and restraint, Williams led the Bucs on a 65-yard scoring drive in 11 plays, taking over five minutes off the clock. Williams had three big completions on the drive. The first two were a nine-yard pass to Isaac Hagins and an eighteen-yarder to Morris Owens that burned a Packer secondary creeping closer to the line to stuff the Bucs steamrolling running game. The last was an eleven-yard touchdown toss to Ricky Bell that was important not only for the points it produced, but the poise Williams showed in throwing it.

On the play the Packers sent an all-out blitz, overwhelming the Bucs offensive line and quickly getting into the young quarterbacks face. Instead of panicking and throwing an ill-advised lob into the secondary, Williams set his feet and threw a pinpoint pass to his tailback moments before being hit by the rush. The 14-3 Buccaneers lead silenced the Green Bay crowd and threw the Bucs sideline into delirium. They were once again dominating a division rival. This time it seemed all the more sweet because they were doing it on the road.

After a three and out by the Packers offense the Buccaneers put a dagger into Green Bay, using only six plays to drive 62 yards in an efficient 2:09. Included in this drive was an impressive, diving catch of a seemingly overthrown Williams pass by Isaac Hagins. The completion was good for sixteen yards and kept the Bucs drive alive. From the Green Bay 19 Bell took a toss from Williams and acting as though he was Paul Hornung following Forrest Gregg and Jimmy Taylor, raced past blocks thrown by Eckwood and Charley Hannah and outran Packer defensive back Estus Hood to the end zone. It was once again the classic "Packer" sweep run to perfection against the team that popularized its use in pro football the way McKay had done so in the collegiate ranks at USC. It gave the Bucs a commanding 21-3 lead.

The third quarter had seen the Buccaneers dominate time of possession, holding onto the ball for over 11 minutes. The fourth quarter saw much of the same only this time the Bucs frustratingly scored no points. After two long drives, the Buccaneers saw O'Donoghue miss field goals of 42 and 47 yards. When the Packers drove the length of the field to score a meaningless touchdown near the end of the game, the 21-10 victory appeared to be much closer than it was. Had the Buccaneers not missed those field goals, the margin of 30-10 would have undoubtedly been much more eye-catching to the rest of the league.

The scoreboard notwithstanding, the Buccaneers had enjoyed a field day against the Pack on both offense and defense. Paced by the play of

Eckwood and Bell, the Bucs eclipsed the team record for rushing set in the season opener against Detroit by gaining 235 yards on the ground. Eckwood and Bell had narrowly missed an impressive double feat, two backs on the same team gaining 100 yards in the same game. Because of the great play of the offensive line, Bell had gained 97 yards on 15 carries and Eckwood 99 yards on 23. These yards, coupled with Williams 132 yards passing, helped to combine for the Buccaneers total offensive yardage of 367.

Rather than celebratory, the atmosphere in the Bucs post-game locker room was defiant. Angered over the Packers choice of the Bucs as the "homecoming" opponent, linebacker David Lewis challenged the rest of the NFL to take notice of the team from Tampa.

"We came here knowing we were the underdogs and all we heard was about their history," Lewis told the Tampa press. "They had a ceremony honoring some past players, but, heck, most of our guys never heard of them. We came to prove we're a good football team. I think Green Bay heard if they couldn't beat Tampa Bay they couldn't beat anybody."

Closing out his post-game comments, the bold Lewis exclaimed, "Maybe somebody will start believing us now."

Dewey Selmon expressed his agreement with Lewis simply and bluntly: "All I want to say is watch out for the Bucs."

Wally Chambers went one better than his teammates, proudly putting a Packer fan in his place as he ran off the field after the game. According to *Times* columnist Hubert Mizell, a Packer fan yelled out at the Bucs "You're lucky!" The old pro Chambers simply raised his index finger and without looking at the man exclaimed, "Tell 'em to read the newspaper." The Bucs were in first place and that Packer fan and the rest of the NFC Central would have to get used to it.

In his post-game comments Coach McKay echoed the sentiments of his players. Eschewing the chance to bask in the glory of a victory, McKay used his forum to poke holes in the prevailing opinion that the Bucs were still just a bunch of bumbling losers on a lucky streak. "You can only be an expansion team for so long and then you become a team," the head coach said. "There's been so much talk that we beat two teams who didn't have their number one quarterback. Well, today we beat a team that had its number-one quarterback, its number-one running back, its number-one receiver and its number-one defense."

McKay closed out his comments by stating that the proof of the Buccaneers ability to legitimately challenge for a division title had just been witnessed on the playing surface of Lambeau Field. "We are as good as the rest of the teams in the division."

CHAPTER 5

Proving It

cKay's belief that the Bucs were as good as the rest of the clubs in the NFC Central Division could have been construed as damning by faint praise. The Bucs 3-0 record was indisputable but the quality of the rest of the division was debatable. The Chicago Bears were the closest team to Tampa Bay with a record of 2-1, while the Packers and Vikings each stood with records of 1-2 and preseason favorite Detroit was 0-3.

Sensing that critics would use the records of the other NFC Central teams as proof that the Bucs were not as good as their record, McKay co-opted the argument. Emerging from his office after studying films of the Packer game, McKay expressed his belief that the first three games were but prologue and that the fourth game against the Rams would be the true test.

"We will have a better idea of where we are on Sunday," McKay said. "I think the Packers have a pretty sound defense and I was happy we were able to move the ball on them. But the Rams will be an even greater challenge. There is absolutely no area in their defense that you can exploit as a weakness. And on offense they have both strong and fast runners, a huge line, capable receiving and good, intelligent quarterbacking."

McKay also let it be known that he was happy with his team's performance but not overly impressed. The coach hinted that he was not allowing his players to bask in the glow of a 3-0 start. McKay wanted them to realize that they had not really won anything yet. "I've been 3-0 before (in college) and since you have to play next week whatever your record you can't get too high or too low. It's a long season and while I want to win every game, my main concern is that we stay healthy and play well."

McKay's statements about playing well belied the fact that he wanted to beat the Rams for reasons other than possible playoff positioning; it was also a matter of professional pride.

The coach had always viewed the Rams as an organization by which to measure the progress of his Buccaneers. They had become his model during his time as coach at Southern Cal. Living and working in Los Angeles during the sixties and early seventies, McKay saw firsthand the work of George Allen and the famous "Fearsome Foursome." Stories of the Rams winning ways shared the headlines of the Los Angeles sports sections with McKay's USC teams. When Allen left the Rams, one of the first people interviewed to replace him was John McKay.

McKay turned down a fifteen-year contract worth $90,000 per year to stay at USC. McKay stated he declined the Rams offer to tend to unfinished business at Southern Cal, which turned out to be two more national championships. The flirtation seemed to stir within McKay dreams of coaching at the highest level and a few years later he made the move to Tampa Bay.

McKay knew that the transition from a pre-eminent program such as USC to an expansion NFL team would be a trying one. Softening the impact was the contract McKay signed. The five-year pact was worth a total of $750,000 plus a $750,000 life insurance policy for McKay and his wife Corky, an annual expense account of $10,000, a $350,000 home and three automobiles.

The first assignment for McKay's team in 1976 was an exhibition game against the Los Angeles Rams at McKay's old office, the Los Angeles Memorial Coliseum. Going into the game McKay tried to lower expectations and realistically assess his team's chances against the Rams. "We are not ready to play the Los Angeles Rams at this time," McKay said to a pool of Los Angeles reporters that once covered him daily at USC. The Bucs proved him right by losing to the Rams 26-3 in a game not as close as the final score would indicate.

While the game was a disaster football wise, it did introduce the National Football League to the wit of McKay. Wired for sound by NFL

Films, McKay's sideline utterances brought to mind a Don Rickle's stand-up routine. Of his team's defensive efforts, McKay was heard saying, "Could we please put in the man who tackles," and "Every time they (the Rams) have the ball they keep it about a week." On his team's overall performance, McKay muttered, "The ones that aren't gutless are brainless."

In fact the only competitive aspect of the game was McKay's futile attempts to keep those on the sideline from creeping onto the field of play and blocking his view. After repeatedly imploring the team to move back, an enraged McKay finally shouts, "If they don't get back, I'll cut them so they'll be down!"

After the game McKay was asked what he felt about Tampa Bay's effort. The answer McKay provided became one of his defining lines. "We didn't block well," McKay said. "But we made up for it by not tackling."

In 1977 the Buccaneers played in Los Angeles again, losing 31-0 in the midst of their record losing streak. In 1978 the Bucs lost at the Coliseum 26-23 on a last second field goal. The game had been hard fought and brutal but it showed McKay that his team had made giant strides in three years even if it was not readily apparent to the rest of the NFL. As far as McKay was concerned, if the Bucs could compete toe to toe with the Rams, they could challenge anybody in the NFL.

McKay wasn't the only one eagerly anticipating the game against the Rams. Owner Hugh Culverhouse and the Buccaneers roster were looking to avenge separate instances of what they perceived to be dirty play. One case occurred in the boardroom and one on the field of strife.

Hugh Culverhouse was one of the most successful tax attorneys in America. After stints as the Alabama assistant attorney general and regional counsel of the Florida Internal Revenue Service, Culverhouse went into business for himself. The Jacksonville firm of Culverhouse, Tomlinson and Mills became one of the most profitable tax firms in the nation.

As his wealth and influence grew, Culverhouse decided to try his hand at professional sports. In 1972 when the Los Angeles Rams went up for sale, Culverhouse made a cash offer to purchase the team. According to Culverhouse the Rams negotiator, Bill Barnes, accepted his offer of $17 million. What Culverhouse didn't realize is that he was soon to become victim of a power play by one of the most powerful owners in the NFL. David Harris' book *The League* chronicles the events that led to Hugh Culverhouse being denied ownership of the Rams with a promise of future ownership.

Baltimore Colts owner Carroll Rosenbloom was growing restless in the small environs of the mid-Atlantic. Rosenbloom had been eyeing the Rams and the lucrative Los Angeles market as a way to increase his wealth and influence. In a bold, and perhaps unethical move, Rosenbloom joined forces with Robert Irsay to outbid Culverhouse for the Rams. Rosenbloom's audacious plan was to "trade" his interest in the Colts to Robert Irsay for control of the Rams. In order for this plan to work, Irsay would have to win the bid for the Los Angeles Rams.

Rosenbloom learned of Culverhouse's $17 million bid and helped Irsay top it with a $19 million offer. Irsay was able to meet this price because he had no intention of owning the Rams. Irsay only had to pay $15 million to Rosenbloom for ownership of the Colts. Rosenbloom accepted Irsay's check and then added $4 million of his own money to purchase the Rams for himself. It was a stunning move that caught many around the league flatfooted, no one had ever "traded" an entire franchise before. The league fathers, a tight-knit group of wealthy entrepreneurs who were primarily interested in keeping Rosenbloom happy and a healthy franchise in the second largest media market in the nation raised little objection to the transaction. Culverhouse, who felt he had negotiated in good faith with the Rams and the National Football League, was outraged. Using all of his legal resources, Culverhouse sued the league and every individual franchise for millions of dollars, citing that they had conspired to prevent him from having a fair chance at acquiring the Rams. He had a compelling case, so compelling that the suits were settled out of court. One rumor had it that part of the settlement involved Culverhouse agreeing to accept lower monetary damages in return for a guarantee of ownership of a future expansion franchise.

That franchise turned out to be Seattle, but only temporarily. The original owner of the Buccaneers was real estate developer Tom McCloskey. After only a few short weeks McCloskey backed out citing financial difficulties. The NFL asked Culverhouse if he would prefer the Tampa Bay franchise instead of Seattle. Culverhouse, a son of the South, recalled that he had agreed so heartily "I almost jumped through the phone."

Over the intervening years Culverhouse buried his hatchet with the NFL and through his tax acumen became a very powerful owner, but he never forgot his L.A. story. Even though Carroll Rosenbloom had passed away and Culverhouse enjoyed an amiable relationship with his widow and new Ram owner, Georgia Rosenbloom, he could be forgiven for wanting to finally beat the team that had almost been his.

As for the Bucs players, they wanted to exact revenge for what they considered a cheap shot against their quarterback in the previous years game. In the first quarter of that 1978 contest Doug Williams was viciously hit by Rams defensive end Fred Dryer after he had released a pass. Dryer's hit was a helmet-to-helmet shot, where the crown of his helmet hit the side of Williams' jaw. The ferocity of the tackle broke Williams' jaw and forced him to miss five of the final six games of the season.

Buc players were infuriated that the officials had not flagged Dryer. Not only had the hit come late, helmet-to-helmet hits were illegal and dangerous. Many on the team felt that had Dryer's hit come against a team that wasn't considered a punch line, justice would have been served. With a year to think about the hit, the Bucs were anxious to settle the issue on the field.

Payback would not be easy, as the Rams possessed one of the most talented rosters in the National Football League. The Rams had been champions of the Western Division throughout the majority of the 1970s and while they had not yet made it to the Super Bowl, the Rams were a dominant team nevertheless. Los Angeles won by employing a suffocating defense that was known for it rugged and intimidating play. With defensive stalwarts such as Fred Dryer, "Hacksaw" Jack Reynolds (who earned his nickname by sawing his car in half after a loss at the University of Tennessee) Jack Youngblood, Jim Youngblood (no relation) and Nolan Cromwell the Rams consistently fielded one of the top defenses in the league.

On offense the Rams were no less dangerous. Led by quarterback Pat Haden, the Rams had a solid passing attack. Wendell Tyler, Lawrence McCutcheon and the wonderfully named Elvis Peacock spearheaded the running game; all were gifted runners who could put up big yards behind the Rams mammoth offensive line. As far as downfield threats were concerned, the Rams did not lack in that department either.

Speedy Billy Waddy was a threat to go deep on any play and consistent tight end Charle Young was a cagey veteran who could easily find seams in the middle of the defense. All of this talent was on its way to Tampa Stadium to see if the undefeated Buccaneers could match up with an elite team.

As if there quest for vengeance combined with the desires of their coach and owner weren't enough, the players were further riled up when they were made aware of some dismissive comments uttered by the Rams head coach. When Ray Malavasi was asked during the week what he thought about the Bucs he had responded that he was not all that impressed. According to Malavasi, the Rams had "nothing to fear about the Bucs," and therefore he and his players weren't overly concerned with stopping Tampa Bay.

To have their undefeated status questioned was nothing new to the Tampa Bay players, they had been hearing it all week. But to have the head coach of your opponent overlook your ability as a player was something different all together and the Bucs planned to show Malavasi a thing or two come Sunday.

Even though the league had accommodated Culverhouse's wishes to move early season home game kickoff times to later in the day, heat and humidity were going to be factors. The temperature for the four o'clock kickoff was 83 degrees with 70 percent humidity. On top of that, violent thunderstorms were predicted for the late afternoon. The storm would cool things off but make a mess of the field in the process.

The Tampa Stadium turf wasn't the only thing that threatened to be sloppy. For most of the first quarter the two teams exchanged turnovers and missed scoring opportunities. When Los Angeles kicker Frank Corrall missed a 47-yard field goal attempt with just over five minutes left in the opening period it looked as though momentum may be starting to go Tampa Bay's way. But then Williams reverted back to a bad habit with catastrophic consequences.

Williams' arm was so strong that he sometimes tried to rifle the ball despite tough coverage. This tendency could lead to interceptions and it did so on this day. Rams linebacker Jim Youngblood picked off a Williams screen attempt to Ricky Bell and raced 29 yards for a touchdown. A frustrated Williams chased Youngblood the entire way and tackled him just as the linebacker crossed the goal line. The only good to come from the interception was that Lee Roy Selmon blocked Corrall's extra point to keep the score 6-0.

As the game moved from the first to second quarter, it was becoming apparent that the Buccaneers were nervous. The team was not playing well and seemed to be wilting under the pressure of playing a high profile team in a game that would go a long way in exorcising the demons of the 26-game losing streak. The Buccaneers needed to produce a big play to get them and their fans back into the game.

Lee Roy Selmon provided just the lift his team needed when he jarred the ball loose from Ram tailback Lawrence McCutcheon. Fellow lineman Bill Kollar fell on the ball and the Buccaneers had a first down at the Los Angeles 27-yard line.

On the first play following the turnover Ricky Bell defied gravity on a cutback run up the middle of the Rams defense. Bell initially ran to the right, saw a hole in the defense and leaned so far to the left on his cut that his shoulders almost hit the ground before he righted himself and burst through to the 15 yard line. On the next play Larry Mucker made an athletic play that almost rivaled Bell's. On the first down play, Mucker ran a corner route in the end zone while being covered tightly by Rod Perry. Williams' pass was perfectly thrown to a spot that only Mucker could get to. Showing tremendous athletic ability Mucker was able to get both feet in bounds and control the ball before being knocked out of bounds by Perry. It was a wonderful throw and catch and in addition to the style points, it tied the game at six apiece. Neil O'Donoghue's extra point was good, and the upstart Bucs had a 7-6 lead and a whole new outlook on the game one-minute into the second quarter.

The defense continued to shut down the Rams but began to do so in a more physical manner. Linebacker Dewey Selmon set the tone for the game on a hit of tailback Lawrence McCutcheon. The pass from Pat Haden was a little off target and McCutcheon could not quite bring it in. As the ball was falling from his grasp, Selmon hit McCutcheon from behind and flung the tailback to the ground in one swift, almost sinister movement. The hit brought the Tampa Stadium faithful to their feet in a standing ovation for the defense. After the hit it was the Rams offense that seemed to become unnerved and they would not be a factor for the rest of the game.

With his defense physically dominating the Rams, McKay decided the time had come for the offense to avenge the pounding Williams had taken in 1978. The head coach didn't order the team to play dirty, but instead McKay sent out a formation whose only purpose was to move the ball down the field through a process of attrition that would batter an opponent and weaken their resolve. Included in the offensive unit that took the field was fullback Johnny Davis, known as Bull by his team-mates because of his blocking technique. Davis was a talented musician off the field but delivered blocks that crashed like cymbals on it.

McKay's shift to power running mode paid off as the Bucs advanced from the sixteen to near midfield. The Rams, unaccustomed to being overpowered by any team, began to show their frustration at being beaten by a team they had once dominated. Cornerback Pat Thomas in particular seemed to take issue with Tampa Bay's physical style. Thomas drew Jerry Eckwood into a fistfight after one play, although no penalty was assessed on either team and then completely lost his cool with back-to-back personal foul penalties for hitting a player late.

Coupled with the hard running of Ricky Bell, Thomas's 30 yards in penalties helped move Tampa Bay to the Los Angeles goal line. On third and goal from the five-yard line Johnny "Bull" Davis blew Rams line-backer "Hacksaw" Jack Reynolds out of the hole and allowed Ricky Bell to high-step into the end zone unmolested. The score and subsequent PAT put the Buccaneers in front 14-6 with 6:32 to play in the first half. The crowd at Tampa Stadium created a deafening roar. This was the big-gest Buccaneer game in the history of the stadium and the fans were seeing their team dominate one of the NFL's elite.

The Rams were unable to move the ball and the Buccaneers took possession with just under three minutes left. As they took to the field, lightning streaked across the sky and thunder shook the air as a violent storm moved through Tampa Bay. The Buccaneers mirrored the ele-ments on this drive as they tore through the Rams. Ricky Bell thundered through holes in the line and just when the Rams thought it couldn't get any worse, Doug Williams unleashed a bolt from his right arm. Wil-liams found a wide-open Jimmie Giles over the middle and hit the tight end perfectly in stride for a 29-yard touchdown. On the play Giles had been double covered by Rams safeties Nolan Cromwell and Dave Elmen-dorf. The two defensive backs simply couldn't keep up with Giles and he easily out-sprinted them to the ball. The PAT was successful and the Bucs headed to the locker room with a 21-6 lead.

The second half saw the Buccaneers defense continue to dominate the Rams vaunted passing attack. The production of the Rams was so poor that Pat Haden was pulled from the game and replaced by Vince Ferragamo. While Haden's benching was a testament to John McKay's defensive system he was hardly overjoyed at seeing Haden struggle. Haden had played for McKay at USC, even lived with the coach's family for a short time. But after three years of suffering through criticism of his 3-4 defense, any pangs of guilt over Haden were probably overridden by pride in his defenders.

On offense the Buccaneers didn't score another point, but managed to kill several minutes off the clock. The I formation running game derisively referred to as "Student Body Left, Student Body Right" was more than the Rams could handle. As the clock ticked towards all zeroes, the rain-soaked fans let out a raucous cheer and the players on the sidelines danced in a manner reminiscent of the franchise's first victory in New Orleans.

The Tampa Bay Buccaneers, one-time owners of a 26-game losing streak and the nation's pigskin punch line for three years, had just dominated the Los Angeles Rams. Whether or not the victory would silence the critics was unimportant. It was time to celebrate.

In his post game press conference McKay was asked numerous questions about where the 21-6 victory ranked. McKay chose to not rate the victory for himself, but instead insisted it was great for his players "Everyone thinks beating the Rams with the game on television in Los Angeles was such a big thing for me," McKay stated. "But I think it was even bigger for our good players. We've got some players on our team who could be stars for any team in the league and this will help them get the recognition they deserve. I think the players should get most of the credit when you win and most of the blame when you lose. I'm not one of those coaches who will tell you, 'We're small and slow and the only reason we're winning is good coaching.' I've always believed that the players deserve the publicity and the credit."

McKay was not alone in praising the team, as his former USC quarterback seemed in awe. "It wasn't our line's fault, it wasn't my receivers fault and I don't think it was my fault," Pat Haden said about the 64-yards passing he had accounted for. "We just couldn't pass down-field against those linebackers. Then, when I completed a dump pass to my backs, the Bucs' linebackers are such good athletes that they reacted and smothered us." When asked what a team could do to beat the Bucs defense, an exhausted Haden replied, "Recover a fumble on the one-yard line."

Haden wasn't the only Ram who was unprepared for the new Bucs.

"They're 100 percent better than last year," said Ram linebacker Bob Brudzinski. "The running backs and offensive line are what make them better."

Defensive lineman Jack Youngblood concurred with his teammate that the Bucs were improved, but he disagreed on the reason. The Bucs second year quarterback was the key difference in Youngblood's opinion. "Doug Williams is really maturing. He has come a long way in one year. He's going to be a fine, fine, fine quarterback. Maybe I should say *he is* a fine, fine, quarterback."

When Tampa Bay players came into the interview room they were more than happy to comment on showing up Ray Malavasi. "I didn't fear anybody out there myself," said an ebullient Doug Williams, whose two touchdown passes had helped to break the game open. "Their coach didn't fear us but like Coach McKay said, he wasn't going to play in the game. It was probably one of the biggest statements. Coach McKay said we respected them. I don't think they respected us."

"Maybe," said Batman Wood, "there was something to fear after all."

Fellow linebacker David Lewis let it be known that the team was inspired by more than just Malavasi's lack of respect, but the lack of respect shown by the national media as well. "Coach Malavasi kept talking about his Big D. Well, our Big D didn't play too bad. We wanted to go right after them, make Pat Haden scramble. Everybody at home was watching. If they don't want to put us on TV, we'll make the playoffs and put ourselves on TV."

The well-prepared Bucs won more than the Rams respect on this Sunday; they also increased their lead in the NFC Central to two full games. The Bucs nearest competitor, the Chicago Bears, had lost to Miami to fall to 2-2. If Tampa Bay could win in Chicago the next week they would have a commanding three game lead over their nearest rival.

Aware of his team's standing in the division, McKay ended his press conference with a confident assessment of his team's chances for the rest of the season. "I don't see anybody on our schedule that we absolutely can't beat. But we must get all our players to the stadium healthy and we have to play completely up to our abilities." As the Rams could attest, when the Bucs were on their game they could beat anybody. The rest of the league would find out a lot more about the Buccaneers over the next several days.

Unbeaten, Untied and Unbelievable

*T*he day after the conquest of the Rams, McKay's team gathered at One Buccaneer Place with the expectation of enjoying the game film. They envisioned sitting in their meeting chairs triumphantly viewing their exploits over and over again as the coaches played and re-played the film. Perhaps there would be a good deal of hooting and hollering as they watched the big plays the offense and defense had made. It could arguably be the best film they would see in 1979, perhaps even better than *Alien* or *The Jerk*, other big films of the year. Their head coach had other ideas and dashed any hopes for an easy Monday by showing them films of their upcoming opponent, the Chicago Bears.

While McKay undoubtedly reveled in the victory, possibly looking for Southern California newspapers so he could witness his old critics eat their words, he knew the Bucs had no time for celebration. Another key division game was on tap and it would be the toughest divisional opponent thus far and it would be far away from the friendly environment of Tampa Stadium.

The Bears were showing themselves to be a young, solid team. Two years removed from a playoff appearance the Bears employed arguably the best running back in the National Football League. Walter Payton held the record for most yards in a single game and had been a thousand yard rusher every year but his rookie campaign of 1975. Possessing speed, power and an amazing sense of balance, Payton was a one-man offense. In 1979 the Bears had put together a solid defense to support Payton and take some of the pressure off of him. The Bears defense ranked first in the league against the run. The Bucs would be in a game that would see two of their strengths, running the ball and stopping the opponent from running the ball put to the test.

One thing working in the Bucs favor is that they had experience with defending Payton, and had actually done an adequate job. In three games versus Tampa Bay, "Sweetness," as the affable Payton was affectionately known, had averaged only three yards a carry. But a back the caliber of Payton was a threat to break a long run at any time and McKay showed his defenders disheartening highlights of the Bears back running rough-shod over the rest of the league including the big day when he almost single-handedly led the Bears to an upset of the Cowboys in Dallas.

While the Bucs were engaged in horror movies, the national media began to make their way to Tampa. At 4-0 the Buccaneers were one of only four undefeated teams in the NFL, the others being Pittsburgh, Miami and Cleveland. With their newfound success the Buccaneers also saw increased scrutiny and press coverage from a national media that was caught flat-footed by Tampa Bay's success. With a 4-0 record the Bucs were no longer an easy team to cover. A reporter couldn't just pawn the team off as a collection of clowns and bumblers, now media scribes would have to do a little bit of homework to cover the team. As the week progressed many media outlets descended on One Buccaneer Place and numerous reporters filed stories with a Tampa Bay dateline.

Rick Odioso, then a 25-year old Assistant Public Relations Direc-tor, was enjoying the fact that he was working for a professional football franchise. When the team raced out to the 4-0 start he and the rest of the PR staff found themselves in high demand. As Odioso recalled years later, it was a busy time but also an exhilarating one.

"These days most teams probably have fifteen people to do what three of us did," Odioso said. "I set up player interviews, wrote press releases and helped to set up player appearances."

"It was pretty exciting. I was new in the profession. I remember Pete Axthelm came down to write a piece for *Newsweek*. He was a well-known writer with some books to his credit. It was pretty exciting to go to lunch with Pete Axthelm."

The most prominent sports publication to cover the Bucs ascension was *Sports Illustrated*. *SI* sent reporter Joe Marshall to Tampa, and his

assignment was to write a profile on the new Bucs. *Sports Illustrated* is
arguably the magazine of record as far as sports are concerned and being
the focus of one of their stories meant that you were considered a legitimate organization and a major league market. In addition to the profile,
Marshall would chronicle the action of the Rams game. While many
had expected the Rams to put the Bucs in their place, the surprise result
of the game provided *Sports Illustrated* with a great angle for a story: a
first-hand account of the upstart Bucs throwing aside years of frustration
and manhandling an elite team.

So pleased with the story were the editors, that they elected to put
the Buccaneers on the cover, another publicity jewel for the team and the
community. The player chosen for the honor was Dewey Selmon. The
photo was a close-up of Dewey's devastating hit on Lawrence McCutcheon after the hapless back had dropped a pass from Pat Haden. Showing
the bruising Selmon riding on the back of McCutcheon, whose legs look
wobbly and whose head is limp, as the ball bounces helplessly away, the
photo captured the physical domination the Bucs had meted out. The
headline above the photo read simply: "Tampa Bay: Unbeaten, Untied
and Unbelievable."

Marshall's article, "Time for Good Times in Tampa Bay," not only
delivered the news that the Buccaneers were experiencing newfound
success, "a real live rock 'em, sock' em football team," as Marshall wrote,
but also attempted to explain how the Bucs had improved so rapidly
while dispelling the conventional wisdom of football experts. Marshall's
view was that while the national press was focusing on the bumbling
Bucs of old, John McKay had put together a complete team right under
everyone's nose. Of particular interest to Marshall was the breakthrough
season of Ricky Bell. The former USC Trojan who had endured two
painful seasons had been an integral part of the Bucs ball control offense
against the Rams and had left the field to a standing ovation. Bell's quote
to Marshall encapsulated his own deliverance from losing as well as that
of his team. Said Bell, "We've had the bad times, and now the good times
are here."

Marshall was also curious to find out how some of the original
Bucs were dealing with winning. Some of the quotes Marshall collected
from the players revealed just how hard it was for the original crew to
continue to keep getting up from all the knock-downs and cruel jokes.

Apparently Buccaneer players had at one time been afraid to admit they were members of the local team. "When the players go out now," Dewey Selmon was quoted as saying, "a lot of them are wearing their Buc T-shirts in public." Added his brother Lee Roy, "I don't have to go to the drive-in window at McDonald's anymore. Now I feel safe walking right into the restaurant."

One thing all the players had in common was the fact that they believed they were playing for a loyal and courageous coach. While the nation was becoming interested in who the Buccaneers were as a team, the players wanted it to be known that they would be less than they were without Coach McKay.

"Getting through the last couple of years took guts on Coach McKay's part because everyone in the whole town was against him," Dewey Selmon told Marshall. "Our team was like the stock market. It was in a depression. He had two choices: sell us out by trading for more experienced players, or ride out the depression with the young ones he had. It would have been easy to shift the blame to us by simply suggesting that we couldn't do the job. But he stuck with us. He stood up and said, 'This is my plan and it'll work.' You've got to give him credit."

While Marshall's article was more of an introductory profile than a revolutionary shift in the national media's perspective of the Tampa Bay Buccaneers, it was a start. For the first time in their existence the Buccaneers had been the subjects of a national story that did not include a laugh track. They were actually the beneficiaries of a positive national profile

The undefeated start also brought long-deserved national attention to arguably the best player on the Buccaneers, Lee Roy Selmon. Selmon had toiled valiantly in relative obscurity for three years much to the cha-grin of his head coach. "Lee Roy always plays excellently," McKay had once stated. "It's too bad he doesn't talk more to get more notoriety. Maybe he should carry a flag and wave it when he makes a good play."

Loquacious was not the word to describe Selmon. Shy and gentle by nature, the knock on Lee Roy around the NFL was that he was too nice a guy to be a dominant player. Teammate Richard "Batman" Wood responded to that assertion with a laugh, "We were all nice guys off the field. Lee Roy was a great guy. But he was relentless; we knew Lee Roy was going to get there. When he played football he was a different person."

Despite three straight seasons of being among the league leaders in sacks, Lee Roy's gentle demeanor still led some to think he was ill suited for a NFL career. A closer look at the defensive lineman showed that there was not a career option in the world that would be ill suited for Lee Roy Selmon.

Lee Roy was the youngest of nine Selmon children. Luscious and Jessie Selmon raised their children in a sharecropping family on a 160-acre farm outside of the small Oklahoma town of Eufaula (pop. 2,355). The Selmon's had little in the way of material possessions, but they were given an overabundance of love by their parents and were brought up with a simple moral credo: remain humble, earn what you get and treat others with respect. Lee Roy in particular seemed to embrace this code.

On the first day of first grade his teacher told Lee Roy that his name should be spelled *Leroy*. Keeping in mind what his mother had said about respecting teachers, Lee Roy agreed and went the rest of his academic career spelling his name the way his teacher had told him to, even when he became an Oklahoma superstar with the Sooners. After being drafted in the first round, Lee Roy finally, somewhat sheepishly, informed the Buccaneers how his name was really spelled.

In addition to the moral code instilled by his parents, Lee Roy was also kept humble as his athletic abilities made him well known in Oklahoma by the fact that he had extremely little free time. Luscious Sr., who had spent so many years of backbreaking work providing for his family had come down with tuberculosis, which meant Lee Roy and his brothers had to do the lion share of the farm work and other jobs to provide income. Waking up before dawn the brothers would do farm chores before heading to school in advance of any other students to sweep out the school among other duties as part-time janitors. Then they would go to classes until early afternoon before heading to football practice. After practice they would head back home and finish up all the farm chores that needed to be done before settling in and completing their homework. It is a testament to their character and teamwork that the Selmon's were able to excel academically and athletically while still running a farm.

That humble nature served Lee Roy and older brother Dewey well and helped to cushion the blow of being selected by an unproven expansion team. Many collegiate stars hope to avoid being drafted by struggling teams, and the Bucs were certainly expected to struggle. Due to his nature the ever-optimistic Lee Roy could only see the positives. Looking back almost thirty years after being drafted Lee Roy concluded that being selected by Tampa Bay and meeting John McKay were momentous milestones in his life.

"I was thrilled to be drafted into the NFL," Selmon said. "Secondly, more exciting than that was when Tampa Bay drafted by brother Dewey, and we had the opportunity to come into the league on the same team. Surely those decisions were the result of scouting by Coach McKay. I started with a great appreciation of him and the Buccaneers for drafting Dewey and myself. Then having known about Coach McKay from his legendary career at USC I was very excited to come and play for him."

Not nearly as excited as McKay was to coach him. During those dark early days of the Bucs, McKay was often quoted as saying, "Whenever I want to feel good, I think about Lee Roy Selmon."

If McKay still wanted to feel good after the Chicago game, Lee Roy and the rest of the Buccaneers defense would have to deliver a great effort to stop Walter Payton.

The sky was crystal clear with brilliant sunshine and a faint breeze blowing off Lake Michigan when the two o'clock kickoff time rolled around. The 75-degree temperature was almost Floridian, meaning the Bucs had caught one break on this early fall Sunday in the Windy City, a metropolis notorious for rough weather year round. The game was to take place in one of the more unusual arenas in the National Football League. Soldier Field, the Bears home since the early seventies, was built in the early twentieth century and combined modern amenities with classic European architecture. With huge Doric columns reminiscent of the Acropolis overlooking an artificial playing surface, Soldier Field appeared to be suitable for professional football or the ancient Olympics. On this day it would be the site of Tampa Bay's attempt to keep their unbeaten record intact against another Central Division rival.

For the second straight road game the Buccaneers were subjected to the indignity of being a "homecoming" opponent. During the summer of 1979 legendary Bears linebacker Dick Butkus had been inducted into the Pro Football Hall of Fame. The Bears management chose the Tampa Bay game as a wonderful opportunity to invite former Bear greats such as Gale Sayers, Sid Luckman and others to Soldier Field to help honor

Butkus at halftime. Much as they had done in Green Bay, the Bucs hoped to ruin the festivities.

Led by another of McKay's former USC quarterbacks, Vince Evans who started in place of an injured Mike Phipps, the Bears first possession of the game was a quick three and out. The first two plays were runs by Payton that totaled only four yards. It seemed as though the Bucs defense was up to the task of controlling Sweetness.

The Bucs first drive was also a quick three play affair that resulted in a Tom Blanchard punt. While the first two drives of the game were not momentous as far as game action was concerned, they were historic nonetheless. With Williams and Evans starting at quarterback for Tampa Bay and Chicago respectively, this game was one of the few in National Football League history where two African-American quarterbacks were starting for both teams in the same game.

Neither team was interested in sociological advancement. The Bears at 2-2 were looking to cut into Tampa Bay's division lead and the rest of the quarter was a slugfest with a pair of excruciating near misses for both teams.

Midway through the first quarter Evans completely fooled the Bucs defense by faking a handoff to Payton. So keyed were they on stopping Payton, the Bucs defense forgot about Bears receiver Mike Cobb, who was free deep in Buccaneer territory. Evans' long pass hit Cobb right in the hands but the receiver inexplicably dropped the ball. The Solider Field crowd who had risen to its collective feet in anticipation of a long touchdown pass fell deathly silent.

The Bucs had dodged a bullet and now their offense had the ball with a chance to take the lead. Settling into a pattern of mixing runs and short passes, Williams led the Bucs from their own 20 down to the Chicago 34 on nine plays. With the Bears defense seemingly on the ropes, Jerry Eckwood took a handoff and promptly fumbled when hit by Bears safety Doug Plank. Fellow Bear Gary Fencik recovered the ball at the 31 and the Bucs most promising scoring chance was over.

In the first quarter both teams had blown scoring opportunities. In the second quarter Tampa Bay would take advantage of one. On first down at the Tampa Bay 39 following a Chicago punt, Jerry Eckwood took a pitch from Williams and headed to the right sideline. What the rookie from Arkansas saw in front of him could have been a vision from Coach McKay's dreams.

Offensive linemen Greg Horton and Greg Roberts escorted Eckwood past the line of scrimmage by throwing key blocks that cleared his path. Eckwood's escort service on this particular play consisted of more than Horton and Roberts however. As Eckwood reached midfield, the remaining Bears defenders converged on him, but receivers Morris Owens and Isaac Hagins, showing that they could do more than run routes, blasted out defensive backs Terry Schmidt and Gary Fencik. Those blocks left Eckwood one on one with safety Doug Plank at midfield. The Bears safety hit Eckwood head on, but Eckwood bounced off the tackle attempt and continued down the sideline. At the twenty, center Steve Wilson, who had sprinted thirty yards downfield to help out his running back cleared out the last remaining linebacker. At the ten yard line Eckwood took another hit, this time from defensive back Virgil Livers, but kept his balance and tip-toed into the end zone to complete a beautiful 61-yard touchdown run. Neil O'Donoghue's extra point made the score 7-0 Tampa Bay.

A football purist would have loved the play as both teams exhibited tenacious desire. On the Bucs side every player who could throw a block did so effectively, and when a Bear defender did get to Eckwood, the rookie ran hard and under control, keeping his balance and fighting off tackle attempts. The run was impressive also because of the effort of the Bear defense. While many teams would have simply given up once Eckwood reached the sideline, Livers and Plank showed the heart that made the Bears the leading defense against the run as they attempted to construct roadblock after roadblock in Eckwood's path.

The touchdown by the Bucs seemed to spook the Bears. On their next drive Vince Evans fumbled the snap from center and Cecil Johnson quickly recovered it. On the very next play Williams looked to capitalize rapidly. With a flick of the wrist Williams found an open Hagins in the end zone. Unfortunately, Hagins was looking directly into the bright sunshine and never saw the ball land right at his feet.

Undaunted, Williams and the offense tried another play to the end zone. For the second time an open receiver couldn't make the play as the usually reliable Morris Owens dropped the pass. While it seemed that Williams had rifled the ball, there is an unwritten rule that if a receiver gets both hands on the ball, he should catch it. Owens' drop forced the Bucs to attempt a field goal. O'Donoghue, who had been one of the rare Buc players to struggle in 1979, missed the kick when the ball bounced off of the right upright. That left the Irishman two for seven in field goal attempts on the season, and coupled with the missed touchdown passes, could have deflated Tampa Bay. Instead it seemed to anger them.

The defense forced another three and out by the Bears and Coach McKay sent in a razzle-dazzle play to get some more points on the board before the end of the first half. Sensing that the Bears were starting to key on Eckwood and Bell, McKay took advantage. Williams took the snap at the Chicago 30 and faked a handoff around right end to Ricky Bell. As the Bears defense flowed to the right side of the field to stop Bell, tight end Jimmie Giles, who was lined up on the right side, sprinted left from his blocking position and took the ball from Williams on a reverse hand-off. Giles headed to the open left side of the field at full speed. Before the Bears linebackers could recover, Giles hit the corner and turned upfield. Only a force out by an alert Bears defensive back at the 17 prevented another Tampa Bay touchdown.

Sadly for the Bucs the old problem of untimely penalties reared its ugly head again when Greg Roberts was called for a holding penalty. The infraction moved the ball back to the Bears 27-yard line. This forced another O'Donoghue field goal attempt. The tall kicker shook off his earlier miss and connected on a 30-yarder that gave the Bucs a 10-0 lead three minutes before halftime.

The Bucs should have taken the shutout into the locker room, but for the first time on the afternoon the Tampa Bay defense gave up big yardage. From the Chicago 30, Vince Evans moved the Bears steadily downfield with long passes to James Scott and Walter Payton. From the seventeen, Evans saw an open Scott in the end zone and hit the receiver in the corner for an apparent touchdown. Officials ruled the receiver out of bounds, and replays confirmed this. On the next play, Evans again saw an open receiver in the end zone, tight end Greg Latta who had gotten behind Mike Washington. This time Evans threw poorly, lofting the ball well over Latta's head. The two incompletions forced a field goal attempt and on fourth down, Bob Thomas successfully booted a 34-yard field goal to cut Tampa Bay's lead to 10-3.

While Tampa Bay went into the locker room at halftime with a seven-point lead, Coach McKay could not have been very pleased. His team was dominating play but had blown multiple scoring opportunities and had been very blasé on defense during the Bears final drive, allowing receivers to run virtually free. Instead of being up 17-0 or 21-0 as they could have very easily been, the Bucs were clinging to their seven-point advantage. If they hoped to stay undefeated, Tampa Bay's offense would have to play much better in the second half, but unfortunately they spent the third quarter and much of the fourth in a funk that cost them the lead.

Leading the Bucs in their attempts to provide the Bears with every opportunity to take over the game were receivers Morris Owens, Gordon Jones and Isaac Hagins. In the first half Owens and Hagins had misplayed certain touchdown throws by Williams. In the second half Jones, the rookie out of Pittsburgh, followed the lead of his veteran teammates. Following a 42-yard field goal by Bob Thomas that had hit the upright but had bounced in unlike O'Donoghue's, the Bucs lead was 10-6 midway through the third quarter. Needing a big play to sustain a drive to answer the Chicago score, Doug Williams looked to his rookie receiver on second down from the Tampa Bay 40. Jones was open over the middle on a crossing pattern and Williams hit him perfectly in stride. Jones who was several steps in front of the nearest Bears defender had an open path to the end zone, but he shifted his gaze to the clear path ahead of him rather than focusing on the ball and dropped it. Jones' drop effectively killed the Bucs drive and kept the momentum clearly on Chicago's side.

While Tampa Bay's offense had been futile in the second half, the Buccaneer defense had gamely kept the team in the lead. Early in the fourth quarter the defense finally gave up a big play to the man they had thus far effectively contained, Walter Payton.

On the first play following yet another Tom Blanchard punt, Evans dropped back to pass from the Bear 35. The Bucs read the pass attempt well as Bill Kollar and Lee Roy Selmon quickly pressured Evans. What Selmon, Kollar and the rest of the Bucs defense didn't realize was that Evans' plan was to attempt the passing equivalent of a long handoff to Payton. As the Bucs defensive line rushed upfield, the Bears offensive lineman, who had simply let the defenders through, raced out left in front of Payton. Evans hit Payton at the line of scrimmage and watched as Sweetness was led down the sideline by a convoy of blockers that looked reminiscent of Eckwood's second quarter touchdown.

The offensive line took care of the linebacking corps of Selmon, Lewis, Johnson and Wood, leaving only cornerback Jeris White with a legitimate shot of stopping a full-speed Payton. Fighting off the block attempt of wide receiver Golden Richards, White hit Payton at the goal line but was run over by the tailback. The touchdown, once again a thing of beauty for football purists because of the effort of both the offense and the defense, gave the Bears a 13-10 lead with eleven minutes to play. It was also shockingly swift and showed off the fact that while a defense could contain Payton for the majority of the day, the runner was always a threat to break a big play at any given moment from any point on the field.

The play also may have planted seeds of doubt in the minds of Tampa Bay fans watching the game on their television sets. Was this the day the Bucs would suffer their first loss? Because the kickoff of the game had been at 2 p.m. EST rather than the customary 1 p.m., viewers of the Bucs-Bears game had been receiving finals from around the league as the fourth quarter progressed and saw that the other undefeated clubs had finally lost. Cross-state rival Miami lost a thriller to the New York Jets 33-27 while the Houston Oilers blew out Cleveland 31-10. As Tampa Bay armchair quarterbacks digested those scores they were informed of the day's biggest upset. The Philadelphia Eagles had upset their Keystone State rivals Pittsburgh 17-14, knocking the defending Super Bowl champions from the ranks of the unbeaten. If the Bucs were to be spared the same fate that befell Miami, Cleveland and Pittsburgh, the Buc offense would have to do something they hadn't done all day: finish a sustained drive with a touchdown.

The Bucs received a boost to their efforts when Bob Thomas failed to properly connect with the football on his kickoff. The ball bounced and squibbed only about 20 yards down the field where Buccaneer blocker Dana Nafziger, a back-up linebacker and kick team specialist scooped up the ball and ran back to the Tampa Bay 46-yard line. With 54 yards to traverse and over ten minutes left in the game, McKay eschewed throwing to his under-performing receivers. Instead the placid coach elected to do what he felt his team did best, run the ball down the defense's throat, even though that defense was the best in the league at stopping the run.

Hitching his offensive wagon to the backs of Eckwood, Bell and his offensive line, McKay watched his team execute one of the most clutch drives in the history of the franchise. Running straight up the middle of a defense deployed specifically to stop him, Bell carried three times, gaining 20 yards, 13 of them on a hard charge up the gut that saw the former Trojan carry several Bear tacklers the last couple of yards. Spent after the run, Bell was replaced by the shifty Eckwood, who zigzagged his way to the Bears' 26-yard line. After six straight runs had put Tampa Bay in scoring position, McKay called on Williams to try a pass to one of his receivers. Showing confidence in players who had had a rough day paid off for McKay as Gordon Jones recovered from his earlier gaffe and hauled in Williams' pass at the 16-yard line.

Having shown the pass, McKay went back to the run and Bell and Johnny "Bull" Davis carried the Bucs to the 8-yard line on back-to-back runs. Facing a third down with two yards to go, everyone in Soldier Field sensed the Bucs would run up the middle to get the first down before attempting any end zone plays. McKay had other ideas, and this time he gave another receiver a shot at redemption.

Williams faked a handoff to Bell, which sucked the linebackers closer to the line of scrimmage, allowing Jimmie Giles some room to work the middle. Williams pump faked in the direction of Giles in the middle of the field, which froze the safeties that weren't sure whether to jump on Giles' route or provide extra protection on the Bucs wideouts. Williams made them pay for their indecision by throwing into the right corner of the end zone to Isaac Hagins who had beaten his defender to the sideline for a touchdown that gave the Bucs the lead. The touchdown reception was a fitting way for Hagins to atone for the sure touchdown he had mis-played when he lost the ball in the sun in the first half.

Neil O'Donoghue's extra point was good and the Bucs led 17-13 with a little over five minutes to play in the game. The offense had answered the challenge of driving down the field on the road against the best rush-ing defense with an undefeated record and their division standing on the line. Now it was the defense's turn to take the Buccaneers home to Tampa winners again.

On the Bears first drive after the Buccaneers took the lead, corner-back Cedric Brown intercepted Evans near midfield. The Bucs offense was unable to run down the Bears throat this time. Just after the two minute warning Tampa Bay was forced to punt the ball back to Chicago. Remembering that they had given up an easy drive during the final minutes of the first half, the Bucs defense was determined not to repeat history this day. On the first play of the drive, Jeris White stepped up and intercepted a poorly thrown pass at the Chicago 45-yard line. White had spent his last few offseason's pursuing his commercial real estate license and on the deciding play of the game, he showed he owned the middle of Soldier Field when it counted most. Out of time-outs the Bears could only watch as the Bucs ran out the clock and left the field 5-0 after a hard fought game. Given the results around the rest of the NFL it could be argued that after five games the Tampa Bay Buccaneers, the same team that everyone loved to watch lose, was now the best team in all of professional football.

The win not only made the Tampa Bay the only undefeated team in the NFL, but the Bucs now held a three-game lead in the NFC Central Division over Chicago. The teams would meet a second time in Tampa come December but for now the players just wanted to crow.

"The Bucs have come of age," said defensive tackle Wally Chambers, who carried a cardboard placard around the locker room adorned with a Buccaneer logo and bearing the inscription **We Are For Real**. "We've thrown that diaper away. We're wearing dress slacks now." The victory was personal for Chambers. He had been a NFL defensive player of the year in 1975 and 1976 while with the Bears. Chambers injured his knees in 1977 and was deemed expendable. Shrugging off doubts about Chamber's health, McKay traded a number one pick for the former standout to provide athleticism to his defensive front wall. So far in 1979 the move seemed to be paying off.

After five games most of McKay's moves seemed to be paying off.

CHAPTER 7

Getting Ahead of Themselves

The Tampa Bay area had supported the Buccaneers through thin and thinner from 1976 to 1978. As the home of the only undefeated team in the National Football League, Tampa Bay became absolutely infatuated with the team. While most of the nation was rocking to tunes such as My Sharona by The Knack or YMCA by the Village People, Tampa Bay stations were being inundated with requests for "Hey, Hey, Tampa Bay the Bucs Know How to Shine" by Jeff Arthur.

Employing the disco beat of the time, Arthur's song was a big hit at Tampa Stadium, but given the 5-0 start by the team it had been enjoying more and more air play over Tampa Bay radio stations. At stoplights, shopping malls or even in offices one could see a group of men and women spelling out the word Buccaneers during the songs infectious opening. Florida orange and red became the colors of Monday through Friday life in Tampa Bay rather than just being the hue found in Tampa Stadium on fall Sundays. For the first time since the inception of the franchise, there was true pride in having a National Football League team in town.

Looking back on the heady first quarter of the 1979 season many years later, *St. Petersburg Times* columnist Hubert Mizell recalled fondly that for the first time in his memory all of Tampa Bay had something to rally around in the Buccaneers' string of victories.

"When the Bucs had success, there was more of a kinship between both sides of the bay, but it would always be limited (to football). That big dose of water is a barrier that, into the 21st century, keeps the Tampa Bay area from ever truly feeling like a single entity." The reason according to Mizell is that most Bay area denizens view a trip across the bay as appealing "as a swim across the English Channel."

In addition to the albeit temporary and gridiron-inspired bonding of all sides of the Tampa Bay area, Mizell and his journalistic colleagues also enjoyed newfound stature as sources of information for the national media on the sports hottest team. "It was fun," Mizell admitted. "Writing about winners is easier than the throbbing life of telling of loss after loss. It was rewarding to see national attention and, being a writer with many pals in that contingent, it was good to have them looking our way and asking me questions about the team I covered."

The Buccaneers possessed the best record in the National Football League and were the darlings of the Suncoast. This status presented Coach McKay with a special problem. He needed to keep his team from becoming overconfident. With the recent national press attention and a thrilling come from behind victory on the road against a division rival, McKay knew that the Bucs could easily forget to focus on their upcoming opponent. The fact that the opponent was the winless New York Giants wouldn't help McKay in stressing how important the game would be.

McKay used the old coach's trick of reverse psychology to keep his team from getting a case of big-head disease. While proud of the victory over the Bears, McKay let it be known the game should have never come down to a dramatic rally. "When you gain 373 yards you should score more than 17 points," McKay asserted.

McKay also took his defense to task even though they had only surrendered one touchdown. "You cannot allow Walter Payton to turn his shoulders and head upfield. You must keep him running sideways. As soon as he turned his shoulders Sunday I yelled, 'Block that kick!'"

McKay was pleased with the publicity that came from defeating teams from Los Angeles and Chicago, the second-and-third largest media markets in the nation. It was gratifying for him to see his players finally receive some recognition nationally. He felt that the Tampa Bay Buccaneers were on the verge of shedding their comic reputation. A win in front of the New York media, the most prestigious and influential contingent in the country, would solidify the Bucs reputation as an elite team.

Concern over how the New York press would perceive the Buccaneers was valid for unlike the previous week, not all the national attention was as polite as the *Sports Illustrated* piece had been.

One naysayer in particular, David Israel of *Gridweek,* put forth the theory that the Bucs were not the NFL's Cinderella, they were merely scullery maids and nothing more. Entitled "Tampa Bay Doesn't Really Deserve to Win," Israel's article laid out three arguments against the Bucs being considered a legitimate playoff team.

The first argument was that the Bucs were the beneficiary of a last-place schedule. Finishing last the previous season meant that the Bucs did not have to play as difficult a schedule as the Bears, Vikings, Lions and Packers. For instance the Bucs did not have to play the AFC East as their division rivals did. Instead of playing the Dolphins or Patriots, two solid playoff contenders, the Bucs played the New York Giants twice. According to Israel this would have give the Bucs a huge advantage.

When the Bucs did play their division rivals, Israel argued, they benefited from the fact that the NFC Central was possibly the worst division in football. The Lions were hurt, the Vikings were old, the Bears were a one-man team and the Packers were horrible went Israel's position. Even if the Bucs were to win the division, they would be quickly squashed in the playoffs when they played a team with real talent.

Lastly, Israel stated that if the Bucs were in the AFC, they would have a losing record. In 1979 the AFC possessed the "elite teams" of the league. With the exception of the NFC's Dallas Cowboys, the AFC had won every Super Bowl in the decade (One by the Colts, one by the Raiders, two by the Dolphins and three by the Steelers). In addition to those teams the San Diego Chargers and Houston Oilers were also thought of as Super Bowl contenders. The Bucs simply did not have the offense or defense to compete against these teams week in and week out claimed Israel. The Bucs not only benefited from a weak schedule and a weak division, they also benefited from being in an inferior conference.

In closing Israel wrote, "It is a travesty to mention the Bucs in the same breadth as the Steelers, the Chargers, the Oilers, or even USC."

Offensive tackle Charley Hannah had been eerily prescient of opinions such as Israel's. In the locker room after the Bears game Hannah had told reporters, "Even though we're 5-0, a lot of people still won't believe we're any good."

If Hannah and his teammates wanted to prove the Israel's of the world wrong, they would have a chance to do so in the media capital of the world.

When the Buccaneer offense took to the field on a gray, blustery day in Giants Stadium they confronted a defense both familiar and unexpected. If imitation is the sincerest form of flattery, the New York Giants complimented McKay by coming out in a 3-4 defensive alignment. After years of hearing how his scheme wouldn't work, McKay was seeing it used against him. The plagiarism may have vindicated McKay as a tactician, but it also would drive him and Doug Williams crazy on this day.

For the first 30 minutes of the contest the Giants' version of the 3-4 befuddled the Tampa Bay offense. Unfortunately the Buccaneer defense chose this day to play one of their worst games in recent memory. Gashed consistently for big yardage by the Giants unheralded running back Billy Taylor, the Tampa Bay defense gave up two touchdowns in the first half.

The Buccaneers offense failed to generate any sustained drives until intermission loomed, and even that one was helped by a Giant mistake. Defensive end Gary Jeter hit Williams late, a personal foul that cost the Giants fifteen yards and gave Tampa Bay a first down near midfield as the two minute warning sounded. The penalty sparked the Bucs and Williams drove the team down the field. A 14-yard touchdown pass from Williams to Larry Mucker capped the drive. Mucker's reception was hardly as pretty as the one he had snared against the Rams two weeks earlier. Mucker was caught somewhat off-guard by the Williams fastball and the ball caromed off his hands, bounced off his helmet and headed towards the ground. Mucker was able to corkscrew his body counter clockwise to stab the ball before it hit the ground. Neil O'Donoghue's extra point made the score 14-7 in favor of New York at halftime.

The lethargy displayed by Tampa Bay in the first half was something McKay had feared all week. Publicity for his players was something he had desired, but McKay knew it could come at a price. The distractions of being on the cover of national magazines and in demand by television and radio reporters might now be taking a toll on the team during a game. McKay could only hope that his team would snap out their collective funk and play to the level they had during the five-game winning streak.

For its part the defense was able to improve their level of play during the second half. Successfully clamping down on Billy Taylor, the Bucs turned their sights on rookie quarterback Phil Simms. Blitzing Mark Cotney from the safety position on numerous occasions, the Bucs caught the young Kentuckian off-guard and kept him from leading the Giants on any drives.

Unlike the defense, the Tampa Bay offense was still the epitome of malaise. Ricky Bell was unable to find running room and the few times Williams had time to throw, his receiving corps would betray him with several drops of easy to catch passes. Early in the fourth quarter a Williams pass attempt to Morris Owens was intercepted by Terry Jackson and returned to the Tampa Bay 31. The Giants did not move the ball, but were already in field goal range. Joe Danelo's 47-yard kick was good and the Giants enjoyed a 17-7 lead with only ten minutes to play.

Desperate to catch up the Bucs continued to throw the ball but to no avail. A touchdown pass from Williams to Giles with less than two minutes remaining gave the team a spark of hope but a failed onsides kick attempt scuttled any chances for victory. For the first time in 1979 the Buccaneers walked off a field losers, 17-14.

"The Giants outplayed us in every way," a calm McKay said after the game. The coach was right. The Giants' offense ran for over two hundred yards and its defense throttled Tampa Bay. "Just say we got out-hit, out-blocked, out-tackled, out-punted and out-coached. Perhaps it was hard to remember that if you don't play well in this league, you'll get beat. That happened to us today."

Asked if the Giants use of the 3-4 defense had caught the team by surprise, McKay admitted that it did but it shouldn't have been that big a deal. "It's our own defense so the offensive line shouldn't be strangers to it. The Giants played it pretty well considering it was the first time they had played it, but anytime you play a new defense you're going to make mistakes. They made some mistakes but we didn't take advantage of them." Little did McKay know that in the years to come many teams in the NFL would start to employ the 3-4.

While McKay was gracious in defeat the Giants gloated in victory. A winless team coming into the game, the Giants still claimed that they had no doubts they would beat Tampa for one simple reason: the Bucs were not impressive. Giant offensive lineman Doug Van Horn said, " We haven't lost to them yet," while teammate J. T. Turner chimed in, "We always beat the heck out of those guys."

What hurt the Bucs more than the scorn of the Giants was the fact that they had flopped on Broadway. McKay hoped that the loss in front of New York's media wouldn't sour the nation on what the Bucs had accomplished so far. "The people who only saw us against New York are probably entitled to think our record is a fluke after that performance. But the people who follow us know we can play much better than that."

Sadly for McKay, the Buccaneers would play their worst game of the season the very next Sunday in front of the people who most closely followed the team. And the reaction of those souls would not be pretty.

After a week of trying to correct the mistakes of the Giants game the Buccaneers took to the field against the New Orleans Saints on a sunny day in Tampa Stadium. McKay had apparently kept his team in loose spirits throughout the week, telling them "Smile, the world hasn't ended." It was also reported that McKay lightened the mood in the locker room immediately following the Giants game by dusting off an old chestnut from his college days. "I told them what I told my USC team that lost 51-0. 'Those who need showers take them.'"

While McKay may have been trying to lift the spirits of his team the New Orleans Saints were determined to crush them. The Saints had never truly recovered from their 33-14 loss to the Bucs in 1977. That loss had cost Hank Stram his coaching job with the Saints and sent the team into a spiral that lasted for most of the 1978 season. One player who escaped the blues of New Orleans had been quarterback Archie Manning, the NFL Most Valuable Player in 1978. In a backfield that included Chuck Muncie and Tony Galbreath, Manning was a member of a talented trio that had improved the Saints rapidly in 1979 and they were determined to make the Bucs pay for 1977.

The Saints game was christened "Orange Sunday" by the Buccaneer marketing department. The point of "Orange Sunday" was to make Tampa Stadium appear to be a sea of Florida orange. Most fans arrived for home games wearing some orange, but for "Orange Sunday," the Buccaneers asked their fans to wear as much of the color as possible. To help with the sartorial salute, the marketing staff handed out orange Buccaneer visors and caps to fans before the game. After a scoreless first half, many in the stands used the caps to ward off boredom but in the second half they used them to shield their eyes from a debacle.

When Ricky Bell raced around end for a 49-yard gain to the New Orleans 23 on the first possession of the second half things looked up for Tampa Bay. When Doug Williams found Isaac Hagins with a 22-yard touchdown pass things started to look even brighter. But then things started to fall apart in dramatically rapid fashion.

The Saints tied the game quickly on a touchdown run by Manning. One series later the Saints took a 14-7 lead on a Tony Galbreath run of six yards. The defense which had successfully corralled the Saints in the first half was showing all the strength of papier-mâché in the second. A few moments later Doug Williams tossed an interception that was returned to the sixteen-yard line by Elois Grooms. As he left the field Williams was cascaded with boos from the sell-out crowd. Fairly or not the fans were upset with how the game was going and chose this particular play to unleash a torrent of invective on Williams. The young quarterback talked briefly with McKay and then stewed on the sidelines. Whether Williams was angry with himself of the reaction of the fans would be left a mystery until the post-game interviews.

With the ball in great field position the Saints went for the jugular. Archie Manning, benefiting from a great rushing performance from his backfield, faked a hand-off and floated an easy touchdown to Henry Childs to put the Saints up 21-7.

The Bucs spirits seemed to sag from the quick touchdown the Saints scored following the interception. The fans sprits were affected as well, but they sure were not quiet about it. In a matter of moments the Bucs had gone from leading by seven to trailing by fourteen. The switch in momentum had been so fast that Buc fans may not have known exactly what or who to boo, starting at first with Williams in particular and now moving on to the rest of the team. What the fans lacked in focus they made up for in volume as they loudly denigrated almost every decision, snap and play that occurred for the rest of the contest.

The volume of the booing increased tenfold when Williams overthrew Morris Owens on fourth down on the very next possession. The conversion attempt on fourth down from deep within their own territory would have been viewed as a shrewd attempt by McKay to get his deflated team back into the game had it succeeded, but the failure to achieve a first down only increased the volume of the fans. When the Saints quickly capitalized with a 20-yard touchdown sprint to make the score 28-7 it seemed as though there would be nothing for fans to cheer about the rest of the day.

That is unless of course the tone of the cheers was sarcastic in nature.

After the Saints kicked-off a loud ovation spread through the stadium when back-up quarterback Mike Rae led the team onto the field. It has often been said that the most popular player on the roster is the back-up quarterback of a team that is struggling. The praise for Rae's insertion into the game seemed to be more of an indictment of Williams than appreciation for Rae's skills. That feeling was proven valid a few moments later.

When the Saints scored on their fifth straight possession of the second half to make the score 35-7 the fans turned their wrath on Lee Roy, Dewey and the rest of a Tampa Bay defense that until this game had been the stoutest in the league. When Rae was intercepted on the very next possession, the fans showed that they showed no favorites by booing Rae as loudly as they had Williams. It was no surprise on this day when absolutely nothing was going right for the team that New Orleans scored yet another touchdown. A seven-yard run by virtual unknown Michael Strachan put the Saints up 42-7.

A meaningless 21-yard touchdown pass from Rae to Jimmie Giles with just over a minute to play made the score a little closer, but the 42-14 defeat still represented the worst showing by the team ever at Tampa Stadium.

Witnessing the debacle from his seat in the press box, PR assistant Rick Odioso learned a valuable lesson about the NFL. Not everything is always as it appears. The day was bright and sunny, with a great deal of heat and humidity. Watching the pre-game warm-ups and the first half of the game Odioso came to the conclusion that the Saints, used to the air-conditioned comfort of the Superdome, were going to be easy pickings for Tampa Bay. "The Saints game was a strange game, boy. That was like wacko. Scoreless at the half and then we score, and they score 42 straight. I remember sitting in the press box, seeing the Saints struggling in the heat in the first half. Football expert I am, I said, 'They're whipped, they got nothing left.'"

If only that had been the case the mood in the Tampa Bay post-game locker room would have been much more pleasant.

Doug Williams was not pleased about anything that had taken place in Tampa Stadium this day. He had played poorly which upset him, but he was also quite annoyed at how he had been singled out for abuse by the fans.

"We've got some good fans and we've got some who aren't worth a damn," Williams declared. "The fans are not taking care of me. The hell with them. Does it bother me? No, I'm going to the bank tomorrow.

"You lose two games and everybody starts booing. If we had won today, those same people would have said, 'we won.' But when we lost they said, 'you lost.'"

Being booed was nothing new to Williams, and for the most part he had exemplified the teaching of Grambling's legendary Eddie Robinson when it came to dealing with hecklers. "You learn to come in and perform and do your duties," Williams recalled looking back on his career. "I was taught early at Grambling that we are in the entertainment business. The fans had a right to boo if they paid to see a game. You can't get caught up in that part of the game. You can't get caught up in whether someone is booing you or cheering you."

Sadly Williams had had to deal with worse than that growing up as a child of the Deep South. As a youth Williams was a witness to acts of intimidation by the Ku Klux Klan, including cross burnings on the street he lived on. Additionally, Williams had a milkshake thrown in his face by an unknown assailant while running an errand for his grandmother downtown.

Trying to escape the pressures of the world on the athletic field, Williams only encountered more racial strife. Zachary, like the rest of the Deep South was struggling with integration. When Chaneyville High School announced during Williams' freshman year that it was integrating, many white families refused to send their children to the school. During his time at the high school, Williams only had one white teammate on the football team. Williams became one of the first blacks in the area to play American Legion baseball, and therefore became a marked man on the field. During one game Williams was repeatedly called "nigger" by players, coaches and fans and was physically assaulted during a play at the plate by the opposing catcher. Williams did enjoy a small modicum of revenge later in the game when he "tagged out" the catcher by hitting him in the face with the ball.

Despite the hostility, Williams persevered and played baseball and football at a high enough level to win a scholarship to Grambling where the legendary Eddie Robinson coached him. While at Grambling, Williams excelled as a deep passer who could scramble and punish any defensive player not prepared to get hit by a quarterback. Under Williams' leadership, the Tigers won four consecutive Southwestern Athletic Conference championships, winning 35 of the 40 games Williams played. After the 1977 season, Williams finished fourth nationally in the Heisman Trophy voting and was named the Most Valuable Player in the East-West Shrine Game and passed for over 250 yards in the Senior Bowl. Despite these glowing statistics, there were many questions and doubts about Williams, which allowed him to fall in the draft where the Buccaneers were only too happy to select him.

Williams' selection by the Buccaneers was truly a storybook come to life for the young man from Louisiana. Growing up he had dreamt of playing for one of two legendary coaches and when it came time for him to pick a school he was worried that if he chose poorly he'd regret it. Ironically his choices were Eddie Robinson at Grambling or John McKay at Southern Cal. Williams chose Grambling, and in being drafted by the Buccaneers was ecstatic to learn that he would be given the rare chance to see two life-long dreams come true.

"I think I was fortunate to get a chance to play for Eddie Robinson," Williams says today. "I was also lucky in the pros. Growing up there were two schools I wanted to play for. If I couldn't play for Grambling, I wanted to play for USC. I know that sounds kind of crazy because at the time John McKay was the coach at USC. I was a USC fan simply because Jimmy Jones had played there.

"Jimmy Jones was a quarterback for USC and John McKay back in the sixties, before African-American quarterbacks were popular at major institutions."

Williams knew how blessed he had been in coming under the influence of both men. In Robinson, Williams had found a life mentor. "I'm glad I had that opportunity (learning under Robinson), because I can truly say he was more than a coach. He was someone we all looked up too and aspired to. Because of the way he handled us and treated us. It wasn't about just football it was about life. It was about supporting yourself."

In the NFL Williams was granted a rare opportunity for a man of color. He would be allowed to grow as a quarterback under a man who cared not about the color of one's skin, but one's ability as a football player. "Truly luck and a dream come true to want to go to USC and play for McKay or go to Grambling and play for Coach Rob and end up playing for both."

During the Saints game the fans and New Orleans defense was making life as a starting quarterback a nightmare. In addition to McKay's tutelage, Williams had a second important personality to guide him. In the Buccaneers offensive backfield Williams could find a soul mate, a man who had experienced first-hand the same angry fans that Williams was enduring.

His name was Ricky Bell.

CHAPTER 8

Run Ricky Run

The torrent of boos that Doug Williams heard during the Saints game certainly would have brought back bad memories for Ricky Bell had he been the type to focus on the negative. Instead Bell saw a chance to guide an embattled teammate through a storm. Bell's positive outlook on life not only kept him on an even keel during two tumultuous seasons in Tampa Bay; it made him arguably the most popular player in the locker room.

Bell was drafted by Tampa Bay with the first overall pick in the 1977 draft. It was a move that stunned fans and pundits. By choosing Bell, the Buccaneers had missed the opportunity to draft Heisman Trophy winner Tony Dorsett out of Pitt. As the fans howled, John McKay explained that he wanted Bell for three reasons. First was McKay's familiarity with Bell from their time together at USC. Second was Bell's status as one of the most beloved players in the USC program. Teammates and coaches praised Bell's unselfishness and McKay knew an expansion team needed that trait more than Dorsett's glamour. Last was Bell's physical stature. At 6'2" and 220 pounds Bell was much larger than the 5'10" 185 pound Dorsett. The power-running that was a staple of McKay's I formation needed a man who wouldn't wear down and the coach felt Bell was better suited for the job than the smallish Dorsett.

That logic didn't completely win over critics. *St. Petersburg Times* columnist Hubert Mizell still thinks the Bucs might have been better served by Dorsett but knew that McKay was adamant about the abilities of his former pupil. "McKay pushed hard for Bell because he coached Ricky at USC," Mizell said. "McKay believed in Bell in the strongest of ways. Surely it would have been more useful for the Bucs to get Dorsett, but John so believed in Bell that I think he would've picked him over Jim Brown or Gale Sayers."

As Bell suffered through injury-plagued seasons in 1977 and 1978 the Tampa Bay fans never let him forget that they had wanted Dorsett. To make matters worse as Bell struggled, Dorsett flourished. Drafted by the Dallas Cowboys immediately after Tampa Bay chose Bell, Dorsett enjoyed back-to-back 1,000 yard seasons and led the Cowboys to two Super Bowls and one world championship. Week after week Bell was reminded of Dorsett's exploits and booed by fans.

To his credit Bell never let the comparisons to Dorsett bother him. He had the maturity to realize that he was never going to be the same runner as Dorsett simply because the men had different styles. "Tony is a great runner," Bell admitted, "I know what I must do. I've never set out to prove I am better than Dorsett. There always can be someone out there who is better than you. Nothing is given to you. You must earn it. Life doesn't owe any individual anything."

Just as his coach had finally lost patience with the criticism and blasted Bill Brundige, Bell reached a boiling point as his rookie season wound down. In week eleven against the Atlanta Falcons the Buccaneers were in the process of being shut out again, 17-0. This was a particularly abysmal loss as the Bucs offense produced only 78 yards the entire game. Late in the game the fans behind the bench were taunting Bell, who was sidelined with an injured knee after gaining only 11 yards. Bell, who had up to this point ignored the taunts, turned to the fans and shouted "Come on down here! If it's that bad, just come on down!" When his hecklers didn't move and increased the volume of their taunts, Bell charged the retaining wall and began climbing up into the stands, intent on throttling his attackers. Teammate George Ragsdale and members of the Tampa Police kept Bell from hitting the fans, and Bell stormed back to the sideline and sat quietly, his face a dark mask of anger for the rest of the game.

After he had a chance to cool down, Bell admitted to the press that he shouldn't have let the heckler get to him. "I know I shouldn't have done it. I've never been a fighter. But it was just the frustration, everything, the whole season . . . saying we'd never win." It seemed that all of the stars were against Bell. In addition to the knee injury, Bell suffered injuries to his ankle and shoulder that caused him to miss significant playing time. Bell's 1978 season wasn't much better than his first and he found himself splitting playing time with rookie running back Jerry Eckwood in 1979.

Eckwood had rushed for more than 100 yards against Detroit and Chicago and narrowly missed the century mark against Green Bay at Lambeau Field. Many players in a situation similar to Bell's may have felt resentment and become a team cancer. But that was not Bell's style. Instead he threw himself into the role of lead blocker for Eckwood on many plays, displaying the selflessness that had so endeared him to McKay. Against Chicago Eckwood hurt his wrist and wasn't able to run as effectively as before so Bell saw his number of carries per game increase. Perhaps revitalized by the team's fast start, Bell responded by running with a power and authority not seen since his days at USC. Bell had been the only bright spot against New Orleans, rushing for 101 yards in the lopsided loss.

During practice in the week leading up to the Packer game Bell spent a good deal of time not just working on plays with Williams, but coaching him through a trying time. "I can honestly say that the guy that kept me out of the tank and kept my head focused was Ricky Bell," Williams admitted many years later. "He told me, 'Hey man, when I came here they were on me like that because they wanted Tony Dorsett.' They didn't want him, but he said, 'You have got to keep your head up.'"

Whatever Bell told Williams seemed to work because when the Bucs took to the field against the Packers both men enjoyed performances to remember.

It was another sunny day in Tampa Bay and a sell-out crowd filled Tampa Stadium to see if the Buccaneers could defeat a division rival and increase their chances of winning the NFC Central. Among the more than 68,000 in attendance was Ruthie Bell, the mother of Ricky Bell. Ruthie had flown in from California to watch her son play and he responded to her presence by giving the gift of a record rushing day.

It became apparent on the first drive of the game for the Buccaneers that McKay decided to ease some of the burden off of Williams' shoulders and place the mantle of playmaker on Ricky Bell. If his first few runs were any indication, Bell was certainly up to the responsibility.

With runs of 19 and 26 yards in his first carries, Bell ran around, past, over and through a Green Bay defense that often had eight men near the line of scrimmage in an attempt to force the struggling Williams to beat them. When the Buccaneers moved inside the Green Bay 10-yard line, Bell proved himself more versatile than any Buc fan had given him credit for when he practically convulsed in an attempt to get Doug Williams attention when he ran a pass pattern into the end zone. The Packers, who probably thought of Bell as one-dimensionally as Buc fans had, neglected to cover Bell out of the backfield and left him all alone. Leaping frantically and shouting at the top of his lungs, Bell got Williams' attention and clasped both hands tightly on a nine-yard touchdown reception that culminated an efficient 68-yard drive. Neil O'Donoghue's extra point put the Bucs up 7-0 and left the crowd at Tampa Stadium buzzing over the one-man wrecking crew in the orange jersey with the number 42 on it. Bell's performance on the first drive was merely a prelude of what was to come.

Gaining three to four yards a pop, Bell kept the chains moving as the Buccaneers continued to grind out yards through the first half. While not all the drives led to points, they did keep the battle for field position well in Tampa Bay's favor and also severely fatigued a Green Bay defense that was growing exhausted by Bell and the heat and humidity.

One drive that did lead to points was vintage McKay. Having run Bell so often that Green Bay was obsessed with stopping him, McKay unshackled Williams and let him go long. Williams responded by connecting on two big passes, 18 yards to Jimmie Giles and 31 yards to Jerry Eckwood. The pass to Eckwood gave the Bucs first and goal at the Green Bay two. A clipping penalty on the next play moved the ball back to the seventeen. Tampa Bay needed somebody to step up to salvage a touchdown chance. On Ricky Bell's coming out day, the former Trojan lifted the weight of his team's playoff chances, the pressure of being an offensive focal point and the hopes of an entire community, along with several would-be Packers tacklers and carried them to the goal line on two powerful runs. Sensing that his star pupil was a little winded, McKay called Williams' number on a quarterback sneak. The Packers' front wall, perhaps gearing up for another Bell onslaught were caught off-guard and Williams snuck through for the touchdown that put the Bucs up 14-0 at halftime.

Bell's performance against Green Bay was remarkable for more than just the fact that he was gaining yards and scoring touchdowns. With every attempt the crowd was cheering him. Considering that he had been an unpopular draft choice who had been injured for two years, this was no small accomplishment. Bell was not only the focal point of the offense, but he was giving the fans what they had hoped to see from Tony Dorsett or Earl Campbell, an elite NFL runner in Florida orange.

In the third quarter the Bucs continued to pound away with Bell. Tampa Bay did not score in the third quarter, but Bell's punishing style was starting to take its toll on the Packers morale. Green Bay consistently failed to move the ball and a turnover late in the game proved to be the final nail in their coffin. With a short field, McKay allowed Bell to continue to showcase his talents. The powerful legs of Bell carried Tampa Bay towards the goal line where a pass play caught the Packers flatfooted. Faking a handoff from the two, Williams dropped back and fired a pass to a wide-open Jimmie Giles in the end zone. The touchdown made the score 21-3, although the contest was a much larger blowout than the score indicated.

Ricky Bell continued to run the ball as the clock wound down on the Bucs' 6th victory of the season, the most wins the team had enjoyed in any year. As the fans celebrated and cheered an announcement came over the PA system at Tampa Stadium. The message informed the crowd that Ricky Bell had set two franchise records on this day. Bell's 28 carries were the most any running back in a Tampa Bay uniform had ever attempted. More impressive than the number of carries was how effective he had been with them. Bell's 167 yards rushing shattered the record of 121 that Jerry Eckwood had notched in the season opener against Detroit. Not a bad day at all for the man many had considered a blown draft choice.

As was his style Bell shied away from accepting any accolades after the game when the media filed into the interview room. Instead Bell made clear that anyone could have had a good day the way his offensive line played. "Hey, it was the whole team that rushed for 167 yards, not me," Bell protested when asked how it felt to set the team record. "I didn't make 167 yards, it was a 'team 167' thanks to incredible blocking."

In his concluding statement, Bell revealed a little of his heart. With one comment Bell let it be known that while he was pleased to be running with success and was ecstatic to see his team and community on a winning ride, he was most concerned with making sure the man who had shown the most faith in him got all the success he deserved. "Coach is happy now and we want to keep him that way."

One striking statistic from the Buccaneers victory was that Doug Williams had only been called on to throw the ball ten times. When he did throw, Williams was highly successful completing six passes for 85 yards and two touchdowns.

If the media suspected that McKay had lost faith in Williams, the young quarterback let it be known that the ball control philosophy had more to do with Bell's success than concerns about throwing the ball. "We had a game plan," Williams said. "We can mix it up pretty good. But there is no sense going away from what you are doing well. We were conservative at times and we probably could have passed. But you never know when a run will break."

With a road trip against the division's dominant team of the seventies just days away, Tampa Bay fans hoped that Bell could break a few long runs through the Northwoods.

The victory against Green Bay was more than Ricky Bell's coming out party; it was a needed boost to the team's confidence. After losing two in a row some doubt had begun to creep in. Recalling the week of practice before the Packer game, linebacker Richard "Batman" Wood said that it was McKay's ability to keep everything in perspective that kept the team on track. "I think we just reached a peak," Wood said of the losses. "Being young and not knowing what we're getting into. We started to get lax a little bit but we found our way back."

"Coach McKay was calm the whole time," Wood said. "Coach just told us to keep our focus and not do anything that would make us lose it."

McKay accomplished this by reminding his team that while the losses to New York and New Orleans had been embarrassing, they had not hurt the team's chances of achieving their ultimate goal, the NFC Central Division championship. The team's 6-2 record included four victories over divisional rivals and McKay knew those wins were most important. He challenged the team to keep their eyes on the prize by striving to win all their divisional games. If the team kept their focus on the division, everything else would take care of itself. McKay reiterated that stance to the press. "Our immediate goal is to win the division. I've thought from the beginning of the season that 10-6 would win our division. If we split our last eight games we'll be 10-6." With four more games against divisional opponents, the players knew which games needed to be won.

According to Richard Wood the players accepted the coach's challenge to win divisional games and had done so against Green Bay. "We knew we had to beat our division teams to get in the playoffs," Wood said. "We knew what we had to do to finish the thing. We knew that if we were going to blow it, it would be because *WE* blew it."

The team would have a chance to lay further claim to the NFC title in Minnesota.

The next leg of Tampa Bay's quest for the crown would be difficult. The Minnesota Vikings, winners of eight divisional titles in nine years, were a proud but desperate team. With the retirement of Fran Tarkenton, the Vikings were suffering through the growing pains of Tommy Kramer. At 4-4 the Vikings were barely in playoff contention but knew that a victory over Tampa Bay would vastly improve their positioning. It would be an intense team that confronted Tampa Bay.

Doug Williams started the day by showing that Bell's influence on him was a positive effect. Playing with confidence and vigor Williams enjoyed one of his best games as a professional against the Vikings. On the first play from scrimmage Williams unleashed a deep pass to Isaac Hagins at the Minnesota 43.

A few plays later Williams went deep again finding tight end Jimmie Giles alone at the ten yard line, giving the Buccaneers a first and goal only a couple of minutes into the game.

On first down Bell ran straight up the middle, delivering just as much punishment as the Viking defenders who tackled him. The gain of seven had the Bucs sitting pretty, but on the next play Jerry Eckwood was tackled back at the five putting the Buccaneers in a passing situation. When Williams dropped back he saw that Hagins had beaten cornerback John Turner to the corner and lofted a pass to him. Hagins was able to haul in the pass, but could not keep both feet in bounds. A golden touchdown opportunity had passed. Neil O'Donoghue, who had not been called on to attempt a field goal in the last three games, salvaged the drive by booting a 22-yard field goal to put Tampa Bay up 3-0.

Although the Buccaneers had missed a chance to score a touchdown, the five-minute drive had shown that Williams was mature beyond his years and ready to lead the Bucs to a championship. Unfortunately a missed opportunity at the goal line would allow the Vikings to stay in the game.

A second deep pass by Williams to Hagins moved the ball near the goal line on the Bucs next possession. On first and goal, Williams again looked for his hot receiver, and although Hagins was unable to haul in the pass in the end zone, he did draw a pass interference penalty against the flummoxed Bryant. The penalty gave the Buccaneers a first and goal from the one-yard line with a chance to quickly take control of this critical game.

On the next few plays the Vikings defense showed why they had helped carry Minnesota to four Super Bowls and six straight division titles. On first and second down Jim Marshall and friends stopped Bell cold at the line of scrimmage. On third down, Williams faked the hand-off and sought to scramble around left end to paydirt. Defensive tackle Mark Mullaney wasn't fooled and tackled Williams just as he got to the line of scrimmage. The first quarter ended after that play, and Williams headed to the sideline to confer with his coach.

McKay had a tough decision to make. The safe option on the road was to kick the field goal and allow his defense to work with a six-point lead. However, the chance to possess a double-digit lead on the road this early in a game against the defending division champions needed to be considered as well. McKay decided to trust his offensive line and go for the jugular.

For the first time in quite a while the offensive line let McKay down. Williams stepped back and rolled to his right on a run-pass option. The pass rush pressured Williams into a hurried throw that fell to the ground behind an open Giles. Just like that the Buccaneers had gone from the possibility of a commanding lead, to owning just a small lead and losing momentum completely to the Vikings.

Kramer, playing like a seasoned veteran rather than a second year quarterback, engineered a long Vikings drive. With Ted Brown and

Rickey Young gobbling up chunks of yardage, Kramer was able to surprise the Bucs by passing when they expected runs. It was McKay's dream drive used to nightmarish proportions against him. By the time it ended with Kramer overthrowing an open Sammy White in the end zone on third down, the Vikings had driven 89 yards in 18 plays and consumed 10:42 off the clock. Rick Danmeier, one of the last remaining straight-ahead kickers, successfully booted a 27-yard field goal to tie the game at 3 apiece.

Moments later the Vikings were on the move again. The tired Buccaneer defense offered no resistance as Kramer led the Vikings two-minute offense efficiently down the field. Utilizing his timeouts and completing short passes to his running backs, Kramer had the Vikings on the Tampa Bay two-yard line with only twenty seconds left when he called his final timeout. From the two, Kramer rolled out to his right and found tight end Stu Voight uncovered in the end zone. Danmeier kicked the PAT and the Vikings went to the locker room with a 10-3 lead. The Vikings in holding the ball for more than twelve minutes in the second quarter looked as though they were ready to start their playoff push on this sunny afternoon. By contrast the Buccaneers in the second quarter had looked very much like a young team that did not know how to play in a game with playoff implications. It was clear that the challenge facing Tampa Bay at halftime was to return to the confident, crisp team that had taken the Vikings by storm in the first quarter before they were stuffed in a goal line stand.

While the third quarter didn't mark the return of the confident, crisp Buccaneers, it did at least see the return of a little bit of swagger on the defensive side of the ball. With a sack by Wally Chambers and an interception by Mike Washington, the defense blunted all of the Vikings possessions in the quarter.

Washington's interception midway through the quarter set the offense up with a first down at the Minnesota 32. The Bucs were unable to garner another first down and McKay used this opportunity to test his kicker. Neil O'Donoghue had been struggling all season, and had seen little use over the last month other than PATs. His short field goal in the first quarter had given the Bucs a lead, but now he faced a much longer attempt that the team needed to succeed if they had any hope of getting back in the game. The pressure to perform could freeze any athlete, especially one who had struggled as much as O'Donoghue had. As he put his foot into the ball O'Donoghue knew this could be a make or break kick for his career. When the 44-yard field goal cleared the uprights, O'Donoghue had not only closed the margin to 10-6, he had proven he could make a high-pressure long-range kick.

Cutting the lead sparked the Bucs defense into dominant mode. Lee Roy Selmon, Wally Chambers and "Batman" Wood, acting as though they were sharks in bloody waters burst though the line and made a crunching tackle on Ted Brown. The nine-yard loss led to a Vikings punt and gave the ball back to the Tampa Bay offense, which went for the deep pass again.

Taking the first snap at his own 20, Williams dropped back to pass and found Isaac Hagins once again running free down the sidelines. By the time Nate Wright caught Hagins, the now unstoppable receiver had run to the Minnesota 27 following a 53-yard pass play. Unfortunately before Tampa Bay could even celebrate Hagin's big catch, Ricky Bell promptly fumbled on the next handoff. It was an unfortunate occurrence for the seemingly star-struck Bell. He had run so well the previous week, fulfilling all of the promise and potential that had led McKay to draft him over Tony Dorsett. Just when it seemed he would be called upon to close the deal on a touchdown drive Bell's fumble seemed as though it could be the momentum killer that sent the Bucs down to a third crushing defeat in four weeks.

The Buccaneer defense would not let that happen on their watch. The defense never let Minnesota capitalize on the turnover, forcing a punt. Tampa Bay's offense came onto the field determined to deliver a dagger to the hearts of the Vikings.

Eschewing the run he loved so much, McKay ordered Williams to continue throwing the ball to the hot Hagins. The receiver responded with yet another big reception, this time a 34-yarder to the Viking 17 in which he beat safety Paul Krause, arguably the best safety in the league. Following a ten yard loss by Eckwood, Williams again found Hagins for another thrilling reception, this one at the two yard line with Bobby Bryant playing the role of perplexed Minnesota defensive back. From the two Bell, atoning for his previous blunder, followed lead blocker Johnny Davis into the end zone for the touchdown that finally put the

Bucs back in the lead. The momentum generated was muted somewhat when O'Donoghue inexplicably hit the upright just as he had done earlier in the season against Chicago. The missed PAT left the Bucs with a precarious two-point lead, 12-10, with just less than fourteen minutes to play in the game.

The missed PAT loomed especially large against the Vikings; a team that was notorious for last minute come-from behind victories. Just the week before, Tommy Kramer had hit Rickey Young with a last second touchdown pass in defeating the Chicago Bears. A confident, gun-slinging Kramer came out on the field in the fourth quarter of games, and the Bucs defense would need to play well to avoid being another one of "Comeback Kramer's" victims.

When Viking punter Greg Coleman pinned the Bucs at their own 3-yard line with a precise coffin corner kick, it seemed inevitable that Minnesota would soon get the ball back in excellent position to attempt a game-winning field goal. Ricky Bell had different ideas.

Proving that not every important run is a ballet-style touchdown sprint, Ricky Bell produced what may have been the most important run of his professional career on the very first play of the Bucs' drive. Taking the handoff from Williams in his own end zone, Bell ran to the right side of the line, saw a crack of daylight and burst through it in a flash. When Bell was finally brought down, he was 27 yards up the field at the 30. The run not only gave the Bucs some breathing room, it demoralized the Vikings and their fans and gave Tampa Bay an important first down with just nine minutes to go in the game. McKay, inspired by his former Trojan tailback, called for a steady diet of runs up the gut of the Vikings. When the drive finally petered out in Vikings territory after burning more than four and a half minutes off the clock, McKay had Blanchard punt. Unfortunately, Blanchard couldn't duplicate Coleman's precision and the ball rolled into the end zone, giving the Vikings a first down with only five minutes left.

Rather than succumbing to the temptation to play the prevent defense, McKay elected to send one of his defensive backs in on a risky safety blitz. Mark Cotney, timing his blitz perfectly with Kramer's snap count, quickly got in the quarterbacks face and forced him to hurry his third down throw. The poorly thrown ball landed well-away from intended receiver Ahmad Rashad, and after Coleman this time failed to

Photo of Ricky Bell Holding Ball Aloft

Ricky Bell celebrates with the sold-out Tampa Stadium crowd after scoring in Tampa Bay's 21-6 victory. Many said the game was McKay's greatest accomplishment in the NFL to that point.

Photo Courtesy Tampa Tribune

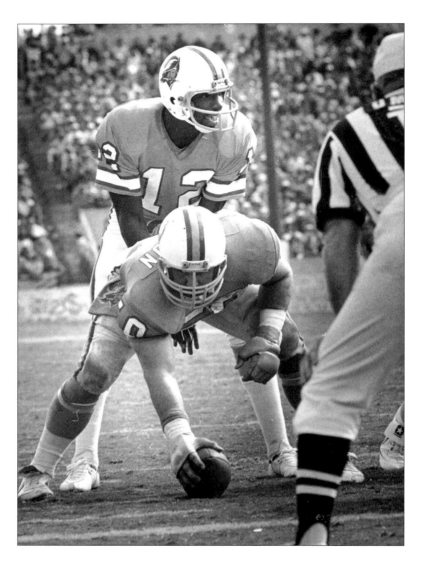

Photo of Doug Williams Taking Snap From Center

Doug Williams calls out the signals against Philadelphia in the Divisional Playoff game. Williams led an epic drive on Tampa Bay's first possession of the game.

Photo Courtesy Tampa Tribune

Photo of Fans in Parking Lot

Thousands of fans rang in the decade of the 80's by camping out for tickets in the Tampa Stadium parking lot before the NFC Championship Game against the Rams.

Photo Courtesy Tampa Tribune

Photo of Lee Roy Selmon on sideline

Lee Roy Selmon, the Gentle Giant who to this day is considered "Mr. Buccaneer" by those that watched him ply his trade. In 1979 Selmon was the most dominant defensive force in the NFL and would end his career in the Hall of Fame.

Photo Courtesy Tampa Tribune

Photo of Ricky Bell running against Kansas City

With the playoffs at stake, John McKay asked Ricky Bell to make the difference. Bell responded by being the Bucs offense in the championship clinching game.

Photo Courtesy Tampa Tribune

Photo of John McKay

Head Coach John McKay. The coach's vision, innovation, patience and humor led the fledgling Bucs to the brink of a Super Bowl.

Photo Courtesy Tampa Tribune

Photo of Doug Williams Tossing Ball on a Sweep

Doug Williams makes the pitch on "Student Body Left," a staple of John McKay's offense since his first years at USC. While not prolific, the Tampa Bay offense successfully pounded opponents into submission on more than one occasion proving that McKay's offense could work in the NFL.

Photo Courtesy Tampa Tribune.

find the coffin corner, Williams and the Bucs offense came onto the field with the hopes of running out the final 3:22 left on the clock.

Bell was able to grind out some yardage, but the Viking defense proved much more formidable than on the previous drive and the Buccaneers were forced to punt the ball back to Minnesota with just 1:13 left. The good news for Tampa Bay was that the Vikings had been forced to use all three of their timeouts.

Tommy Kramer was able to overcome a sack by Lee Roy Selmon on the first play of the drive and complete a pass to Ted Brown at the Tampa Bay 39 with just one second to go in the game. With memories of the dramatics from the previous week's victory over the Bears, Viking fans stood up in unison as Kramer unleashed a Hail Mary towards the right corner of the end zone as time expired. A mass of purple clad Vikings and orange clad Bucs all jumped up for the ball with Jeris White and Curtis Jordan proving to be the better high jumpers. The two defensive backs batted the ball out of bounds securing the Bucs' victory and solidifying their claim on first place in the NFC Central Division. They had traveled to the Northwoods and had slain the Vikings in their own den.

After the game McKay expressed gratitude for the win but let the players know he expected this from them in every divisional game. "The victory sure puts us in a better position than if we had lost. But we'll have to fight like this in every game. It puts us in a good position because we can do some bad things now and not worry too much about it." With a 7-2 record the Bucs now enjoyed a three-game lead over Minnesota and Chicago and looked to be well on their way to winning the division that in the pre-season only McKay had felt they would win.

Focused as he was McKay did lighten up just enough to admit the thrilling finish had been more exciting than he had thought comfortable. "This team may be the death of me, we don't make anything easy. But if this had happened last year, the team wouldn't have come from behind. I don't think this team will panic. I just think they have more confidence."

Ricky Bell agreed with his coaches assessment, "We found a way to win. We weren't exactly overpowering down there on the goal. That's maturity, winning and playing as we did."

Doug Williams, who had enjoyed perhaps his most efficient day as a professional, throwing for 267 yards, gladly pointed out that in a battle of two highly motivated teams the Buccaneers had come out on top on the road. "This game we needed and they needed, and I think we wanted it more."

While McKay and his players were focused exclusively on the NFC Central Division crown, fans around the Bay Area noticed that their beloved Buccaneers were joining a pretty elite circle of teams. In a rematch of the previous season's Super Bowl contestants, the Pittsburgh Steelers had out-slugged the Dallas Cowboys 14-3 at Three Rivers Stadium. The loss dropped the Cowboys' record to 7-2, which meant that the Tampa Bay Buccaneers were now tied with America's Team for the best record in the National Football Conference.

Bucs players were so absorbed with winning their division that it may have escaped notice that they were contenders for home field advantage throughout the playoffs. Would this knowledge prove a distraction to McKay's plans for focusing on the division? As the team was flying high, both literally and figuratively, on their way back to Tampa, John McKay would be faced with the challenge of keeping his players heads out of the clouds and focused on maintaining their stellar play. This had been the one aspect of the season that McKay had struggled with. While McKay had done an excellent job of preparing the Bucs for every team they faced, he was having problems keeping them grounded in the face of success. For the third time this year, that problem would rear its ugly head.

CHAPTER 9

Turmoil and Triumph

Has Commissioner Rozelle issued some kind of directive saying we're the champs?" McKay asked as he met with the local media during his Monday press conference. "I'm not aware of it and unless he does, we still have seven games to play. We could lose them and not win our division."

McKay was not intending to be a wet blanket or curmudgeon; he instead was trying to head off a potential problem. The entire Tampa Bay area had come down with an acute case of playoff fever. The symptoms were flattering game summaries in the local papers and fawning broadcast packages on the evening news. Fans were also affected, as evidenced by the hundreds who jammed the phone lines to call-in shows putting forth their views on everything from how the Bucs defense could stop the Steelers offense in a potential Super Bowl match-up to wondering when the Bucs front-office would start printing up playoff tickets.

McKay saw the epidemic spreading through the community and wanted to keep it from infiltrating the locker room. Against New York and New Orleans the Bucs had shown their inability to balance media demands with their football responsibilities. The two losses had cooled the coverage of the team and the Buccaneers had returned to their winning ways. As the presumptive favorite to win the division the media attention had re-started and McKay hoped his team would show they had learned from their previous experience.

According to Lee Roy Selmon one way in which McKay attempted to quell playoff fever was by not allowing the players to talk about the playoffs. "McKay told us to approach the rest of the season with a one-game-at-a-time attitude," Selmon said.

Another topic that was forbidden was talk of vindication. McKay worried that if the players focused on proving themselves to the media rather than winning the game that they might press too hard and make critical errors. It was a logical decision but it was hard for at least one Buccaneer to conform to it.

Richard "Batman" Wood admitted many years later that while he abided by McKay's decision, it was hard for him to ignore a term associated with the Bucs of 1979. "We were not a Cinderella team," Wood protested about being thought of as a lucky team. "We were a football team destined to be winners. You got tired of hearing it. We've been playing together for four years. We were not a Cinderella team. We developed ourselves into winners. It took some time, but I knew Coach McKay would put it all together. It was our time."

In addition to media requests, community leaders were also vying for the attention of Buccaneer personnel. While this added to the distraction that McKay worried about he knew it was something that had to be dealt with. McKay couldn't cloister his team in a convent, so he trusted them to use their better judgment when dealing with the outside world.

On the Sunday of the Viking game in Tampa the Ronald McDonald House Telethon was broadcast locally. WTVT, Tampa Bay's CBS affiliate, had agreed to air the telethon before and after the Buccaneer game in the hopes of helping to raise the funds necessary to complete the construction of a Ronald McDonald House for Tampa Bay's All Children's Hospital in St. Petersburg. A philanthropic endeavor of the McDonald's Restaurant Corporation, The Ronald McDonald House is a home where the families of seriously ill children can reside during the recovery process. Modeled after the first such home to open in Atlanta, the St. Petersburg house would be located adjacent to All Children's Hospital and would be able to house eleven families at a time.

Rather than broadcasting the CBS halftime show "The NFL Today," WTVT instead aired more of the telethon. The introduction to the halftime segment of the telethon starred Lee Roy Selmon. Taped earlier in the week after a mid-week practice, an obviously tired and sweaty Selmon spoke of all the good work and benefits of the Ronald McDonald house. Not content to just read from cue cards, an involved Selmon pleaded with viewers to call in a pledge to support an important civic addition to the Tampa Bay community before sending the program back to the studio. When the telethon returned live sportscaster Andy Hardy appeared on camera with a partner for this portion of the telethon, injured punter Dave Green.

Hardy and Green did not talk about the game during this time, other than to re-assure viewers that the complete second half would be shown in its entirety. Instead Green spoke of the importance of the Ronald McDonald house and also requested that viewers call in a pledge of support. The short halftime segment of the telethon also featured taped appeals from Richard Wood and Jeris White. Another segment featured Lee Roy touring the facility construction site and conducting an interview with Ronald McDonald House president Sherwood White.

In explaining his activism many years later, Selmon expressed gratitude at being approached. In his mind, giving back was a great opportunity to show that he planned to be more to the Tampa Bay area than just a football player; he wanted to be an active member of the local society.

"It's a case of just being a citizen in a community and joining hands with others to try and make a difference," Selmon said. "They asked if I would consider getting involved and doing some promotions. It was fun to do. It was a great way to get involved. It was nice to try to make the community the best community it can be."

The appearance in the telethon did more than raise funds; it showed the Tampa Bay players that they were viewed differently now. When they had been losing game after game, no one wanted their endorsement. In 1979 they were sought after for commitments big and small.

One of the many duties PR Assistant Rick Odioso was responsible for in 1979 was to help arrange player appearances at Buccaneer Booster meetings. Since the team represented all of Tampa Bay, there were fan clubs everywhere from Longboat Key to Crystal River and all points in between. These clubs would have luncheons or dinners and were always on the lookout for a player to come up and speak to the fans for a little while and sign autographs. During the 26-game losing streak, there hadn't been too many takers but Odioso noticed that the demand had increased considerably in 1979.

"There were more demands for players in '79, but not like today. We had booster clubs that we would try to get players to each week in the smaller towns."

According to Odioso, one of the benefits for the players taking the time out was that the team would provide them with a little something for their efforts. "The players got paid $50 by the booster clubs, and that was some money back then. The largest contracts in the league were only around $100,000 a season." That was considered superstar money, so someone making close to the league minimum of $25,000 to $30,000 a season was probably thrilled to get paid to eat chicken salad and sign autographs. The players were fast learning that winning meant a lot more than just playoff positioning; it meant a whole different level of relating to the community.

The Buccaneers had handled the distraction of the telethon well as their victory over Minnesota had proved. But could they keep up their dual roles for the season? As Lee Roy Selmon remembered it the team tried their best to keep the distractions to a minimum but admitted that 1979 was demanding. In spite of the demands, Selmon thought that year was a lot more fun than any previous season because of the requests. "We were just a team of guys having fun," Selmon recalled.

Selmon also recalled that the leadership of the team kept the players head level for the most part. "The leadership on our team kept us focused. The things being written about whether we were real or not didn't take us away. That leadership started with Coach McKay getting us ready to play."

Selmon continued, "We couldn't get too swept up with the kudos and congratulations. We appreciated our fans support and energy. Getting the fans involved in the title chase is what was most fun in the season. But when it came time to come into One Buc Place, we knew we had to stay focused. The season was long and in order to achieve your goal you have to get ready to play physically and mentally." Against the Atlanta Falcons it looked as though the Bucs off-field requests may have caused them to lose some of their mental focus.

To keep their new winning streak alive the Buccaneers would need to defeat one of the more enigmatic teams in the league. The Atlanta Falcons had arguably been the Tampa Bay Buccaneers of the 1978 season. Having endured over a decade of at best mediocre football, Peach State football fans had seen their Falcons ride a strong defense and an improved offense to a playoff berth. The "Grits Blitz," as the Falcons defense was nicknamed, had pressured passers and pounded runners in 1978. With players such as Wilson Faumuina and Rolland Lawrence, the Falcons defense was strong against the pass and run. On offense Steve Bartkowski had quarterbacked a balanced attack led by running back Bubba Bean and receivers Wally Francis and Alfred Jenkins. The Falcons finished 9-7 and hosted one of the brand new Wild Card games in the latest addition to the NFL post-season. The Falcons defeated the Philadelphia Eagles 14-13 and took the eventual NFC champion Dallas Cowboys to the limit before falling 27-20 at Texas Stadium.

Drafting an exciting running back out of Auburn, William Andrews, and a USC tailback by the name of Lynn Cain, the Falcons were expected to win the NFC West in 1979. Things had not gone according to plan for head coach Leeman Bennett and the Falcons found themselves losers of six of their past seven games. The Falcons were hoping that a win over the current surprise team of the league would help kick-start their season and propel them back into the division race. It would be a desperate team that the Bucs faced for the second-straight week. Unfortunately Tampa Bay wouldn't be able to reproduce the success they had in the similar situation the week before.

Good weather and a warm reception greeted the visiting Bucs as they lined up for the kickoff at Atlanta Fulton County Stadium. The Bucs took to the field before a healthy contingent of Buccaneer fans who had made the eight-hour drive up Interstate 75 to witness what they hoped would be an easy Tampa Bay victory and in the first quarter, it seemed that is just what they would receive.

Facing the worst defense in the NFC Williams decided to let it fly during the opening fifteen minutes. From his own 35, Williams let loose a bomb the likes of which Atlantans hadn't seen since Sherman marched through. The high arching pass flew more than fifty yards in the air and was caught at the Falcon 18 by Morris Owens. Owens took the pass in stride and raced to the one before being tackled by Rolland Lawrence. The 64-yard strike electrified the Buc partisans in the crowd and set up Ricky Bell's one-yard plunge for a touchdown on the next play. Just like that the Bucs were up 7-0 and those who made the long trip up from Tampa looked forward to a celebration during the drive back to Florida.

The defense held the shutout throughout the first quarter and the offense looked to double the advantage when things started to fall apart. With the Falcons blitzing on almost every play, McKay ordered maximum protection from his line and backs and called for another deep pass play. This time Williams dropped back from the Atlanta 48 and lofted another perfectly timed pass, this one in the direction of Isaac Hagins. Hagins, who had tormented the Vikings the week before, tormented his teammates instead on this play. The pass hit Hagins in stride and the receiver put both hands on the ball, but inexplicably the ball popped out and landed on the turf incomplete. A potentially commanding two-touchdown lead was now by the boards.

Moments later Hagins had even worse luck as he fumbled a pass from Williams near midfield. Falcons defensive back Tom Pridemore scooped the fumbled ball up. The alert Falcon then ran 31 yards to the Tampa Bay 21. Realizing that momentum was starting to slip away, the Buccaneer defense managed to hold the Falcons to a short field goal by Tim Mazetti and kept the lead at 7-3 as halftime approached.

Tampa made it to intermission still holding their four-point lead, but as the first half wound down it became apparent that momentum had shifted in the game After an early spark the Bucs had become lethargic and the Falcons took advantage in the second half.

Tampa Bay tried to establish a running game with little success. The Falcons had blitzed Williams silly in the first half and now the same blitzes clogged the running lanes. Ricky Bell found the going hard and Jerry Eckwood found it even harder, coughing up the football at a most inopportune time.

Jerry Eckwood, who had been having troubles adapting to a running style designed to protect the wrist he had injured against the Bears, fumbled on a running play at Tampa Bay's own 28-yard line early in the final period. The ball was quickly recovered by Atlanta and Falcon quarterback Steve Bartkowski used both the running and short passing game to defeat the Bucs defense. Tampa Bay gave up the yards grudgingly, forcing the Falcons to use seven plays to move the short distance to the end zone. Bartkowski found tight end Jim Mitchell with a four yard touchdown pass to give the Falcons their first lead at 10-7 with a little over eleven minutes to go in the game.

The Bucs offense gained little when given the opportunity and the overworked defense finally wore down. With a little over two minutes to go Tampa Bay finally gave up a big play when Bubba Bean, subbing for an injured Lynn Cain, raced 60 yards through the heart of the defense for a touchdown to put the Falcons up 17-7.

With the game out of reach the Buccaneers were able to score a touchdown in the final minute, a twelve-yard pass from Williams to Jimmie Giles, to cut the lead to 17-14. McKay ordered an onside kick, but Falcon special teams player Ray Easterling recovered the attempt. Even if the Bucs had recovered the kick, they would have had only fifteen seconds to move into field goal range. Coach McKay left the field knowing that it should have never come down to such a scenario.

"We played poor and Atlanta played better than we did," McKay summarized in his post-game conference. "We had a chance to blow them out and we didn't. We didn't think they were going to score in the second half unless we put the ball down for them." The coach didn't have to finish his thought, everyone knew he was talking of the ten points that resulted from the Hagins and Eckwood fumbles.

To his credit Isaac Hagins, whose dropped pass and second quarter fumble had been two of the most prominent mistakes in the game, came out and faced the assembled media. One week after being the hero of the Viking game Hagins offered no excuses on his horrible day in Atlanta. "I just dropped it," the speedy receiver said when asked about the sure touchdown that got away. "I had them beat pretty good. I only got one hand on the ball. It didn't even hit my fingers so I guess I took my eyes off it. I didn't concentrate on the ball all the way in. I was thinking too much touchdown at the time. I was in the end zone or close when it slipped through my hands.

"I guess it will haunt me for awhile, probably for the whole week. But I won't let it bother me when we play Detroit."

As for his fumble, Hagins was unsure what had happened because of the speed of the play. "I was trying to put on a move. A guy had me by the legs and a linebacker came up from behind and hit me."

Tampa Bay's defeat was the third time on the season that they had lost to somebody with a losing record. Coming after the players had

spent the week celebrating their status as the standard bearer of the NFC
was an especially bitter pill to swallow. Lesser teams might view such a
loss as a reason to panic, but the tone of the Tampa Bay players showed
a disappointed but focused group. Perhaps George Ragsdale, the spunky
special teams ace, put it best when he tried to put the loss in perspective.
"We just weren't the Bucs everyone loves in the second half. But we are
7-3. Teams lose games. We lost. It's not the end of the world, like it seems
to be to everybody but the players. We feel bad but now we just got to
work harder for Detroit next week."

Ragsdale comments showed just how much the players had bought
into McKay's belief that they could contend for the NFC Central title.
Previous Buccaneer teams may have been shaken by a loss but this team
appeared different. They were embarrassed by the loss but thoughts in
the locker room turned immediately to Detroit because the players knew
it was a key divisional game.

McKay kept the focus on Detroit throughout the week. Due to a
unique scheduling quirk the game at Detroit would be Tampa Bay's third
straight road game. Heading into the season McKay viewed this as a significant challenge facing his team. "Two weeks ago we would have been
satisfied to win two out of three on this road swing. If we can defeat
Detroit we will have accomplished that." The victory over Detroit would
also be Tampa Bay's sixth divisional win and provide them with almost
all the tie-breaker advantages over Chicago should the Bears shorten the
Bucs' two-game lead.

With a chance to take a momentous step toward the division crown
the Buccaneers had a spirited week of practice. They would need all of
that spirit and focus on Sunday to stage one of the greatest comebacks in
team history.

Through the first three quarters of play at the Silverdome the 1-
9 Lions played like the playoff contender that many had thought they
would be, particularly on offense. The former Fighting Blue Hen from
Delaware, Jeff Komlo riddled a surprised Buccaneer defense with laser-
like shots to his receivers. The main beneficiary of Komlo's career day
was Fred Scott. The fleet Lion receiver torched various members of the
secondary for 148 yards on nine catches. Scott's number of receptions

and receiving yards were both the most ever given up by a Tampa Bay defense to any one in receiver in a single game. One of Scott's receptions was good for a 14-yard touchdown in the third quarter.

Scott's touchdown, combined with a seven-yard touchdown run by Bo Robinson in the first period gave Detroit a 14-6 lead late in the third quarter. For the second straight week the Buccaneer offense seemed to be stuck in neutral as they were only able to muster two Neil O'Donoghue field goals despite consistently winning the battle for field position. Two weeks after setting the Minnesota Viking secondary on fire, the Bucs receiving corps were rapidly becoming non-factors.

With the lack of a consistent passing attack, the Lion defense jammed the line of scrimmage and made life miserable for Ricky Bell and Jerry Eckwood. Bell in particular was suffering through a miserable day, as he would finish with only 25 yards. Bell would see his number rarely called in the fourth quarter as McKay was forced to put the game on the shoulders of his young quarterback.

For the second week in a row Doug Williams enjoyed little success. Against Atlanta his receivers had betrayed him with drops, today against Detroit Williams struggled to find open receivers. The one thing Williams didn't have to worry about was the confidence his teammates had in him.

When asked what made Doug Williams so special, Lee Roy Selmon answered that his former teammate had a magic about him that was hard to describe. "Doug was the type of player where everybody knew we have to give him an opportunity because he can make things happen. (Doug) was very knowledgeable of the game and caught on to Coach McKay's offensive systems very, very fast. He elevated everybody's play, which really is the sign of a leader. When he was on the field the offense picked up a notch. If we can get half a second more of protection for him, he'll get things done. That was true on the defensive side of the ball as well. We felt like hey, if we can get the ball in the offense's hands more, he can make things happen."

Evidence of the gist of Lee Roy's comment a quarter of a century later could be found in the fourth quarter of the game against Detroit. Trailing 14-6 with less than five minutes to play, the Tampa Bay defense provided Williams a chance to get something done.

After running in place for most of the day, Williams led the Buccaneer offense on a smart drive before bogging down around the Lions

ten-yard line. With only 3:56 to go in the game everyone watching the
game back in Tampa Bay expected McKay to go for a touchdown, but the
iconoclastic coach had other ideas. Knowing that it was going to take at
least nine points to win anyway, McKay ordered Neil O'Donoghue out to
try a short field goal.

O'Donoghue's 28-yard field goal was good and the Bucs cut the lead
to 14-9 but many a scribe and armchair quarterback were left wondering
about the call. McKay obviously had confidence in both his kicker and
his defense, but wasn't the coach putting a lot of pressure on the defense
to stop the Lions cold in order to get the ball back to the offense? The
move would also put a lot of pressure on the young shoulders of Doug
Williams. The second year quarterback had led come from behind victories at Baltimore and at Chicago, but that had been when the offense had
been playing its best. How would Williams and his struggling offensive
teammates respond to having to score a touchdown in a must-win game
with over 65,000 people screaming their heads off in the closed confines
of the Silverdome? Only time would provide the answer.

O'Donoghue kicked the ball back to Detroit and the Lions took
over deep in their own territory determined to run out the clock and
take revenge on the Bucs for the beating Tampa Bay had administered
on opening day. On the second play of the drive McKay's confidence in
his defense was rewarded when a defensive leader and an unlikely hero
stepped up to make a big play.

David Lewis, who was fast becoming the impact linebacker the
coaches dreamt he would be, blasted into Lion halfback Lawrence Gaines
and jarred the ball loose. Dana Nafziger, subbing for an ailing Cecil
Johnson, quickly pounced on the ball at the Lion 23. Nafziger, whose
specialty was long-snapping, not linebacking, was more than happy to
have the chance to make what at the time was the biggest defensive play
of the season. The turnover gave the Buccaneers an excellent chance to
steal a game that they had long been in danger of losing, quite a change
from the team that a week before had lost yet another game it should
have won. Nafziger gleefully ran from the field, celebrating with his
defensive teammates and eagerly anticipating Doug Williams' efforts to
win the game.

Williams wasted no time in showing that he was up to the challenge of making the play when the game was on the line. Dropping back

to pass, Williams patiently allowed his receivers to run their routes as the offensive line provided him with ample time. As he raised his right arm up by his ear, Williams saw Larry Mucker break into the end zone with Lions cornerback Walt Williams right by his side. Knowing that he would have to throw the pass high to keep the defensive back from knocking it away, or worse yet intercepting it, Williams fired the pass about seven to seven and a half feet off the ground. Mucker, knowing that Walt William's back was turned to the quarterback and unaware of how high the pass was, slowed down just enough so that his defender lost his balance for a split second. That second was all Mucker needed as he leapt high and snared the pass in the end zone as Walt Williams made a futile attempt to jump while off-balance. The 23-yard touchdown pass was a textbook example of a quarterback and receiver reading each other's mind on the run and it gave the Buccaneers a dramatic 16-14 lead with only 3:20 to go in the game.

The good news for McKay was that he had been proven right. The bad news was that the Bucs had scored so quickly that the Lions now had a great deal of time in which to attempt to drive themselves into range for Benny Ricardo to possibly attempt a game-winning field goal.

With Jeff Komlo continuing to play as though he were the second coming of Bobby Layne, the Lions started to do just that. Following O'Donoghue's kick-off Komlo calmly led the Lions down the field, continuing to complete passes to his favorite target on the day Freddie Scott. As time continued to wind down, Komlo drove the ball into Tampa Bay territory, closer and closer to field goal range. On Komlo's last pass of the day, the Tampa Bay defense made a dramatic stop.

With thirty seconds left on the clock, Komlo found receiver David Hill over the middle at the Tampa Bay thirty-yard line. Just as Hill was turning to head down the sideline Mike Washington blasted him. The force of Washington's hit knocked the ball loose and a mad scramble ensued. Several members of the Bucs and Lions had a chance to recover the ball as it bounced from one pair of desperate hands to another. Finally, Curtis Jordan secured the ball at the 34 giving the Bucs possession and the chance to end the game. While Jordan continued to clasp the ball, Morris Owens led a jubilant Buccaneer offense onto the field to run out the clock. Three snaps later the Buccaneers walked off the field 16-14 winners. A team that had won only seven games in three years of existence before 1979 now had their eighth victory of the season and knew they had achieved it by never giving up when things seemed bleakest.

Richard "Batman" Wood fondly recalled the game-winning touchdown thrown by Doug Williams. Looking back on it many years later, Wood saw it as just another example of what the young quarterback brought to the team.

"Doug was not only a great athlete, a great quarterback and a good man, he was a great leader," remembered Wood. "Doug had that winning persona that we needed on the offensive side. He brought confidence to that unit. Doug was a winner period. Doug was just a winner."

Commenting on the ten points scored in the final four minutes of the game, Coach McKay proudly gave credit to the quarterback that he had staked the season on. "We couldn't have done it two years ago," McKay admitted. "As long as he (Doug Williams) is in the game, we have a chance to score. It was a struggle and we stumbled a lot, but, well, we won."

That Larry Mucker had been the man to make the game-winning catch was all the more amazing considering he had almost been a no-show for the game. Two hours before kick-off Mucker found himself still at the team hotel. The young receiver, who had been driving assistant coach Abe Gibron crazy all season by being late for the team bus, finally saw his tardy ways backfire on him. Coach Gibron, a gruff, giant of a man, was in charge of herding players on to the team bus during road trips. The defensive line coach had been incensed at Mucker ever since the receiver had missed the team bus when the Bucs were in Chicago. On this morning in Detroit, Gibron, seeing that Mucker was once again running late ordered the two buses to pull away from the Hilton without his split end. "I'm tired of baby-sitting for you, Mucker," Gibron was overheard saying.

The dismayed Mucker, watching the two buses heading off had a momentary bout of panic. How was he going to get to the Silverdome in time to join warm-ups and get prepared for kick-off? Fortunately a third bus, reserved by the team to transport the local press and travel staff, was loading just as Mucker forlornly stood in the exhaust of the players' buses. Swallowing his pride, and preparing for the ribbing he would receive from the press and his teammates, Mucker hitched a ride with the press and rode to the stadium.

Fortunately for Mucker and the Buccaneers, it wasn't the best pattern he would run all day. Shaking off the tongue-lashing he received in the pre-game locker room, Mucker's game winning catch was the culmination of a quarterback's confidence in his arm, a receiver's crafty ability and the unspoken communication between the two.

Mucker recounted that while the play may have looked spectacular, it worked the exact same way it had when he and Doug had run it over and over in practice. "Doug just throws the ball and I try to out-jump the defensive back. I felt it was going to be a touchdown. I stopped and jumped. If I look back early, he looks back. We practice and practice the play. I know the timing of the ball."

Doug Williams, the man who had made the clutch throw, was much less loquacious about the big play than the outspoken Mucker. "Larry made a great effort to get it," said the understated quarterback.

With a record of 8-3 the Buccaneers were guaranteed not to have a losing record for the first time in franchise history. Over the next seven days they would see themselves vaulted to a level that even the most optimistic of Buccaneer fans would have never dared dream.

CHAPTER 10

Winners at Last

The statistical line on Doug Williams for the victory over Detroit looked rather pedestrian. The second-year quarterback had completed 17 of 34 passes for 182 yards. But on a team coached by John McKay the quarterback wasn't expected to put up gaudy numbers. McKay believed that the most effective way to move the football was through the running game and that passing should be used only to try to spread the defense to make running easier. McKay wanted a strong-armed quarterback who could throw deep and eschewed controlled-passing games.

"Passes completed is a statistic that means nothing," McKay once told *Football Digest's* Bob Oates. "My quarterback will never have a 60% completion percentage. I want big plays and points not completions. You've got to keep throwing deep to score points in this league and that means a lot of incompletions. Some teams complete a short pass and the crowd cheers and its now second down and eight yards to go. Well, then we have them just where we want them. I want a big play quarterback."

A benefit of such a philosophy was that it freed up Williams to just play. In only his second year, Williams was still learning to read defenses and harness the power of his right arm. As the years went on Williams would become a master of the passing game, but in 1979 he was content to play McKay's way. "We weren't a very complicated offense," said Williams.

"If you knew Coach McKay it was pitch right, pitch left, slam it up the middle. When we passed it was try to find one of the receivers deep and if not scramble until you find someone open."

When the running game bogged down though, as it had against Detroit, a McKay quarterback needed to be able to deliver in pressure situations and Williams had done just that. The third come-from-behind victory Williams had led in 1979 cemented his status as a legitimate NFL quarterback and further endeared him to his teammates.

Performing on the field is only one aspect of a quarterback's role on a team. He is also expected to be the team leader. Coming to Tampa Bay as a rookie in 1978 Williams knew that he would be viewed as a leader and he was not afraid of the challenge. "When you walk on the field as a quarterback in the NFL you are automatically handed the job of leadership," Williams said. "I felt like that job comes with the position I play. I think the quarterback plays a major role in how the team performs because everyone looks up to the quarterback."

Being handed the leadership mantle and earning it are two different things and in 1978 Williams earned it in a very painful fashion.

Williams broken jaw at the hands of the Rams had still not healed by the day of the season finale against New Orleans. Tired of standing on the sidelines Williams received clearance to start despite his jaw still being broken. Wearing a specially designed facemask containing extra bars to protect his jaw, Williams showed his teammates how committed he was to them. Ignoring the pain Williams threw a touchdown pass to Jimmie Giles in the 17-10 loss.

Williams was hit several times by blitzing Saints defenders, jarring his jaw and sending tremendous bolts of pain throughout his body. The young quarterback refused to give in to the pain and as a result left his teammates in awe. "Right then and there," Ricky Bell told the press after the game, "if anyone has any doubts about Doug Williams' courage they have to be dispelled. The man just doesn't know what it means to stay down. He doesn't know what it means to fail. He's a winner in every sense of the word."

Many years later Lee Roy Selmon saw Williams' decision to play in the 1978 season finale as the catalyst for the 1979 season. "Those type of things are what elevates the play of others," Selmon said. "When you see your quarterback taking those kind of hits to get a first down, you go 'Wow! This guy is putting it on the line.' It brings people's play up to another level. Those are things you like to see in a team."

Williams agreed with Selmon's assessment. "I broke my jaw but came back and played after losing twenty pounds. I think what that did for the football team was tell them that we have a tough sucker at quarterback. This is the type of guy I want to go to war with. I think that helped us as a team."

When asked how he was able to call plays with a broken jaw, Williams chuckled softly as he explained he was the beneficiary of McKay's offensive philosophy. "The wire was removed but I still had rubber bands holding my jaw in place. I guess I mumbled well enough to be understood. Our offensive system wasn't that complicated. If I was playing today in a west coast offense I wouldn't be able to play, not from a physical standpoint but because I wouldn't have been able to communicate."

Williams chose to let his status as team leader remain subtle. He was not a holler type of leader, preferring to use a look or tone of voice to convey what he wanted done on the field. According to Lee Roy Selmon, Williams' style worked well. "In his own way Doug led vocally," Selmon said. "He didn't jump up and down and scream when something needed to be said. If something needed to be said he just said it. If we needed to be re-focused in practice, he re-focused us."

Joining Williams in the quiet ways of leadership was Ricky Bell. Beloved in the locker room for his enthusiasm and positive outlook, Bell's teammates were happy over his successes in 1979. Bell was on pace to become the first runner in Tampa Bay history to gain more than one thousand yards. In 1977 and 1978 Bell had struggled with injuries and appeared to the outside world to be one of the least likely candidates for team leader. According to Lee Roy Selmon though Bell earned his teammates respect for the way he practiced.

"You knew he was going to show up everyday for practice or a game ready to go," Selmon recounted. "Ricky brought great leadership to the team. I admired Ricky a lot in practice. He practiced like he played. During our team drills he would get the ball and run all the way to the goal line, no matter where we were on the field. That gets to be contagious. It makes you look at your own practice habits. I found myself thinking that maybe I should run my pursuit angles all the way to the sideline rather than just three-quarters of the way."

"It's those types of things that are above and beyond that Ricky brought to our team," Selmon continued. "So when you think about what type of person he was, the character of him on and off the field, he was a winner. He was a winner all the way around and just what we needed."

After the re-match with the Giants the Buccaneers as a team would be winners all the way around.

The first quarter of the game would prove to be maddening to McKay and his team. Each time Tampa Bay had the ball Ricky Bell would run roughshod over the Giants on his way to gaining 93 yards in the first quarter. All of the Giants possessions ended quickly as the Tampa Bay defense harassed Phil Simms and shut down the unsung hero of the previous game, Billy Thompson. However, every one of Tampa Bay's long drives would end because of either an untimely penalty or on a dropped pass by one of Williams' receivers. There was a sense of restlessness among the record crowd of 70,261 at Tampa Stadium. Were these young Bucs, who as a team only averaged 25 years of age, going to lose again to the Giants? As the first quarter ended, the Buccaneers held a yardage advantage of 122-35 over New York but were tied 0-0 as the second quarter began.

Following a punt by the Giants Dave Jennings, the Buccaneers started at their own 22 and overcame their earlier blunders to put together a "McKay Drive" for the first time in a few weeks. Fueled by Ricky Bell running with power and confidence through holes the size of the Holland Tunnel, the Bucs churned their way to the New York 46. From there Doug Williams made his first big play of the day. With the Giants linebackers crowding the line in a desperate attempt to stop Bell, Williams dropped back and found a wide-open Jimmie Giles in the middle of the field at the New York 29. After catching the ball, Giles used his surprising speed and power to move the ball to the New York 15, physically running over a surprised Steve Odom before finally being tripped up by Brad Van Pelt.

Two plays later Williams threw high into the end zone, seemingly over the head of his intended receiver Larry Mucker. But Mucker, who had made an incredibly acrobatic catch against the Giants in the previous game and didn't have to worry about missing a team bus for a home game, outdid that catch by leaping several feet into the air to snag the ball. The catch gave Tampa Bay a 7-0 lead and electrified the Tampa Stadium crowd. The eleven-play, seventy-eight yard drive had consumed just over seven minutes and seemed to unnerve the Giants.

Phil Simms in particular seemed rattled on the next Giants possession. With Tampa Stadium's denizens at full roar, and Lee Roy Selmon and company consistently getting in his face, Simms looked like the rookie he was for the first time against Tampa Bay. Dropping back to pass from the Tampa Bay 48, Simms was blindsided by Cecil Johnson at his own 40. Simms lost control of the ball on the hit and it bounced into the waiting arms of fellow linebacker David Lewis who quickly hit his stride and outraced everyone to the end zone. The 39-yard run with the fumble recovery gave Tampa Bay a 14-0 lead as the two minute warning sounded. A confident team headed to the locker room at halftime and the Tampa Stadium crowd hoped that same team would return in the second.

When the game action resumed in the second half the enthusiasm of the fans was dealt a blow when Steve Odom returned Neil O'Donoghue's kick 75 yards to the Tampa Bay 20. Only a saving tackle by a hustling Billy Cesare prevented a full catastrophe. Just like that the Buccaneers were in danger of losing control of a game they had been dominating. The Tampa Bay defense had been showing continued improvement over the course of the season and chose this time to show their fans, their coach, the New York Giants and all of football America that they were at a level equal to the Steel Curtain of Pittsburgh.

The Buccaneer defense prevented the Giants from fully capitalizing on Odom's big return by stuffing the Giants running game. The Giants were forced to settle for a short Joe Danelo field goal. While in other situations the Giants may have found some confidence from getting on the scoreboard, the Bucs defensive stand seemed to end the competitive aspect of the game. The rest of the contest would merely prove that when the offense executed to John McKay's specifications, the Buccaneers were arguably one of the most dangerous teams in the National Football League.

Desperate to staunch the Bucs momentum Giant head coach Ray Perkins instructed Joe Danelo to try a squib style onsides kick. Instead of kicking the ball just ten yards down field and trying to outfight the

Tampa Bay special teams for the ball, Danelo kicked the ball about 20 yards over the first wave of blockers heads into a dead zone between the blockers and the returners in an attempt to allow the Giants gunners to race to the ball before the Bucs knew what hit them. When executed properly the squib kick catches the opponent off guard, when executed poorly it gives your opponent great field position. Unfortunately for Perkins and his Giants, Danelo's squib wasn't very effective and the Buccaneers took possession at their own 35 and quickly set about building an insurmountable lead.

Two Ricky Bell runs raced the Buccaneers out to New York's 42. On first down Doug Williams dropped back to pass and for the second time in the game found an acrobatic Larry Mucker for the score. Mucker had outraced cornerback Terry Jackson to the five-yard line and had to slow down a little bit as Williams slightly underthrew the ball. Mucker caught the pass and quickly hopped into the end zone in a running style similar to a member of the Russian Ballet. The 42-yard bomb once again ignited a crowd that, shark-like, could sense blood in the water. O'Donoghue's PAT gave Tampa Bay a 21-3 lead with just five minutes gone by in the third quarter. The touchdown also earned Mucker a nickname from broadcaster Curt Gowdy, calling the game for CBS. Noting that five of Mucker's eleven receptions had been for touchdowns, Gowdy christened the speedy receiver "Six or Nothing" Mucker.

The Tampa Bay defense quickly provided their offensive counterparts with another opportunity to showcase their skills when they held the Giants to a three and out on the next possession. On the ensuing drive the Bucs showed their offensive maturity by converting three third and longs. The first, a third and 10 from their own 19 saw McKay cross-up the Giants by running a sprint draw to Bell against a defense expecting a pass. The result was a 25-yard run by Bell, who wasn't even touched until after he crossed the Tampa Bay 40.

Two plays later on third and 12 from his own 42, Williams stood strong against the Giants blitz and found Isaac Hagins over the middle at the New York 43. Following a false start against Greg Roberts, the Bucs faced another third and 12 from the New York 45. This time Williams found Jimmie Giles, proving himself as a primary target, at the New York 30. The drive eventually stalled out but was partially redeemed by Neil O'Donoghue's 40-yard field goal that upped the lead to 24-3.

As time wound down the Buccaneers offense played with an extra bit of intensity as they saw the chance to establish a new team record. With 1:05 left in the game, Johnny Davis scored on a 4-yard run to make the score 31-3. The final score marked the largest margin of victory in team history. It also gave the Buccaneers their ninth victory in 1979, meaning they had secured the first winning season in the history of the franchise. With the players and fans celebrating throughout the stadium, CBS technicians hastily escorted one of the new leaders of the Buccaneers offense near the tunnel for an impromptu televised interview.

Ricky Bell was chosen for an on-field interview during the CBS post-game show. Suddenly thrust into the role of national team spokesman, Bell handled the duties with aplomb. Asked how he felt about the Buccaneers sudden ascent from the bottom to the top of the league's standings, Bell replied, "I am elated at how far we've come in such a short period of time." Ricky Bell, with his 152-yard performance against the Giants had shown he was an elite back and no longer had to live in Tony Dorsett's shadow.

Teammates in the post-game interviews with the local media expressed elation for Bell. "Ricky Bell went through some tough times here," said linebacker David Lewis, who had made like Bell when he sprinted 39 yards for a touchdown on Phil Simms fumble. "We're real close, both being from Southern California. Ricky is working his butt off, really playing great football. But deep inside, with all the Dorsett stuff and all, he wonders what people really think of him in the area."

Another player close to Bell was Richard "Batman" Wood who had known Bell since the running back's freshman year at USC. "I first met Ricky when he got a job at Big Five Sporting Goods," Wood recalled, chuckling. "I was working there for the summer and I remember he was a bright-eyed freshman."

With the luxury of hindsight, Wood viewed Bell as being above the unfair treatment he received from the fans and press in 1977 and 1978. According to Wood, Bell never got fair treatment those first two years because, "He wasn't Tony Dorsett or some type of Heisman guy."

According to Wood though, not being a Dorsett type was the perfect thing for the Bucs and for Bell. "We needed the type of running back who brought something to the table, a power guy. Tony was more shifty, a slasher. Ricky could slash, but he could also bring it with power and we needed that type of guy."

What endeared Bell to Wood and the rest of his teammates was that the young back never let the criticism stop him from putting in the work to be the best he could be. "It never affected him," Wood said of Bell's critics. "Because he knew he was a great player. He was also a great guy."

In addition to platitudes for Bell, players and coaches also commented that it was particularly sweet to have such a complete and dominating performance against a team that had mocked and tormented them only weeks before. Rather than come into the game determined to jaw back at the Giant players, members of the team said they followed Coach McKay's advice to let the Giants talk all they wanted while Buc players focused entirely on their play. The result was an easy victory and very little noise from the Giant sideline as the game wore on.

"We didn't talk to them at all," explained Dewey Selmon. "We let our play on the field speak. I figured a lot of talk would be silenced by our plan and now they have a long ride back to New York to contemplate."

Coach McKay's football philosophy had no room for players who thumped their chests or engaged in a running commentary during the course of the game. To McKay that style of self-aggrandizement was disrespectful to the game. He had heard the comments Giants players had made during the earlier game and came up with a brutal solution: hit them in the mouth and they'll shut up. As far as he was concerned, his team had executed that plan perfectly.

"We were just magnificent," said an unusually effusive McKay. "The talking is over and we don't have to listen to all that nonsense. We were a better team today. We figured we could run. We put Ricky Bell and Johnny Davis up there with a two tight end offense and said 'Stop us.'"

The final score had shown that the Giants couldn't.

The fans showed their appreciation throughout the game. The Bucs had stood up for themselves and secured a winning season. The loud ovations did not go unnoticed by some of the Giants, who were impressed with how the Bucs and their fans seemed to be enjoying the fact that their almost symbiotic relationship was based on winning for the first time rather than losing. "When you have an entire city behind you, when they are really behind you, you're going to be tough to beat," said one Giant.

The loudest cheer of the day may have come on Lewis' touchdown run. Lewis admitted he was unsure what to do after he had scored for everything had happened so fast. "When I got into the end zone, I didn't know how to act. I hadn't scored a touchdown since 1971, when I was at Lincoln High School in San Diego. So, I just sort of flipped the ball over my shoulder."

Lewis may not have known how to celebrate a touchdown, but the loquacious linebacker was sure of one thing. "We're going to make the playoffs, nothing is going to stop us now."

What had been viewed as an unsupportable boast by Coach McKay in the pre-season seemed to be becoming a stark reality. With a record of 9-3 the Tampa Bay Buccaneers were tied with such luminaries as the Pittsburgh Steelers for the best record in the National Football League.

Having the best record in all of professional football was the result of the players continuing to focus on what McKay had set out as the goal before the season began: the NFC Central Division championship. With back-to-back games against Minnesota and Chicago in the next two weeks the chance for Tampa Bay to clinch the title was firmly in their grasp.

Richard "Batman" Wood said it wasn't hard for McKay to get the team focused on the title. In addition to wanting the championship the players were also interested in asserting their right to be thought of as a true member of the Black and Blue division. "All the games were taken personally," Wood recalled. "Beating the teams in our division, Chicago, Detroit, Green Bay and Minnesota, teams that had basically beaten us consistently. Reminding them that we are going to be a focal point of this division."

When the Chicago Bears were stunningly shut-out 20-0 by the Detroit Lions on Thanksgiving Day, the Bucs found themselves needing just one victory to assure themselves the crown. The thought of winning a division championship was particularly sweet to players such as Wood, who had been a member of the 0-26 Buccaneers. Wood wanted the title for more than just himself. He also wanted it for the one man who thought he had the talent to be a linebacker in the NFL, John McKay.

Richard Wood had earned the nickname "Batman" as a linebacker for McKay at the University of Southern California. A fan of the comic book hero as a boy, Wood introduced himself to his Trojan teammates as Batman from Gotham City. Wood had introduced himself in that manner in an attempt to break the ice as a freshman and the name stuck. Wood's enthusiasm, personable nature and on-field performance endeared him to his teammates and they gladly indulged his alter-ego moniker.

Wood had also introduced himself as an offensive player, but soon after donning the persona of the Caped Crusader, the New Jersey native found himself switched to middle linebacker. The move paid off, during his three years as a starter Wood was named All-American twice and helped the Trojans earn a national championship in 1972 and 1974. Drafted by his hometown New York Jets, "Batman" looked forward to a career of battling ball-carrying archenemies weekly.

Wood only spent one year with the Jets and was traded to the newly christened Buccaneers for a seventh round draft choice before the 1976 season. The knock against Wood was that he was injury prone, a reputation that the linebacker bristles at to this day. "I had no injuries," Wood said. "I was hurt, but that didn't keep me from playing. I played in every game. It was nonsense that I was injury prone. I missed one game my entire career."

"That's why I was traded for a seventh round draft choice. They said I was injury prone. I think that was an excuse to get rid of me. They wanted a big group of linebackers to play under Walt Michaels."

Size was also a concern that some in the league had about Wood. At 225 pounds he was lightning quick but some scouts worried about his ability to shed blockers and stand up to the constant pounding of the pro running game. McKay scoffed at the notion that Wood was too light. "How can a man that weighs 225 pounds, sometimes 230 and is built like a rock be too light?"

Wood spent the next three years proving McKay right and the doubters wrong by showing a versatile repertoire of linebacking skills. In stopping the run Wood was without peer on the Tampa Bay defense, evidenced by his status as the Bucs all time leading tackler. With speed and a strength not seen in many men his size, Wood could fight off offensive linemen, let alone a back or receiver, in pursuit of the ball carrier. Wood was the fastest Buc linebacker from sideline to sideline and was relentless at the point of attack. Against the pass Wood used his speed to clamp down on tight ends, backs and receivers coming over the middle. In fact he led the NFL in interceptions by a linebacker with four in 1977, return-ing one for a touchdown in the historic first victory over New Orleans.

"I think he is the best inside pursuit linebacker in football," McKay beamed. "He catches running backs on the sweep from behind and con-fronts offensive schemes that usually don't try to even block his position away from the ball. He's plenty tough at the point of attack and is excel-lent on pass coverage."

In addition to playing ability Wood also distinguished himself through his sartorial style. Realizing the team and the Tampa Bay fans needed something to have fun with and rally around, Wood, with the help of assistant equipment manager Frank Pupello, donned a football uniform that caught everyone's eye. In addition to his game jersey, the linebacker wore elbow pads and shoes emblazoned with the Batman logo. Bucs fans became enamored with the linebacker in the superhero garb who seemed to be in on nearly every tackle. Batman paraphernalia was a common sight among the Buccaneer faithful.

What most in the Bay Area didn't realize is that it was the "Boy Wonder," Frank Pupello, who presented Wood with the wardrobe and not the other way around. "He kind of surprised me," Wood recalled about Pupello's hand in the evolution of Batman. "It was 1978, we were playing in Cincinnati. I come to my locker and he has all these bats drawn on my pads. I say, 'Frank, you know that stuff is illegal man?' And he says, 'No, I talked it over with the official and he said they'd be okay.'"

"Next thing you know, that was it. Everyone thought I was a hot dog. But I didn't think about that. I thought about the Batman legend. How great it was for me and kids, I wasn't going to make it (the legend) look bad."

"You can't do that now," Wood mused. "After the 1982 players strike, Pete Rozelle said you couldn't do that anymore, so I stopped. But I never got in any trouble with the league for the pads. When they said you couldn't wear them anymore, I took them off. I felt bad about it, but everyone still called me Batman."

While he eventually had to shed his cape, Wood was enjoying his role as a super-hero on the Bucs defense. In 1979 he and his teammates had become winners for the first time and the dream of the playoffs was about to become a reality.

Unbeknownst to Wood and the Tampa Bay Buccaneers was that the next three weeks would see that dream become a nightmare.

CHAPTER

11

Hitting a Wall

*T*hose fans that couldn't get a ticket for the game and settled in to watch the pre-game show were reminded what was at stake in the match-up against the Vikings. *The NFL Today* came on a half-hour before the kickoff of all CBS football telecasts with live shots of all the stadiums hosting a game with studio host Brent Musburger providing a voice-over introduction with his trademark "You are looking live at ... " opening. The bigger the game the earlier in the rundown Musburger introduced it. On this Sunday after the introductory music a shot of a sold-out Tampa Stadium greeted the national viewing audience with Musburger announcing, "You are looking live at sold-out Tampa Stadium where they are oiling the goalposts." The scene then shifted to a stadium employee on a stepladder rubbing STP engine lubricant on the cross bar of the goalposts. The unusual application of engine lubricant to the posts was in case the crowd stormed the field to celebrate the NFC Central Division championship. With the posts greased, fans would be unable to shimmy up the sides to tear down the posts, which would be needed for the following week's game.

With the national exposure during the first few moments of *The NFL Today* it was clear that this game would be the most important Sunday in the history of the Buccaneers. John Madden, the former coach of the Oakland Raiders and a newcomer to broadcasting making one of his first appearances with play-by-play man Pat Summerall, stated that the Bucs needed to treat this game as a must-win. The Bucs, according to

Madden, had to forget that they had four tries to win the division and instead should focus on winning it outright today. By clinching the spot now Madden stated, the Bucs could use the final three weeks to rest up key players and practice for the intensity of the NFL playoffs.

For the first fifteen minutes of the game it seemed as though the Tampa Bay Buccaneers were keen on doing just that.

The Tampa Bay defense rose to the challenge presented to them when Minnesota's Jimmy Edwards returned the opening kickoff 75 yards to the Buccaneer 20. Forced to defend a short field just seconds into the game, the Buccaneers defense held the Vikings to a mere three yards in three plays and left the field with a giant sense of accomplishment when Rick Danmeier missed a 35-yard field goal. The defensive stand ignited the sell-out crowd and they continued their deafening roar the rest of the opening period.

Following a Viking fumble on their next possession, Doug Williams showcased his arm strength against Minnesota as he first found Morris Owens on a 25-yard pass to the 23 and followed that up a few plays later with a 28-yard laser to Jimmie Giles at the 2. Leaving all thoughts of subtlety aside, McKay called on his warhorse, Ricky Bell, to run straight up the gut. With all the nimbleness of a jackhammer, Bell bulled over several would be tacklers and fell into the end zone to give the Bucs a 6-0 advantage. The lead would remain six points as the Vikings, known throughout the league for their kick-blocking ability, rejected Neil O'Donoghue's PAT attempt.

The Buccaneers next drive benefited from the sudden re-emergence of Morris Owens as a key contributor. The popular wide receiver had been Tampa Bay's only consistent offensive weapon their first three years. In 1979 Owens suffered a sub-par season by his standards. That changed for the better against Minnesota as he contributed catches of thirteen and twelve yards. Combined with Bell's hard running, Owens' receptions kept alive a drive that approached the length of a Cecil B. DeMille epic motion picture. As the drive got closer to the end zone, the Bucs started to miss some golden chances for a touchdown that could have put the game away early.

Having moved the team to the five-yard line Williams saw an open Jim Obradovich in the end zone but led the second tight end just a bit too far. On the following third down play from the five, Williams overthrew open rookie Gordon Jones for what could have been the decisive six-point play. Tampa Bay instead settled for a 20-yard field goal by Neil O'Donoghue, no small accomplishment considering the Viking front wall once again surged through Tampa Bay blockers.

The 18-play, 82-yard drive had taken over 8:54 off the clock, but failed to put the Vikings away early. The Vikings, out of the running for the playoffs with a record of 5-7, spent the last two minutes of the second quarter spoiling what many in Tampa Bay had expected to be a day of celebration.

On the first play after the two-minute warning the Vikings faced a third and 21 from the Tampa Bay 26 when Tommy Kramer completed a devastating pass. Scrambling out of two sure sacks by first Wally Chambers and then Randy Crowder, Kramer lofted a pass towards the far corner of the end zone. Cornerback Mike Washington seemed in perfect position to intercept the pass, but it sailed through his hands and into the waiting arms of Terry LeCount for a touchdown that defied logic. The Tampa Bay defense had been in the position to make several big plays on this one vital down. The fact that the Bucs had missed two sacks of Kramer and an interception on the Vikings touchdown was improbable. That the Vikings had scored a touchdown was crueler still. When Danmeier's PAT sailed through the uprights cutting the lead to 9-7 one could have heard a pin drop in Tampa Stadium.

Just moments later, a funereal atmosphere would envelop the stadium and not leave for quite some time. Following a three and out by the Tampa Bay offense the Vikings hit on a second big play. Kramer caught the Bucs in all-out blitz from the Tampa Bay 33. Ahmad Rashad caught Kramer's outlet pass at the 20, avoided a poor tackle attempt by Mike Washington and jogged the remaining distance to the end zone. Grumbles turned to full-throated displays of disgust as the Vikings PAT made the score 14-9. In a span of just moments the Bucs were trailing a game that they had been dominating and the sold-out crowd grew restless. A thunderstorm generated a downpour as the teams headed off the field, only adding to the misery felt by Buc followers.

The fans misery only grew in the second half. George Ragsdale fumbled the opening kick-off giving Minnesota excellent field position.

While the defense was able to hold Minnesota with out a first down the Vikings were able to increase their lead in what can only be described as a cruelly ironic manner. Rick Danmeier's 44-yard field goal try appeared to be short from the start, and as it descended it struck the cross bar at the bottom of the goalpost. Rather than bouncing backwards however, the ball rolled over giving Minnesota an additional three points and a 17-9 lead. Immediately the football announcers and the fans in the stands could only think of one thing: the crossbars were coated with oil. Had the stadium's maintenance crew's use of STP as a way of preventing the goalposts from being torn down in any way helped the ball creep over rather than bouncing back? While it was impossible to determine, it certainly felt as fate had determined to keep the Buccaneers from clinching a playoff berth.

Things only got worse. A great Buccaneer drive, climaxed by Johnny Davis' powerful 16-yard touchdown run was trumped by another breakdown by the Buccaneer special teams. Tom Blanchard's punt was blocked by Robert Steele deep in Tampa Bay territory making it easy for Tommy Kramer to find Ricky Young on a three-yard screen pass for a touchdown. That made the score 23-16 as the third quarter mercifully came to a close.

The special teams weren't done with making mistakes. A field goal attempt by Neil O'Donoghue that would have trimmed the lead to four was blocked, the third blocked kick of the day. That block put a great deal of pressure on Doug Williams when he led the offense on to the field with 2:23 to play. Needing to move the team 75 yards to tie the game, Williams carried the hopes of the Tampa Bay area on his shoulders. Lost in the controversy that came moments after the game is the fact that the young man once again rose to such a challenge Showing the gritty determination that had made him a team leader the year before, Williams combined with Ricky Bell to produce the most courageous drive in team history. On first down he found Bell on a screen to the 34 right before the two-minute warning.

With precise strikes to Isaac Hagins and Larry Mucker, Williams guided the team to the Minnesota 47 with 1:34 to play. Williams took the next snap, avoided the pass rush and scrambled through an open field to the Minnesota 35 before ducking out of bounds with 1:25 to go in the game.

An incompletion to Larry Mucker was followed by a 15-yard sideline strike to Jim Obradovich at the 20 with 1:12 to go. With each yard gained, Williams became more confident and the fans grew louder and louder as they cheered on the young quarterback. Following another incompletion to Mucker, Williams found Bell again over the middle at the 11 and quickly called timeout to stop the clock with 54 seconds remaining.

Williams headed to the sideline to confer with his head coach. It is quite possible that Williams and McKay had a hard time communicating because of the noise in Tampa Stadium. The crowd that moments before had been ready to mutiny over the sloppy play of their team was in a state of near-delirium as they witnessed the coming of age of their scrappy signal-caller. Doug Williams, the man who some had thought was not seasoned enough to be an NFL quarterback was showing an amazing grace under pressure as he made play after key play.

On the sideline McKay called the next two plays for his quarterback. From the eleven the Bucs called a quick draw to Bell to secure a first down at the Viking 8, which meant the clock was still ticking. Since McKay had called two plays, Williams quickly assembled his team at the line and took the center snap as the Vikings were emerging from their defensive huddle. The speed with which the play occurred caught the Vikings flat-footed and Williams rifled a pass into the waiting arms of Morris Owens in the end zone. The wild cheering of the fans quickly turned to boos however as referee Chuck Heberling signaled that the Bucs had committed an illegal motion penalty. The snap had come so fast that receiver Isaac Hagins had not had a chance to set himself before the play began, negating the touchdown and moving the ball back to the 13.

The boos were still showering the field when Williams threw the ball out of the end zone on the following play to avoid a sack. The clock stopped on the incompletion, meaning the Bucs now had just 27 seconds left to tie the game.

As the next play unfolded, Williams once again was under an intense rush, this time by the ageless Jim Marshall who was playing in his twentieth professional season. Williams was able to run away from Marshall's rush to the right side. On that side of the field he saw his safety valve Ricky Bell near the goal line. Rather than throw a pass, Williams instead lifted up his left arm and gestured to Bell to turn around and clear a path as he sprinted towards the end zone himself on a keeper.

Bell complied and blasted away Viking defensive back Tommy Hannon with a devastating block. Williams concluded his sprint by vaulting over Bell and Hannon at the goal line, somersaulting through the air and landing on his head in the end zone. The Viking lead was now just one point, 23-22 with 17 seconds left.

Tampa Stadium exploded with sound as the fans, which must have felt as though they had been on one of Busch Gardens' famous roller coasters, reacted to the touchdown. Part of the cheer was for the score, but a great deal of it was for the determination shown by their quarterback who had sacrificed his body to score the touchdown. The affection showered on Williams was in stark contrast to the booing and invective that had been hurled on him earlier in the season when he struggled so greatly against New Orleans. Whether Williams was able to comprehend the cheers at the time is unknown because he needed help leaving the field, as his awkward landing had left him quite shaken up and woozy. With Williams needing assistance, back-up Mike Rae started to warm up on the sideline for the potential overtime period that would come after Neil O'Donoghue made the PAT.

NFL Films, figuring a game in which the moribund Buccaneers could clinch a playoff berth was of historic importance, had several cameras and microphones on the sideline. The microphones caught John McKay imploring his offensive line to block. "Block! Block! Block!" McKay shouted over and over as the kicking team took the field.

An excited hush fell over the crowd as Neil O'Donoghue lined up for the PAT that would tie the game and send the most important game in franchise history into overtime. As the ball left the kickers foot Buccaneer players joined hands, coaches prayed, fans closed their eyes in excitement, reporters and cameramen readied their recording devices and . . . .

BLAT!

That was the sound of disappointment in the guise of the Vikings inexplicably blocking yet another kick. This time Wally Hilgenberg batted down the attempt. For what seemed like an eternity nothing in the stadium moved or made a noise, such was the shock that had fallen on everyone associated with the Buccaneers. As time started to move again, the only sound that could be heard were the faint cries of joy coming from the Minnesota sideline. After recovering, the fans unleashed a reign of vitriol upon their hometown team. Moment's later Viking tight end Bob Tucker recovered the ensuing onside kick and the deed was done much to the dismay of everyone who wore Florida orange, red and white. The Tampa Bay Buccaneers who had just engineered one of the greatest pressure-packed drives in recent history, had lost their chance to win the NFC Central Division because they had twice been unable to execute one of the simpler plays in football, the extra point.

The fans that had planned to turn the post-game into a holiday festival unleashed all of their frustration on the team as it left the field. While it was not the fault of the team that the fans had set their sights so high, the Bucs were going to be the ones to pay for the feeling of disappointment swirling around like the rain at Tampa Stadium. Expecting to see their reign as the fans of the worst team in professional football end, Buccaneer fans were bitterly callous to the team as it trudged, with heads down towards the locker room. Fans booing over an ending such as this would have been easily endured by McKay, but as he got closer to his locker room he became enraged by the racial insults from a small gathering of idiots. McKay engaged in a shouting match with a particular heckler and had to be led from the field away from the line of fire.

Former PR Assistant Rick Odioso bore witness to the confrontation. "The fan that he (McKay) was mad at said some terribly racist things. He yelled out 'We've got to watch a n----r quarterback, a n----r team and at halftime you even gave us a n----r band!' McKay didn't like that at all. He was frustrated by the loss, but I don't think a lot of people understood the nature of the incident."

Perhaps still incensed over the callous comments of a smattering of small-minded men, McKay's demeanor was darker and angrier than anybody that followed the Bucs was accustomed. "We stunk," McKay growled. "We blocked bad. We played terrible on defense and our kicking game made up for it by being absolutely horrible."

Gone was the sly humor, replaced by a series of lacerating barbs. "We were idiotic, absolutely foolish. I saw nothing that delighted me."

One week later McKay saw even less that pleased him.

The Chicago Bears had stepped up their play in previous weeks. Notwithstanding the embarrassing loss to Detroit on Thanksgiving Day, the Bears had stayed in the Bucs rearview mirror just two games out of first place. Knowing a loss to Tampa Bay would end their season, the Bears came to Tampa Stadium ready to wage a rough and tumble campaign to show the upstarts from the South what the Black and Blue Division was all about.

The tone for the game was set in the first quarter by both defenses. Walter Payton was corralled by the Bucs aggressive defense while Doug Williams was constantly harried and hit by the Bears front four. As in the week before the Buccaneer special teams would provide the visitors with the chance for victory.

Late in the first quarter Tom Blanchard had his punt blocked by Bruce Herron at the ten-yard line. Chicago's Lee Kunz recovered the ball at the Tampa Bay one-yard line. This was the fifth Buccaneer kick to be blocked in just two games. Shocked silence filled the stadium just as it had done the week before. On the sideline John McKay suddenly looked much older than his 55 years as he tried to comprehend why his team had suddenly become unable to execute the simplest plays in football. The Bucs defense, which had stymied the Chicago offense throughout the first quarter, was unable to hold the great Payton at the goal line. Payton's one-yard dash through the middle of the defense gave the Bears a 7-0 lead as the first quarter expired.

Bucs fans that had seen their high hopes dashed in much the same fashion the week before once again unleashed a torrent of boos in the direction of the Buccaneers. Coupled with the cheers of the visiting Bear fans, the noise was almost deafening as the Bucs offense took the field. Coping with a suddenly hostile home crowd in addition to the Bears fierce pass rush, Doug Williams finally showed some nerves as he embarked on his worst performance of the season.

On the drive immediately following Payton's touchdown, Williams was once again harried, harassed and finally sacked by Alan Page. Page and the rest of the Bears defense were so effective at getting pressure on Williams that the young quarterback developed "happy feet," dancing in the pocket and not setting in a proper throwing stance because he felt that his offensive line couldn't protect him. This led to many bad throws by Williams as he consistently overthrew or underthrew his intended receivers. The pass rush also led Williams to make some bad decisions as well.

On Tampa Bay's first drive of the second quarter Williams threw deep to Jimmie Giles in Bear territory. The tight end was tightly covered and Bears cornerback Terry Schmidt easily intercepted.

The Bucs defense held the Bears without a first down and quickly got the ball back for Williams and the offense. Sadly, Williams gave the ball right back and lost his composure in the process. After a pair of solid Ricky Bell runs moved the ball to mid-field, Williams underthrew Larry Mucker and the ball was intercepted by Chicago safety Gary Fencik. Fencik returned the ball to the Chicago 45 before being tackled. As the teams unpiled, pushing and shoving occurred with Doug Williams and Alan Page standing toe-to-toe yelling at each other. A penalty flag was thrown. A personal foul was called on Doug Williams of all people. Replays showed that after the pass was intercepted, Williams, who had been hit on the attempt, was about to be blocked by defensive tackle Mike Hartenstine. Perhaps becoming a little shell-shocked, or else just angry at the physical contact, Williams grabbed Hartenstine's facemask and flung him to the ground. Alan Page, standing up for his teammate had gotten in Williams' face and started to argue with him. Williams' flare-up only exacerbated the turnover as the penalty yardage moved the ball to the Tampa Bay 40-yard line.

The personal foul on their quarterback seemed to set off a chain reaction of bone-headedness among the Buccaneers. On the very next play Mike Washington was called for unnecessary roughness as he bodily threw Mike Williams out of bounds after a short gain on a reception. This gave the Bears a first down at the Tampa Bay 19. An additional infraction could have been called on Tampa Bay as Randy Crowder got in the face of referee Fred Silva to dispute the penalty and had to be dragged back to the huddle by his teammates. Before the Bucs could compose themselves, Chicago Quarterback Mike Phipps found Mike Williams again, this time for a touchdown. The PAT by Bob Thomas gave Chicago a 14-0 lead with five minutes to go in the half.

Williams showed that he still hadn't calmed down when he threw his third interception of the half on the very next possession. On the attempt to Jim Obradovich, it looked as though Williams was trying to do too much to make up for his previous mistakes. Obradovich was open in a seam along the left sideline, but Williams put too much on the throw, sailing it high over his tight ends hands and into the waiting arms of Alan Ellis who happily returned it to the Tampa Bay 34. Tampa Bay was now in danger of being blown out at home in a crucial game and if not for the play of Lee Roy Selmon that just might have happened.

On first down Walter Payton took the handoff and was immediately engulfed by Lee Roy for no gain. On the next play Payton tried to run away from Lee Roy to the opposite side, but Selmon, showing tremendous speed, caught Payton from behind with one arm and with the other stripped the football away from him. Cedric Brown pounced upon the ball at the 36.

The Tampa Bay offense was once again stopped without a first down and the Bucs kicking team narrowly averted yet another disaster. For the second time in the game Dana Nafziger sailed a high snap back to Tom Blanchard. Blanchard was able to snag the ball, but had to run away from Bear special teamer Bruce Herron, who was eager for his second blocked kick of the day. Blanchard avoided Herron and punted the ball while on the dead run. In either a case of tremendous skill or tremendous luck, Blanchard's running punt rolled to a stop at the Chicago 31. The Bears were quite content to let the clock run out on the first half and headed to the locker room with a two-touchdown lead.

In the third quarter Tampa Bay's offense finally began a long, determined drive that saw the offensive line physically defeat the Bear front line. Up to this point the deepest the Bucs had driven the ball was to the Chicago 48, but on this drive they made it from their own 38 to midfield in just three plays as Ricky Bell began to benefit from solid run blocking. From midfield Doug Williams dropped back and found an open Isaac Hagins at the Bears 35. Two plays later Williams hit Jimmie Giles for a first down at the Chicago 25 and Buccaneer fans came alive for the first time in the second half, awakened from their stupor by the first sustained drive of the game for Tampa Bay.

Two more blasts by Bell moved the ball to the Chicago 17, presenting Tampa Bay with a third and two. With the Bears' thinking run, Williams dropped back to pass and saw Jim Obradovich open at the 10. As he had done all day, Williams threw a poor pass that fell just short of the reserve tight end. On fourth and two McKay, perhaps fearful of his kicking team, decided to go for a first down. It was a brave move, but McKay's field general never got the chance to make any kind of a play. From the moment the ball was snapped Williams was under an intense pass rush, as the Bears linebackers blitzed up the middle. Williams had no choice but to throw the ball away early and it fluttered harmlessly to the ground far away from any Buccaneer receiver.

As the ball lay on the ground, the Bucs offense trudged dejectedly from the field, still behind by two touchdowns.

After a fourth interception by Williams McKay decided that the young man had had enough. Mike Rae replaced Williams at quarterback and fared no better as Gary Fencik quickly intercepted him. The theft was Chicago's fifth of the day and sealed the shut-out for the Bears. The Bears frolicked off the field, their 14-0 victory having moved them to within just one game of the NFC Central lead and keeping their playoff hopes alive. The Bucs, on the other hand, were forced to contemplate that for the second straight week they had let a chance to clinch a playoff berth at home slip through their fingers.

As far as the fans were concerned, their emotions were much more muted than the week before. Perhaps it was because the Bucs were very rarely in the game or maybe it was because they were still suffering an emotional hangover from the week before. Whatever the reason, there was simply an eerie silent murmuring as the Tampa Bay team headed to their locker room. In an interesting note the team exited through a canvas covering that had been added during the week to prevent a repeat of the heated exchanges between McKay, Buc players and fans after the Minnesota game. On this day it was unnecessary as nobody was in the mood to do anything but mope.

The loss was tough for the team to handle, but particularly Williams. He had suffered through his worst performance as a professional, completing only five of nineteen passes for 60 yards while being sacked twice and throwing four interceptions. To add salt to the wound on one of the interceptions Williams had given the Bears extra yardage by being hit with a personal foul penalty. For the second time in the year the young quarterback had been yanked out of the game and replaced by Mike Rae. Compounding the indignity of being benched was the fact that both occasions had happened at home in front of a sell-out crowd that had come into the game with high expectations.

Williams seemed resigned to the benching, stating that he understood McKay's decision. Like any true competitor Williams hated being pulled, but showed increasing maturity in accepting the decision as for the good of the team rather than an indictment of his play. Williams even admitted that he would have benched himself given his performance and held no grudge against McKay. "I'm human, we're all human," Williams said when asked about how he felt about his efforts. "We had a bad day, all of us. A lot of interceptions were anticipated. The ball just went into the wrong hands."

McKay wouldn't let his quarterback take the whole blame for the loss. "Our pass protection was non-existent today," McKay said.

The offensive line had been a surprising bright spot of the 1979 season. Possibly the weakest link of the entire team from 1976-1978, the line had undergone a major overhaul in 1979 and seemed to have turned the corner. Under the tutelage of former Cincinnati Bengals head coach Bill "Tiger" Johnson, the line had helped Ricky Bell become the first 1,000-yard rusher in team history and for the most part had kept Doug Williams upright. Tackles Dave Reavis and Charley Hannah, guards Greg Roberts and Greg Horton and center Steve Wilson had been anonymous yet instrumental cogs in the teams overall improvement. In the last two weeks though they had been party to blocked kicks and constant quarterback pressure. Against Chicago they also suffered a loss when Charley Hannah went down with a leg injury. He was replaced by Darryl Carlton, a little-used back-up from the University of Tampa. Carlton, like the rest of the offense, had struggled a fact not lost on McKay.

"When things go bad, they go bad," McKay said. " Why we looked like a high school team . . . no, I take that back . . . like a sandlot team. We just played lousy."

Members of the Tampa Bay defense were particularly upset with the loss because they had effectively shut the Bears down. The Chicago offense was only able to generate 164 total yards of offense. The two touchdowns they had scored came courtesy of Buccaneer mistakes that had given them an extremely short field, such as starting at the one-yard line following Blanchard's blocked punt.

David Lewis encapsulated the feelings of the defensive unit when he commented to the press following the game. "To hold them to 164 yards and to lose was very frustrating," said a perturbed Lewis.

The livid linebacker was not ready to give up on the season and scoffed at the thought that the Buccaneers were merely playing at the level to which the NFL had become accustomed. "We're not living in the shades of the past," Lewis said emphatically while admitting, "I feel like we've got to show more pride than what is being shown. This is where character comes in."

One week later against San Francisco Williams would struggle again, tossing five interceptions. The defense would offer up an embarrassing effort as they were pushed around by the 1-13 49ers. The 23-7 loss to San Francisco combined with Chicago's 15-14 victory over Green Bay placed both teams in a tie for first place in the NFC Central Division. The championship that had once seemed Tampa Bay's for the taking was now very much in jeopardy. If the Buccaneers lost to Kansas City the following Sunday and the Bears defeated St. Louis, Tampa Bay would miss the playoffs.

Doug Williams remains flabbergasted at the three-game losing streak during this crucial stretch of the season. The team had been so confident heading into the final quarter of the schedule that the thought that they could lose three in row was almost laughable.

"All we had to do is win one game out of four to be in the playoffs," Williams painfully remembered. "The way we had played earlier there was no doubt in our mind that we could take two, or three or all four games."

The offense in particular had struggled during two of the three losses. Williams recalled that the offensive difficulties had done nothing to affect team chemistry. David Lewis' comments had been pointed at the entire team and not just one unit. According to Williams this was because in 1979 there was more respect in the locker room than in today's NFL.

"I think unlike today, one of the reasons there are splits between offense and defense is because of the salary cap, the money and all that stuff.

"Back then we were playing for the fun, we weren't making a lot of money. We were playing for the glory of the game. Back in 1979, we honestly felt like we may not be the best team talent wise, but we had a bunch of guys that felt like we were going to get it done."

Another reason for the chemistry is that McKay had set up an offensive and defensive unit that knew well not only their responsibilities, but respected the philosophy of the other unit. "There was no rivalry. We knew what our defense was as far as what they could do, and how they played.

"And they knew what we were. We weren't a wide-open, three wide-out, split the tight-end out, one back sophisticated type of offense. We were going to hand to Ricky Bell, get tough yardage, hit Jimmie Giles every now and then, hit a deep one every now and then. The defense was going to play their behinds off and we were going to keep it close and eventually find a way to win it. So everybody was on the same page when it came to team."

But at this particular moment the team was in danger of losing out on the playoffs. To prevent such a calamity from taking place John McKay was going to need to summon all of his coaching experience. All season long McKay had made the right moves at the right time. In the pre-season he had told them they could win the NFC Central Division championship and they had played as though they believed him. A 5-0 start had made the team into celebrities and he had managed to keep them focused. Back-to-back losses to New York and New Orleans had failed to dampen their enthusiasm because McKay told them to keep their eyes on the prize. Wins in Minneapolis and Detroit had proved McKay's style of football could work in hostile environments. But now after a three-game losing streak the wheels seemed to be coming off the bandwagon. Fair or not the week leading up to the finale against Kansas City would be seen as a test of McKay's ability to coach in the National Football League. He needed the game as much as his players.

John McKay needed one more win.

From Worst to First

*C*hokeneers.

That was the term coined by *Tampa Tribune* columnist Tom McEwen to describe the state of the Tampa Bay Buccaneers following the third of three straight defeats with a championship on the line.

The insinuation of McEwen's term was clear. The Tampa Bay Buccaneers were in danger or perpetrating one of the greatest collapses in NFL history. If the Bucs lost to Kansas City on Sunday and the Bears defeated St. Louis, Tampa Bay would not only lose out on the NFC Central Division title, they would miss the playoffs entirely.

In the face of such circumstances, John McKay didn't flinch. Instead the coach honestly assessed what he and his team faced. "If we defeat Kansas City we will go into the playoffs as the NFC Central Division champion with second standing in the conference for home field advantage which I consider quite an accomplishment for a fourth-year team no matter how it is achieved. And should we lose, a season of overall improvement will still be one of great disappointment at its conclusion. We are faced with a great emotional difference for the outcome of our season based on this game and the character of the players and coaches will be tested in the week ahead.

"Our team has played with great intensity earlier this season in games we deemed especially important. We defeated our first six division opponents, including four on the road and beat the Rams and Giants, two teams

I think are pretty sound, very convincing. So we have the ability to do it if we want it and I would think we certainly would want it. I know I do."

One player that McKay believed had the ability to win the title was Doug Williams. On Tuesday the coach let it be known that Williams would start against Kansas City. The young quarterback had suffered two horrible games in a row but McKay admitted that Williams had been victimized by the offensive system more than anything else. McKay believed in high-yield, low-percentage passes and this often put Williams in an untenable situation. McKay hoped to help Williams out as he had at mid-season by unleashing Ricky Bell.

"If you feel your quarterback is having a bad day, you should go to your running game," McKay admitted. In the past two games the Bucs had inexplicably used Bell sparingly and the offense suffered for it.

"We have some ideas—some things that will take the pressure off the quarterback. But I just have the feeling he will play well."

McKay's faith in Williams seemed to embolden not only the quarterback but the entire team as well. The Tuesday practice after McKay solidified Williams' starting status was as intense as any that had been witnessed at One Buccaneer Place. The offensive line and defensive line engaged in stalemate after stalemate as they put extra effort into their physical drills. Ricky Bell, continuing his habit of taking all hand-offs to the end zone, zipped around and through Lee Roy Selmon and company when his front wall was able to provide the room. Doug Williams threw crisp strikes to a corps of receivers that ran solid routes under the watchful gaze of Coach McKay. It looked to all witnesses that the Bucs of the first five weeks of the season had suddenly re-emerged at the practice facility. Perhaps all of David Lewis' teammates had taken the linebackers words to heart and had looked at themselves closely in the mirror. It appeared that they hadn't liked what they had seen and were determined to show all the doubters in Tampa Bay and beyond that the time had come to step up and take a playoff spot by brute force on Sunday.

A pleased McKay, his spirits buoyed by the intensity his young team was showing, openly stated that the Bucs would win on Sunday. "Well, this is certainly the biggest game in the history of the Buccaneers and I'm predicting we will win. We are in a big one. You can never win a big one without being in one."

The only thing McKay admitted to worrying about was his special teams. If the game came down to a kick as the Minnesota loss had, the coach knew that he would be counting on a group that had been unreliable lately. He good-naturedly warned of what that would mean for his kicker.

"We would have to kick and if Neil O'Donoghue missed he better get on a slow boat to Ireland."

When the Buccaneers arrived at Tampa Stadium for pre-game workouts they learned that they would have to do battle with not only the Kansas City Chiefs to earn a historic playoff spot, but they would need to overcome the elements as well. A torrential rainstorm had swept into the Tampa Bay area earlier in the day dumping a tremendous amount of water. Traffic getting to the stadium was a nightmare and as the hearty souls who were hoping to see history filed to their soggy seats it appeared that there would be no let-up in sight.

In the press box on the top rim of Tampa Stadium, *St. Petersburg Times* columnist Hubert Mizell and his peers had a panoramic view of the mayhem the water was causing on the field and in the stands. "It rained so hard that Tampa Stadium's aisles became mini Niagaras. Water was gushing and people slipping. On the field it was a quagmire and clearly if either the Bucs or Kansas City could score just once it was probably going to be enough."

Quarterback Doug Williams viewed the elements as just one more hurdle he and his teammates would have to jump to make the playoffs. But what a hurdle it was. "To be playing football on that day, in the monsoon on a lake," Williams sighed. "(Those were) probably the strongest odds of all time (against us)."

Defensive lineman Bill Kollar's observation before the game was that the field was holding up well but there was a lot of water coming not only from the sky but also from the stands. "Boy, you talk about a rainstorm that was second to none," recounted Kollar. "It was really tough. The water wasn't standing bad (on the field), but it was rushing down from the stairs."

Lee Roy Selmon's perspective from field level provided him a view of a football field with more water on it than he had ever seen, but he and his teammates shook off their awe and focused on the task at hand. "The field was just really filled with water. We didn't want that to happen, we wanted a nice day at home. We still believed we could win, we had felt that all season long. We didn't know what the rain would do. But the conditions were what they were. It became a defensive battle, back and forth."

Footing proved to be of no concern to the Buccaneers defense on this day as they put on a clinic regarding the topic of team tackling with the Chiefs acting as their reluctant subjects. During the first fifteen minutes of play the Kansas City ground attack was stuffed as running back Ted McKnight found little if any daylight to run through. The lack of daylight was due to Lee Roy Selmon elevating the level of his play in this most important game of his young life. Throwing aside linemen, tight ends and fullbacks, Selmon, joined by teammates Wally Chambers, Bill Kollar and Randy Crowder took turns introducing McKnight to the soggy Tampa Stadium turf.

With his ground attack stopped, Kansas City coach Marv Levy turned to quarterback Steve Fuller to move the football. Fuller found the going even more difficult than McKnight. With the running game not working, Selmon and company refused to bite on the play action pass that was such a staple of Levy's offense and instead ran straight through their blockers and met at Fuller for multiple sacks and hurries. When the first quarter ended the Chiefs had not left their end of the field: in fact they hadn't moved the ball at all.

Lee Roy Selmon explained that the Bucs employed a different strategy than might have been expected given the soggy conditions. The Bucs' defense was based on an attacking, gang-tackling style. When the footing on a football field becomes questionable however, most defenses try a more conservative read and react style. McKay decided to experiment with a different strategy and according to Selmon it made all the difference in the world.

"We still played our defense and the defensive calls allowed us not to read and react so much as to get to spots in the defensive scheme," Selmon said. "I thought that put us in positions to make plays better than trying to read, then react and take a step and maybe lose your footing. Our coaches did a good job of scouting Kansas City and putting us in a position to play a good defensive game."

Unfortunately for the Buccaneers their offense was not enjoying any more success than their counterparts from the Show Me State. As the first quarter began to wind down the Bucs started to put together a string of Ricky Bell runs that got them down the field efficiently. Literally leaving Kansas City defenders in his wake, Bell carried the ball, and his team, down to the Chiefs' 15-yard line before the drive stalled. With the rain coming down harder than it had at anytime during the game Neil O'Donoghue trotted onto the field to attempt a 32-yard field goal.

Seeing their team with a chance to grab an early lead in a game played in deplorable conditions the drenched faithful in the stands started to chant the song "The Bucs Know How to Shine." The execution of the specialty teams once again torpedoed the opportunity for taking early advantage. The snap from center Steve Wilson to holder Tom Blanchard appeared to be solid, but the punter couldn't handle the slippery football and was forced to simply fall on the ball. Blanchard was then quickly engulfed by a horde of Kansas City players and a solid chance for a score was wasted.

As the first quarter ended and the second began, the elements directly led to the second scoring opportunity of the day to be wasted. After crossing the midfield stripe Williams handed off to Jerry Eckwood on a power sweep. With tight end Jim Obradovich leading the rookie around the corner it appeared that Eckwood had a path to the end zone forming. Suddenly the wet football started to slip down Eckwood's wet arm and before he could adjust his grip it bounced against the padding he wore to protect the wrist he had injured during the first Chicago game. The ball fell to the ground and a mad, wet scramble ensued with members of both the Chiefs and Bucs hydroplaning several yards down the field as they dove after the loose ball. Kansas City's M.L Collier was the one man able to control his sliding enough to recover the ball at the Chiefs 34.

A few moments later the Chiefs were able to get into field goal range and sent out Jan Stenerud to break the scoreless tie. On the attempt Lee Roy Selmon decided that turnabout was fair play considering how many kicks by the Buccaneers had been blocked in the previous three weeks. Bowling over the blocker in front of him, Selmon crashed into the Chiefs backfield and rejected Stenerud's kick. The block kept the game scoreless as intermission began.

When the Bucs were in the locker room at halftime they probably
could not have helped but to hear that the Bears were having little trouble
handling either the St. Louis Cardinals or the blizzard like conditions of
Soldier Field. Walter Payton was putting on a bravura performance as
the Bears raced out to a large early lead. Knowing the talent the Bears
possessed as well as how poor a team the Cardinals were, the Bucs now
knew that these final thirty minutes would make or break their reputation as professional football players.

That realization didn't translate into an offensive explosion as the
worsening weather overwhelmed the drainage system at Tampa Stadium.
This led to the formation of several pools of standing water in various
spots on the gridiron. With both defenses playing well and the field a
virtual swamp, neither offense was able to advance the ball very far and
the fourth quarter arrived with the score still deadlocked at zero.

The fans in the stands started to develop a sense of unease, making
their mood almost as dark as the skies around Tampa Bay. The sense of
dread was further enhanced as the scoreboard showed the Bears continuing to pour it on the Cardinals. To add to the drama, the audience for
the game was about to become much larger.

When the Bucs got the ball at their own 35 early in the fourth quarter the NBC television network cut into the regional coverage of other
games and sent most of the football-watching nation to Tampa Stadium
to see if the owners of the longest losing streak in the history of the NFL
could crash the playoff party. The timing of NBC was fortuitous because
on this drive the Tampa Bay Buccaneers showed not only their hearty
fans, but also the entire nation that they did indeed have the will of a
champion.

Ricky Bell, who had been the Bucs offense for most of the game,
started the drive by blasting through the middle of the line to secure a
rare first down. That initial first down of the drive seemed to inspire his
teammates and the offensive line started to create bigger and bigger holes
in the Kansas City defense as the drive progressed. Continuing to ride
the legs of Bell the offense drove towards Kansas City territory before
McKay bravely threw a change-up at the fatigued Chiefs.

The coach ordered Williams to run a naked bootleg to gauge how
seriously the Chiefs were going to take the Buccaneer passing attack.

Taking the snap from center, Williams rolled out to the side and saw that the Chiefs came up to attack him rather than dropping back into pass coverage. Williams was able to make a short gain on the play but more importantly it gave McKay an idea. It was logical that on a day when the ball was soaked and heavy the Chiefs wouldn't fear a throw from Williams thinking that the conditions would prevent the young quarterback from making an accurate throw. McKay filed that away for a moment and sent Bell up the middle for a few more plays.

Facing third and three from the Kansas City 47, McKay decided to put the drive on the shoulders of Williams. Williams took this opportunity to rise to the challenge and rewarded McKay's confidence. After faking a handoff to Bell, Williams dropped back to pass and saw that the Kansas City defense was coming forward thinking he would either run another bootleg or throw a screen pass because of the elements. Instead Williams lifted up his right arm, ignored the heaviness of the waterlogged ball and rifled a pass to Jimmie Giles. The Chiefs seemed momentarily stunned by not only the audacity of the play call but the fact that Williams was able to pull it off. Giles raced through the shocked secondary before he was tackled at the 30.

Following the throw McKay fed the demoralized Chiefs a steady diet of Bell up the middle until he faced a third and six at the twenty. The cautious call in this situation would have been to continue to run Bell up the middle and if he didn't get the necessary yardage, have O'Donoghue attempt a field goal in the area of 37 yards. With the rain still pounding, McKay threw caution to the wind and called for another Williams pass. Once again the emboldened Williams executed the play perfectly against a perplexed Kansas City defense that had to wonder how in the world this second year quarterback was able to complete such important passes in such horrible weather. The shot to Giles moved the ball to the Kansas City 9.

McKay's faith in the ability of Williams to make the play regardless of the weather still touched the quarterback many years later. "You have to understand that when a ball is that wet you cannot squeeze it," explained Williams. "If you squeeze it, it's going to get away from you. You have to place it in your hand and almost shotput it to where you have to have it. I was glad that Coach McKay felt that to win this we have to put it in Doug's hands."

Three runs by Bell later the Bucs faced fourth and goal from the Kansas City two and it became time for McKay to make his most important decision as Buccaneers coach: go for the touchdown or attempt a field goal by the erratic O'Donoghue.

McKay showed faith in his beleaguered kicker and called on the Irish immigrant to kick the Bucs into the playoffs. It seemed to be a divine decision for as O'Donoghue trotted onto the field the rain let up for the first time all day. The horrible storms that had hit Tampa Bay had caused some to lose power and they weren't able to see what the rest of the nation saw. Instead if they had a transistor radio they tuned it to WDAE and heard Mark Champion, the voice of the Bucs, call the thirteenth play of the most important drive in franchise history. What they heard at first could have caused massive heart failure.

"Neil O'Donoghue awaiting the snap from Steve Wilson. It is a low snap!" Champion said with a touch of panic in his voice. Wilson had tried his best to dry off the ball but all the towels had become soaked by the rain. As a result the center had no choice but to lob the ball back due to the lack of grip. The ball bounced a bit but unlike the earlier attempt, holder Tom Blanchard was able to get the ball down cleanly. What Champion told the radio audience next sent the entire Tampa Bay area into convulsions of ecstasy.

"The kick is up. . . . It's good!" O'Donoghue, a player many had wanted to deport, had stepped up to prove to his teammates, his coach and perhaps more importantly, himself, that he could be counted on when it mattered most. The Tampa Bay Buccaneers were in the lead 3-0. It was too early to celebrate as the Chiefs still had over eight minutes to tie the game or worse.

The defense had been brilliant throughout the game, blunting the one legitimate Kansas City scoring threat and holding the Chiefs to just four first downs so far. Could they step up now and protect the lead or would this tremendous effort be wasted by a fourth consecutive missed opportunity? An entire nation was watching to find out the answer.

O'Donoghue, perhaps riding an adrenaline high, uncharacteristically boomed the kick-off through the end zone for a touchback. The Chiefs started at the twenty and gained next to nothing as Ted McKnight and Steve Fuller were both battered and bruised by the defense.

The Chiefs punted the ball back to the Bucs with 7:42 to play thinking that they would get one more shot to spoil Tampa Bay's season. Ricky Bell had other ideas.

With a lead to protect, Bell and his offensive teammates executed flawlessly. Starting at their own 44-yard line the Tampa Bay Buccaneers showed an entire nation that John McKay's offense could succeed in the National Football League. With each chunk of yardage ripped off by Bell and company, more and more time burned off the clock as delirious fans counted the seconds down. By the time the drive reached the Kansas City twenty it became apparent that the Chiefs were not going to get the ball back and the realization that the Tampa Bay Buccaneers were going to be Central Division champions sent the fans and the players into near pandemonium.

When Doug Williams took the final snap of the game and knelt down, Mark Champion gave the unfortunates who couldn't see the game on television a taste of the atmosphere at a jubilant Tampa Stadium. "The players are really whooping it up on the sideline, it is quite a sight to see," intoned Champion as Ricky Bell helped to carry Coach McKay off the field in a celebratory gesture that may have held more meaning for those two men than any of the national television audience could have possibly comprehended.

"A bunch of kids down there," Champion continued. "They deserve it. The Tampa Bay Buccaneers are the NFC Central Division champs." Fans in the stands danced with delight but were barred by the Tampa police department from storming the field because of the danger posed by the slippery steps, waterlogged field and a sea of inebriated humanity. Instead Buccaneer fans chanted "goalpost" over and over again and happily serenaded Buccaneer players with many renditions of "Hey, Hey Tampa Bay! The Bucs Know How to Shine!" The players in turn interrupted their celebrations among themselves to run towards the retaining walls to exchange high fives, shoulder slaps and primal screams with the fans. Doug Williams and Wally Chambers were seen stripping off some of their football equipment and hurling it into the stands to an appreciative throng. The last four weeks had tested the relationship between town and team, but on this day everyone involved chose to ignore the emotional outbursts, demanding expectations and hurt feelings to re-ignite a love affair that had started in 1976, survived 0-26 and was now being consummated with the teams first-ever championship. The Bucs had gone from worst to first and that was the most important thing.

Looking back on the victory many years later, PR Assistant Rick Odioso couldn't help but chuckle at the way the weather turned around. "It rained a lot, but the sun came out right after the game. Had it been a four o'clock game, it would have been played in sunshine." Instead the setting for the game was straight out of Hollywood, making the clinching victory all the more memorable.

The ending may have been exciting for the fans and television audience, but Richard "Batman" Wood said he and his teammates were even more juiced because of what was at stake for them. "3-0, you couldn't ask for a better culmination of the season," Wood remembered. "The excitement of the season from beginning to end, just total excitement. When Neil kicked that ball, it was like . . . . WHEW!!!"

Wood laughed, "I kept saying to myself, 'Is it that hard to be a champion in professional football?' I finally realized it was. You have to be on top of your game all the time." On this day the Buccaneers defense was on top of its game for 60 full minutes and the result was the NFC Central Division championship.

From his view high above the stadium floor, Mizell enjoyed watching the celebration, not as a fan but as a member of the Tampa Bay community. "Spectators stayed tough (despite the two inches of rain that fell during the game). They had been through the 0-26 and didn't want to miss the sweetest moment in Bucs history. When the winning field goal squished through the uprights, the feeling was as lifting as anyone will ever feel at a Super Bowl."

As the celebration moved to the locker room, word soon spread about how important this victory had been. The Chicago Bears had defeated the St. Louis Cardinals 42-6 at snowy Soldier Field. If the Bucs had lost the game, they would have been eliminated from the post-season. Instead they had won and it was time for a party in the locker room.

Cameras from NFL Films captured an uncharacteristically ecstatic John McKay, soaked to the bone by a combination of rainwater and Coca-Cola (the NFL had forbidden alcoholic beverages in the locker room) whipping a towel over his golf hat-clad head. "Gentleman, who picked us to be last?" asked the giddy coach to a series of laughs from his players. "We is the champs!" the coach bellowed to thunderous applause. With those words the good times truly rolled.

One by one players took time out from their revelry to take part in interviews with the assembled reporters. After three weeks of apologizing for their play, Buccaneer players seemed to revel in the opportunity to brag and engage in a little "I told you so" with the rest of the National Football League.

"We could have played in overtime, we could have played all month, and Kansas City would not have scored," offered Danny Reece. The cornerback wasn't necessarily exaggerating. The Kansas City offense had managed to gain just 80 yards on the entire afternoon, accumulating only four first downs along the way. The only legitimate scoring threat the Chiefs had enjoyed after Doug Williams interception was quickly blunted by Lee Roy Selmon's block of a field goal.

The defensive back also took a jab at some of the older and established teams like the Bears and Redskins who now had to sweat out making the playoffs while the upstart Bucs were in. "Now we know we won't have to go home and know that the rest of the NFL is laughing at us. Now the Bucs are in and the rest of the league can say, 'Oh No!' Now they have to watch us on television. Hah!"

As for the final score, not a single member of the team viewed it as an ugly victory. They all thought it was the most beautiful game they had ever played in. "I don't care if it was 3-0, or 10, or point-five to nothing. We are the champs!" exclaimed fullback Johnny Davis. "Hey! It was like the night before Christmas Saturday night and Sunday was Christmas."

Those sentiments were echoed by some of the members of Davis' offensive line.

"Wasn't a big score, but it was a big win," said guard Greg Horton.

"Biggest football thrill of my life," agreed center Steve Wilson. "We've been through the good times and the bad times. Now the good times are back. Three to nothing is as good as 30-0."

Wilson's snap to Tom Blanchard on the game-winning field goal had added to the drama, but the man who put the ball through the uprights defended the center and let it be known how clutch the special teams had been when the game was on the line.

"We had talked on the sideline about a slower snap so it would be easier with all the wet," said Neil O'Donoghue. "I was prepared for anything that might go wrong. As long as he (Blanchard) could get it down, I figured I could hit it good. I held up kicking a second while Tom got the ball down and then I hit . . . . I saw it go through."

Punter Tom Blanchard admitted he had not been as confident as O'Donoghue on the strategy of a slow snap and came onto the field green to the gills. "Yes, I was particularly nervous as we prepared for the second field goal attempt," Blanchard said amid the din of the locker room.

"I understand it slipped in my hands, but I don't remember," Blanchard continued, sounding as though he was so blinded by adrenaline that he couldn't recall the field goal and may not have been able to recognize the play if he saw it on tape. "I know it took a little longer and I was concerned, you know how we have been. Another mess-up would have been a disaster. But Neil got through quickly and got the ball up high quickly."

If Blanchard and O'Donoghue's teammates had any inkling of how dangerously close the game winning field goal had come to being missed, they didn't let on. Chances are they were more than happy not to think of what might have been and instead focused on what was: the Buccaneers were champions. That fact seemed to overwhelm many.

"This is the happiest moment of my career," proclaimed defensive end Wally Chambers, who had been on some horrible pro teams. "I haven't been on a championship team since my senior year in high school. This is it. This is the highlight of my career. This has got to be the max."

The sentiments of safety Mark Cotney spoke for all original Buccaneers, "Oh man, what can you say?" said a tired but elated defensive back. "It's my personal high in football. I didn't go to Oklahoma or Alabama. I went to a small school, Cameron State. I've always loved to play football because I love the game. We played our hearts out the first years and now, well the good Lord's been good to us. He was out there on the field with us today. This is all a credit to the coaches and fans that stuck with us."

Perhaps the man with the greatest behind the scenes impact during the week of preparation for the clinching victory sat in a heap in front of his locker, still in full uniform well after some teammates had already showered and changed. Linebacker David Lewis, who had stepped up and challenged his teammates to elevate their games and had then gone out and led them by example, wore a subtle smile of exhausted contentment.

While not nearly as voluble as he had been a week before, the words chosen by Lewis spoke to the heart of what the Buccaneers had just accomplished and what it meant.

"It's great, it's super, it's the ultimate," began Lewis. "It was do or die. It was like being an actor and the curtain was either going to go up or down.

"I played for losing teams here and this makes it that much sweeter. (Coach) McKay and the rest of the coaches kept the faith and the five year plan is working out – mark it down.

"You talk about great Pittsburgh, great Houston and great Dallas, but the Tampa Bay Buccaneers are the only team to win a division championship in just four years. All that talk about not being able to win the pressure game. We wanted this game, I wanted this game bad, real bad. We're in the playoffs and that's what I care about."

After he had finished his ruminations the tired athlete was asked if he was going to wear his uniform home.

Lewis wearily replied, "I might." Then he reconsidered, "Naw. Can't wear it home, it would mess up my car."

Thanks to the triumph over Kansas City, Lewis would have at least one more chance to slip on his Florida orange number 57 jersey.

Time may have diminished some of the crispness of the memory for Lee Roy Selmon but not the luster. Looking back on the locker room scene following the victory over Kansas City, Selmon knew that he and his teammates had done something that would never be replicated.

"We were just so excited," he said. "I was so excited for our team. That was a team effort to make it to the playoffs. To be a part of the history. It's the first time. It's history. To celebrate as players, coaches and fans, it's a once in a lifetime experience. You realize you'll never be in that position again. You make the playoffs again, it's not the first time. So it was very special for a lot of reasons. It was the culmination of a lot of hard work for Coach McKay and the players, especially those who had been there for four years."

The victory did more than just clinch the NFC Central Division championship and a playoff berth; it also meant that a playoff game would be played in Tampa. With a record of 10-6, the Buccaneers were one game ahead of the NFC West champion Los Angeles Rams and therefore claimed the right to play at least one game at home in the playoffs. The Bucs opponent in that game wouldn't be determined until after the Wild Card round the next Sunday.

On this night no one in Tampa Bay cared about possible opponents. The time had come to celebrate a championship. The Buccaneers were in and the rest of the league would have to deal with it.

CHAPTER
13

Snubbed

Although John McKay had let loose with some uncharacteristic celebration following the victory over Kansas City he had quickly slipped off to the side to allow his players to bask in the limelight. The day after the game during his Monday post-mortem the usually glib coach gave a heartfelt account of what the win meant for him. Eschewing puns and one-liners, McKay surprised all in attendance when asked to rank the accomplishment of winning the NFC Central Division with the other milestones of his career.

"I don't think I've ever been happier for a group of football players," McKay started, obviously a little emotional. "I've never felt such elation as I did after the win over Kansas City that gave us the division championship. The elation wasn't for me but for the players, especially the players like the Selmon brothers and Richard Wood and the rest who had been here since the first year. No players have ever had to suffer through what they did."

Considering that his resume included four collegiate national championships and two Heisman Trophy winners, McKay's admission that this was the happiest he had been as a coach only highlighted the regard in which he held his players. By the same token those same players who may have been cast aside by a more impatient or unfaithful coach were only too happy to have given him such a moment.

One in particular was Richard "Batman" Wood. Wood had won two of McKay's national titles at Southern Cal and had seen the coach through all 26 losses of that notorious streak. According to Wood, the NFC Central Division Championship was a testament of McKay's coaching ability and strong will. "I understood what he was talking about," Wood said of McKay's unexpected praise. "You have to look at that season and the three previous seasons. Look at what he had gone through as a football coach. You look back at his career and how successful he was."

"Then in pro football it was hard," Wood continued. The way McKay was treated by the national media appalled Wood. "That was sad, but coach hung in there. You could tell it was frustrating to him. Hell, it was frustrating to me and a lot of the others like Lee Roy Selmon, Mark Cotney, Mike Washington and Cedric Brown. A lot of great players were there those first two years.

"For us to persevere and stay close and not fall apart at the seams, like some teams do when guys don't care about each other. We cared about each other and it showed on the field." It also showed in the way McKay praised his champions on the Monday following the Kansas City game.

The one player who more than any other had been the greatest beneficiary of McKay's tutelage and gridiron nurturing was Ricky Bell. After two years of injuries, heartache and frustration, Bell had put together a season for the ages. Bell's statistics on the year solidly placed him in the upper echelon of the NFL's running backs. 1,263 yards on 283 carries for an average gain of 4.5 yards and seven touchdowns. Not measured in the statistics was the impact Bell's running style had on demoralizing opposing defenses. That was never more apparent than in the season finale when Bell almost single-handedly ran off the last seven minutes of the game as he rushed for a total of 139 yards on the day.

Bell's mere presence also forced opposing defensive coordinators to spend most of their time looking for #42 on the field. This allowed Doug Williams to continue his development as a professional quarterback. When the running game was really clicking Williams had hurt defenses several times with long passes. In the end he had enjoyed possibly the most successful second year of any quarterback in league history. Williams' statistical line showed a completion percentage of 41.8% (166 completions in 397 attempts) for 2,448 yards and 18 touchdowns. While his completion percentage was low compared to other quarterbacks and he had piled up a great many interceptions during the late season three-game losing streak, Williams had executed McKay's offense exactly the way the coach had demanded. Williams had executed it so well that he was now the youngest quarterback to lead his team to a division title and big things would be expected from him in his third year.

Williams' appreciated Bell's contributions to the offense and states plainly that the Buccaneers would not have been the same team without him in 1979. According to Williams, Bell's hard charging running style not only inspired his teammates but was necessary to keep many crucial drives continuing. A perfect example was the clutch run from his own end zone during the victory in Minnesota. Without that play, the Buccaneers would have been forced to punt from deep within their own territory in a tight game. Instead, the Bucs were able to run a good chunk of time off the clock to preserve the victory. "We rode Ricky Bell," Williams admits. "We literally rode Ricky Bell. I can honestly say 700 to 750 yards were Ricky yards after his first initial hit."

Ricky Bell's practice habits also made him a team leader in addition to his game day performance. Because of his statistical line, work habits and status as a team leader Bell was overwhelmingly voted the Most Valuable Player of the 1979 team by a panel of local sportswriters. The man who had once been the symbol of all that was wrong with the worst team in professional football now found himself the symbol of all that was good with the surprise team of the NFL.

In his typical understated style, Bell thanked the press for the award and then gave the praise to his coach and teammates almost as quickly as he burst through the line of scrimmage throughout the season.

"What makes it the greatest honor I've ever received is that we have so many great athletes on our team, especially on defense," Bell said. "Guys like Lee Roy Selmon and David Lewis and Richard Wood. I feel like those guys are being cheated because they're the ones who held the team together for three to four years now. I can't speak highly enough of those guys. The defense has done it for us all year long. There have been so many times when the offense has struggled. But the defense has been fantastic."

When asked if the award was all the more sweeter because of his struggles during the first two years of his professional career, Bell admitted that it was, especially because he had needed to grow up a lot as a man.

"Of course it is," Bell began his long and thoughtful answer. "It's been tough, what with all the injuries, all the losses, all the setbacks, being the Number One pick in the league.

"Truthfully, I expected to come in here and rip up the league, but it just doesn't happen, especially with an expansion team. But we've come such a long way in such a short period of time.

"The first couple of years it was difficult to believe I could do it. I couldn't do anything right. But the drive was always there, it was never missing, and I knew eventually I'd do it. I never got down, not when people were booing, never. All we needed was to get the guys who are winners, leaders, guys like Doug Williams and Jimmie Giles and Steve Wilson and all the others.

"When we got the right guys, we developed a winning attitude. Now we're for real. It makes you forget about all the tough days. Each victory now means a lot more than it ever did. We were at the bottom of the barrel and now we're headed to the top.

"Man, it's unbelievable, but I believe in the unbelievable. I couldn't ask for anything more. Today is the most rewarding day in my life."

The team as a whole was finding the experience of being a playoff participant rewarding in many ways. One way was that they were getting a few days off. A division championship meant that the Buccaneers would be off for one full week while the Wild Card teams battled to see who would be their opponent. However, the players were so sky-high emotionally, that they couldn't stay away from One Buccaneer Place even though McKay had dismissed them for a few days to prepare for Christmas with their families. They were coming to the facility so that they could make the feeling last and when they spoke to reporters they spoke like little kids who had found a bicycle under their tree on Christmas morning.

Much like his head coach Ricky Bell also viewed winning the NFC Central Division Championship as the greatest football accomplishment he had been connected to.

"Even at Southern California, I never felt like I do now," Bell said. "There a winning tradition was already present when I arrived. Here, we're building something. It's a lot more rewarding. Now we'll be on national TV at least once and, who knows, maybe more. Maybe we'll get to the Super Bowl."

It wasn't just the stars of the team that were feeling the high. Role players were coming into the training facility just to be where the electricity was. Special teams player Tony Davis, who was in his first year as a Buc after three years in Cincinnati, may have described the feelings of the team most accurately and eloquently.

"All the chances we had of winning and making it until (the finale), it's an indescribable feeling," Davis said by his locker. "I just feel honored to be a part of this team although I don't play that much.

"I remember the first day of camp. It was 102 degrees and the humidity was 90 percent. 'How can I play football in this weather?' I asked myself. And look at me now. We're division champs."

The players weren't the only ones who wanted the delirious high of the championship to last forever. For the first time that anyone could remember people were dreaming of a Florida orange Christmas rather than a white one and children would go to sleep with visions of souvenir Buccaneer jerseys and helmets dancing through their heads. The most sought after Buccaneer related gift this Christmas season however was a ticket to the Divisional playoff game.

Season-ticket holders received first priority when it came to tickets to the home playoff game the weekend after Christmas. For those who weren't season ticket holders purchasing a ticket meant spending the night at the Bay Area's newest campsite, the Tampa Stadium parking lot.

Thousands upon thousands of fans pitched tents, unfurled sleeping bags and lit camp stoves to cook their dinners the night before single tickets went on sale. The next morning when the box office opened at 8 o'clock there was a line snaking all around the edifice of the stadium. The ducats went before evening selling at a rate of 1,100 per hour, and many fans left disappointed, although not too horribly disappointed. They would still see history made in Tampa; they would just have to do it in the same manner as the rest of the United States, on CBS.

The good times and good feeling temporarily subsided as the week before the Wild Card round ended. Post-season awards were announced and the Buccaneers were rudely reminded that while they may have won a division championship they still had not won much respect as a team.

When the voting for the NFC Pro Bowl rosters was announced only one member of the Tampa Bay Buccaneers was named as a member,

Lee Roy Selmon. Being selected to the Pro Bowl was considered a great honor because your peers in the league chose roster spots. Lee Roy had undoubtedly deserved the honor, leading the team with 11 sacks and an astounding 60 quarterback pressures, all while being double and triple teamed by opposing offensive lines.

While Lee Roy's great season was being richly rewarded with a mid-winter trip to Honolulu, his defensive teammates were shockingly ignored. Despite achieving a historic triple crown, leading the league in total defense by allowing the fewest points (237), yards (3,949) and yards per play (3.89), the rest of Selmon's teammates were left without recognition from players around the league.

Selmon was stunned by the development and used the notoriety he received in his selection to stump for national recognition for his overlooked and under appreciated teammates.

"One player can't make a team the Number One defense in the NFL," Selmon told the *Tampa Tribune's* Jim Selman. "It takes all 11 players and a good offense to have a good team. This honor reflects on the type of people we have."

Coach McKay agreed with Lee Roy that it was wrong for the number one defensive unit to only have one Pro Bowl representative. McKay had a sneaking suspicion that nobody believed that a Tampa Bay Buccaneer unit should be rewarded because they were still perceived as a group of bumblers and losers.

"I'm glad to see Lee Roy make it," said McKay. "Disappointed for the others? Yes. I won't say who else I thought should be there. But we had several other players I thought had played well enough to be chosen.

"I am pleased with our season and resent the people who are trying to detract from it because of our schedule or the way we finished. This team pulled together and won the game it had to win to get into the playoffs. I think our division is stronger than anyone gives it credit for and we will do our best to represent it well in the playoffs."

McKay's defense of his team was appreciated in the locker room. Richard "Batman" Wood, left off the Pro Bowl roster even though he led the number one defense in tackles (158) said that he and McKay talked about the oversight and determined to set the record straight on the field. "I think it (being left of the Pro Bowl roster) was a snub period. We had enemies everywhere. You just got to look past it and say, 'I played on a great football team and had a great season.' McKay and I spoke about it and said we just got to go out and win the Super Bowl."

Later in the week Lee Roy received yet another honor, being named first team All-Pro by the writers of the Associated Press. Lee Roy was selected over perennial choice Harvey Martin of the Dallas Cowboys, and joined Jack Youngblood of the Los Angeles Rams at defensive end. Once again, he was the only Buccaneer named to the first team as Wood and Lewis were overlooked. Even more shocking than their omission from the Pro Bowl or the first team All-Pro rosters was that neither Wood nor Lewis were named to the second team All-Pro roster. One Buccaneer was named to the second team All-Pro roster and he had something in common with Lee Roy, he was a Selmon. Dewey Selmon was voted to the second team All-Pro roster at linebacker joining Jim Youngblood of the Rams and Randy Gradishar of the Denver Broncos.

Dewey seemed almost apologetic in accepting the award. While he had an outstanding season, recording 125 tackles and causing two fumbles, he had not had as many tackles as Wood (158) or as many big plays as Lewis. Nevertheless, Selmon was still deserving of recognition but wanted it known that he should not have been chosen over his teammates.

"I definitely have not had the year Richard Wood and David Lewis have had this year. As linebackers go, Richard Wood probably is the best of all the inside linebackers in the league. And pound for pound and potential for potential, David Lewis is the best outside linebacker."

Dewey continued, "We have not been on national TV, so the sportswriters have not seen Richard and David play. Maybe they will get the exposure they deserve in the playoffs."

Defensive players weren't the only ones snubbed by post-season awards. Despite rushing for a career high and being the focal point of the team's offense, Ricky Bell was not named to the Pro Bowl and was not selected to either the first or second team of the Associated Press roster. He was overshadowed by Walter Payton, Earl Campbell, Ottis Anderson of the St. Louis Cardinals and Wilbert Montgomery of the Philadelphia Eagles.

When some of the less prestigious awards came out, two Buccaneers received recognition. David Lewis was named All-NFC linebacker and guard Greg Roberts was named to the All-Rookie team, the only honor to any member of the offensive line that had paved the way for Bell and had allowed Doug Williams to only be sacked 12 times, the best in the league.

As some of his teammates were finally rewarded, the week of honors for Lee Roy continued. In addition to his Pro Bowl selection and the Associated Press honor Lee Roy received the highest individual honor on the defensive side of the ball. To the delight of everyone in the Tampa Bay area, Lee Roy was voted the NFL Defensive Player of the Year for 1979. The scope of the recognition was enormous. With candidates such as L.C. Greenwood, Jack Lambert, Jack Ham and Joe Greene of the Pittsburgh Steelers, Randy White of the Dallas Cowboys and Mike Reinfeldt of the Houston Oilers, Lee Roy had won out over an impressive list of candidates.

The award meant that the nation was becoming aware of a fact that fans in Tampa Bay had known since 1976, the most dominating defensive force in all of professional football resided in Tampa Stadium. Lee Roy, a man who would rather face three offensive linemen than talk about himself, was overwhelmed by the honor. His reaction was notable not only for its humility, but for the way he expressed something no one in the country had ever thought possible, pride in being a member of the Tampa Bay Buccaneers.

"I can't say it's a dream come true because I never dared to dream of such a thing," an awed Selmon admitted. "Why, everything this year is like a story somebody sat down and wrote maybe like I sat down and wrote it.

"I felt that way from the start of the franchise and when they drafted my brother Dewey, well a feeling came over me I still don't have words for, that we could stay together in the pros.

"And now we have what we have and I have a fine wife and daughter, a fine home, and we all have our health, we have this great team, these wonderful fans, why, who' d live anywhere else?

"God's been good to Lee Roy Selmon."

Even long after his playing career ended, Selmon couldn't help but think that his teammates were the reason for his receiving so much recognition. "I tell you it was quite humbling (winning the awards). I have always approached team goals as the biggest goals. The biggest accomplishments I key on are our team goals. Win as many games as we can, get as far as we can, try to win a championship. That's what we want, that's what I would like to see more than anything than having an individual award. It was a team award. We had great players and coaches that I had the privilege to play with. Had it not been for those players and coaches the individual awards would not have happened."

Selmon's bevy of post-season honors acted to quell some of the pain his teammates may have felt in being snubbed. To a man they all said that individual awards weren't as important as team goals and that the goal now was to get to the Super Bowl. However, they were keen on using any disappointment they did feel as a motivating factor heading into their playoff match-up with either the Eagles or the Rams.

Any pain they may have felt for themselves was wiped away by the pain they felt for their head coach when the greatest snub of the post-season award process was perpetrated. The NFL Coach of the Year was announced last and John McKay, who had guided a team that had once been 0-26 to a division championship in just two years, had not won. To make matters worse the man who was named Coach of the Year, Jack Pardee of the Washington Redskins, hadn't even led his perennial playoff team to the post-season. Washington lost in a must-win game in the season's last weekend while McKay's team won their pivotal contest. More embarrassing than not winning, McKay wasn't even the runner-up or third place candidate. He finished fourth behind Pardee, Dick Vermeil of Philadelphia and Don Coryell of San Diego.

If he had finished second, McKay would have probably been fine with the decision, after all he had once said to the Tampa Bay media, "I don't desire the honor, and I don't think you should try to judge talent in awarding it. The best coach is usually the one who wins the most. Last year the Steelers won it all and that makes Chuck Noll the best. The year before it was Tom Landry."

Surprisingly the 1979 winner was not a coach who had won the most, it was a coach who didn't even qualify his team for the playoffs although they had been to the post-season several times in the decade. Additionally, Vermeil and Coryell coached teams that had been to the playoffs the year before and had only achieved maintaining the status quo. There was no doubt in most Tampa Bay followers minds that McKay was being punished for succeeding with a team that was supposed to lose and doing it by proving that his style, long viewed as "not professional" could thrive in the NFL.

For the first time the iconoclastic coach, who had freely admitted he did not care for the politics of the NFL, lashed out over the lack of respect he received from his peers and the sportswriters across the nation. Losing the award was not what bothered him. What made McKay angry was that the powers that be in the NFL were so obstinate about what they felt was the right way to run an NFL team that they couldn't admit that they had been wrong about McKay, his coaching style or his football strategy.

"I think I take the biggest bum rap in the country. The reason is they're so damn jealous that a college coach came in and did it," McKay said at a press luncheon where he ripped NFL coaches and national sportswriters.

He lamented that nothing the Bucs did would satisfy the national media because they had already ordained Tampa Bay a laughingstock and were either too lazy or stubborn to change their tune. "We can't get a national image because I didn't play in the NFL. I had other things to do. It just kills them (that we have won) so every time they get a chance . . . (to insult the team), they do.

"That is our image and we are not going to shake it, unless we go to the Super Bowl. No, if we do that they'd say we were lucky. It is inborn in the National Football League about college coaches. That's as it has been for years. They try to make the game a mystique. I told you when I came in and I tell you now, there is nothing unusual (about pro football)."

McKay also admitted that he was treated as a pariah among his fellow head coaches because he hadn't gone up through the ranks of NFL assistants as most of them had. That lack of respect irked him to no end. "Only ones that have treated me worth a damn are Don Shula, Chuck Knox, Dick Vermeil and Marv Levy. I think it all started with my salary. Hell, I wasn't looking for a job, I had a job."

Another reason that McKay felt he was constantly belittled was that he didn't look or act like a typical NFL coach on the sidelines. McKay's lack of emotional outbursts on the sideline, his golf hat and sunglasses, his unorthodox relationship with players and the press and his strict adherence to the offensive philosophy that had served him so well at USC alienated him from his peers and national press.

"I heard there were complaints about me saying we stunk. We did. And note I said 'we.' I include me, the coaches. These players have my 100 percent support but the one thing you better do is play. I will praise them when they play well and won't when they don't. On the sideline when something happens I normally don't yell, I don't do anything."

After getting worked up, McKay did calm down enough to state plainly that his national recognition was really not important after all. He had proven he could do it, his players had proven they were worthy of the NFL and that was truly all that mattered to him.

Looking back on how far the team had come, McKay allowed himself to be proud.

"The biggest mistake that you can make when you become a head coach someplace is the desire for victory too quickly," he said. "If you make that mistake in the pros you make trades and in college you cheat in recruiting. We could have made some trades and won four, five or six games a year but we wouldn't ever have come close to getting in the playoffs.

"I have to thank Mr. Hugh Culverhouse for giving me the time. I don't think there is another owner in football who would have been so patient. We knew in 1976 that with the exception of a few players like Lee Roy Selmon and Richard Wood we weren't any good. But I couldn't just say it at the time. It wouldn't have been fair to the players.

"I read everything I could find about how the various teams had built themselves and only one thing was clear. You had to have a lot of your own draft choices on the team. Those teams win and the others don't."

McKay had followed that advice to the maximum, as the 1979 Central Division champions included 21 players from their first four drafts, four free-agents from college and ten others who had signed as free agents with the Bucs after spending only one season or less with another professional team. This meant that the roster of the Buccaneer was filled from top to bottom with players who only knew how to play professional football the McKay way and had done so very well.

McKay continued, "Another important thing is to stick with the same leadership and same plan. Teams like Dallas have been successful with the same management and the same philosophy over many years. Other teams have changed coaches, front office and offenses like underwear and they haven't gotten anything done."

This philosophy was the reason McKay stuck with an offensive and defensive system that was ridiculed during his first three years in the league, but it was also the reason both the offense and defense had been so successful in 1979. The players knew what to do and when to do it, and that equated with a division championship.

McKay's philosophy in never changing leadership was also the reason he didn't bench Doug Williams for the finale against Kansas City. With the season on the line, McKay knew that the team would react better under a familiar hand than that of someone they weren't as used to. Williams had rewarded McKay with a solid effort and a post-season clinching victory. The coach admitted that Williams was the "X" factor the Bucs had needed to implement his offense.

"Biggest thing was to make a trade that gave us a quarterback who could do it for us. Doug Williams has had some bad games lately but he has had some great ones. There is a lot more pressure on the quarterback than anyone, including the coach. He has proved to be a good quarterback."

As he left the luncheon, many reporters wished McKay a Merry Christmas and thanked him for his candor. Not to leave the luncheon on a down note, McKay did have to let a one-liner fly when asked what he wanted for Christmas.

"I think my wife is getting me a fur coat." Then McKay said what he really wanted, "Three wins in a row and never look back."

McKay's feelings that he was an object of scorn throughout football were not merely the ramblings of a paranoid man. The most popular player on his team and a leading member of the Tampa Bay press corps also felt that the coach was a target although for different reasons.

"I was very disappointed for Coach McKay," said Lee Roy Selmon after his playing days were over, "because he had done a good job. He had done some things perhaps others in the NFL didn't appreciate. Like he brought in the 3-4 defense which others said wouldn't work. But he said we were going to run it and we ran it. It became very successful and some other teams started playing the 3-4 scheme.

"Why he wasn't chosen I don't know, but he was certainly deserving from the year he had with us coaching that team that year. I truly believe his enjoyment was in seeing us go as far as we did."

When asked about McKay's reputation as a coach 25 years later, Hubert Mizell lamented that the Bucs' first coach may have just been too honest when it came to the simplicity of football and his detractors would never forgive him for that. "McKay was in some ways unconventional," the *Times* columnist remembered. "He refused to speak in coaching idioms like 'Backs against the wall' or 'There's no tomorrow.' John, explaining his colorful and interesting talk, told me, 'Back when I was an assistant at Oregon in the late 1950s, and still wasn't sure I didn't prefer joining the FBI and becoming an agent rather than staying in football, I promised myself that I would never lean on clichés.'"

Mizell continued, "Some media, especially after McKay moved to the NFL, found him a difficult challenge. Truth was, John felt happier and more comfortable in dealing with local reporters, guys he got to know. He thought, with reason, that many national media persons came to Tampa with an agenda to make the old USC coach look less than appealing.

"I loved dealing with him, especially having one-on-one sessions in his office when both of us would usually wind up in powerful laughter. He was creative, entertaining, gutsy and intriguing."

Even without Coach of the Year hardware, McKay enjoys the support of his quarterback to this day. "John McKay was straightforward, to the point," Doug Williams says. "If you are not getting the job done he is going to ship your ass out. He'd tell you that. At the same time he was able to put together enough decent athletes, enough players to put them in a position to make the playoffs."

While McKay and his players were rightfully feeling unappreciated by the NFL for all they had accomplished, they did receive a vote of confidence from the most important voice of all. Commissioner Pete Rozelle didn't care about coaching credentials or end of year awards; he was concerned with the business of the NFL. During his year-end review, Rozelle told the national press that the success of the Tampa Bay Buccaneers, no matter how it was pooh-poohed, was good for business and he for one wished them the best of luck.

"You know as crazy as things have been in the NFL this year, just think that the Bucs have to win only two games to get into the Super Bowl. Obviously anything can happen."

It was this "anything can happen" optimism that Rozelle wanted to see spread throughout the NFL. Having visited other teams around the league Rozelle knew the important role the Bucs had played in revitalizing hopes in all NFL cities.

"The fans in Detroit," Rozelle gave as an example, "are saying they get their quarterback next year plus good draft picks and look what Tampa Bay did.

"Tampa Bay's achievement should be great encouragement to have-not teams and from where I sit that's exactly what we want."

As amazing as it may have sounded, Rozelle's message was clear. The Tampa Bay Buccaneers, the laughingstock of the league, was now the model franchise heading into the new decade and the rest of professional football better get used to that idea.

The week of speculating about whom the Buccaneers would play in the divisional round of the playoffs was put to rest on December 23rd. The early game on Wild Card Sunday pitted the Chicago Bears against the Philadelphia Eagles at Veterans Stadium. In the first half the Bears executed all the phases of the game well. That sound fundamental style had made them one of the hottest teams in the league. Walter Payton scored two touchdowns and the Bears defense clamped down on Ron Jaworski and the Eagle's offense to lead 17-10 at intermission.

The second half saw Walter Payton forced to leave the contest when he aggravated the shoulder injury that had forced him out of the second Tampa Bay game. Without their offensive focal point, the Bears didn't score another point the rest of the way. Meanwhile Ron Jaworski got hot and fired two of his three touchdown passes in the second half, including a 63-yard strike to Billy Campfield that sealed Philadelphia's 27-17 victory.

The result of the Wild Card game meant that Coach McKay knew he would have to get his team prepared to stop a very potent offense in the Philadelphia Eagles. In the second half Jaworski had dominated the game against a Bears defense that was in almost every way the equal of Tampa Bay's.

For now football was put on the back burner and the Tampa Bay area focused on Christmas. It was a short respite, for as soon as the last package was unwrapped and the last leftover was put in the refrigerator, the rest of the week would be spent in eager anticipation of December 29th.

CHAPTER 14

Party-Crashers

Saturday, December 29, 1979 was a typical winter day Tampa Bay style. The skies were clear blue, the sun was shining brightly and a faint breeze circulated through the air as temperatures reached into the mid-seventies. It was the type of day referred to in the Tampa Bay area as a "Chamber of Commerce" day, where the weather corroborated with the natural landscape to showcase just how beautiful and inviting the Bay Area is.

Weather such as this had been attracting tourists by the millions to spend a few weeks of every year escaping the dreary environs of the Snow Belt by relaxing on the Suncoast beaches. On this day Tampa Bay's natural beauty would take a backseat to its football team as a carnival atmosphere surrounded Tampa Stadium.

All the pomp and circumstance of playoff football was on display. CBS's Brent Musberger, Jayne Kennedy, Irv Cross and Jimmy "The Greek" broadcast *The NFL Today* live from the corner of an end zone. One Buccaneer in particular, Doug Williams, had eagerly anticipated the arrival of the crew of *The NFL Today* to Tampa.

According to Williams, earlier in the season when Kennedy had taped a profile of equipment manager Frank Pupello, she had made a wager with Williams concerning Tampa Bay's chances of making the playoffs and now had to come through on it.

"I think everyone thought Jayne Kennedy was the prettiest woman ever on this Earth," chuckled Williams. "She promised me if we made it to the playoffs that she would cook me dinner. So we made it to the play-offs and I was ecstatic. It was the first time I ate broccoli and cheese and Jayne Kennedy cooked it!"

On Saturday the hosts of the pre-game show thought it was the Bucs that would be cooked. The announcing team of Curt Gowdy and Hank Stram agreed with the pre-game panel. It was a given that the Buccaneers had no chance to beat the favored Eagles.

As the nation watched *The NFL Today* and the fans in attendance worked into frenzy John McKay was in the locker room with his team. Richard "Batman" Wood recalled that the team and coaching staff were not in awe of Philadelphia and in fact felt as though they were about to administer a whooping that no one in the country could anticipate.

"You wouldn't want to play us on this day, I can guarantee you that," Wood vividly explained. The negative media coverage and the lack of post-season honors led to a defiant clubhouse. Wood recalled that while there was no yelling or screaming, that was just not McKay's style; there was a palpable feeling of intensity and anger coursing through the team and coaching staff.

"Coach McKay was pretty pumped up himself, he was kind of excited," Wood recalled. There had been a lot of talk throughout the week about the Bucs chances, but now was the time for action. "Talk is talk," Wood remembered feeling. "The point is that you are playing a pro football team. There are players who just talk but we were ready. Everyone was against us except those in the stands wearing orange.

"A lot of emotions, there were a lot of guys ticked off. They had to play us for four quarters, but we said that they would not leave the field that day with a win."

Quarterback Doug Williams was not one of the players ticked off. Instead the young man from Grambling, perhaps still savoring the broc-coli and cheese dinner cooked up by Jayne Kennedy, was quite relaxed.

"I felt good going into that football game," recalled Williams. "We were kind of like the gunfighter, because all of the pressure was on Phila-delphia. We were such an underdog we had nothing to lose. Therefore we were loose."

As the 12:30 kickoff time approached John McKay probably looked around at the faces of his players and took in the realization of what had been accomplished by this small band of men. Just two years after ending a 26-game losing streak that had made him and his team the butt of national jokes, the Tampa Bay Buccaneers were about to play for the right to advance to the NFC Championship Game. McKay had shocked quite a few people when he had said he was prouder of this group of men than any he had coached. Now in this time and place, they looked to him before the biggest game of their lives.

There was Doug Williams, who in only his second year had not only debunked the myth about the inability of an African-American to be a professional quarterback, but had also become one of the youngest men ever to lead a team to a division championship.

There was Lee Roy Selmon, the first draft choice in franchise history and the foundation that McKay had chosen to build his team around. Selmon had accepted the tremendous responsibility of being the focal point of an expansion team and had excelled both on the field and in the community. 1979 had been Selmon's coming-out season and he was no longer just McKay's rock, he was a pillar for all of Tampa Bay as well.

There was Dave Reavis, Greg Roberts, Darryl Carlton, Greg Horton, Steve Wilson and an injured Charley Hannah. They were a mixed group of rejects, rookies and out of position players who had formed one of the NFL's best offensive lines in 1979.

There was Neil O'Donoghue the Irish kicker who had persevered through the blocked kicks and had rewarded McKay's confidence in him by kicking a game-winning field goal through a monsoon from a muddy field when the entire season was on the line.

There was Dewey Selmon, Cecil Johnson, Richard Wood and David Lewis a quartet of talented linebackers who had been the dominant playmaking force on the number one ranked defense in all the National Football League.

There was Wally Chambers, Randy Crowder and Bill Kollar, three defensive linemen who had overcome injury, personal demons and professional disappointment to join Lee Roy Selmon in his quest to stuff the run and punish opposing quarterbacks.

There was Mike Washington, Curtis Jordan, Jeris White, Mark Cotney, Danny Reece and Cedric Brown who together formed the most underrated secondary in the league.

There was Jimmie Giles who in only his sixth year of organized football had become the most productive receiver in Tampa Bay history. Joining Giles were Larry Mucker, Morris Owens, Isaac Hagins and Jim Obradovich as a group of under-appreciated receivers who had struggled at times but made big catch after big catch during the season when it counted most.

And finally there was Ricky Bell, the running back who had always been known for who he wasn't rather than who he was. In 1979 Ricky Bell out-rushed Tony Dorsett and had accomplished something Earl Campbell hadn't, he had been the offensive force that led his team to a divisional championship. By doing so Ricky Bell had become the undisputed heart of the team.

As they filed out of the locker room and onto the field many of the players probably dedicated themselves to winning the game not just for themselves or for the Tampa Bay area, but for their coach as well. The sarcastic, silver-haired cigar-smoker in the funny golf hat had endured ridicule and potshots for three years. Without his patience and selflessness in bearing the brunt of all the criticism for their lack of execution, the Bucs may have never have ended that first losing streak. To truly thank McKay for all he had done for them and restore him back to his proper place as one of the sports truly gifted coaches, the Buccaneers knew they would have to win today's game.

"Coach McKay and the staff had us so well prepared," recalled Lee Roy Selmon. "I thought the excitement was generated during that period of time (filing out of the locker room)."

"It didn't take much," Selmon said, chuckling over the adrenaline that he and his teammates felt coursing through their systems moments before the biggest game of their lives. "Let's go play, get 'em out on the field," those were the pre-game comments of McKay that Selmon recollected. "We win we go on, we lose we go home, and we had worked too hard, we were eager to get out of the locker room and get the game started."

Added Bill Kollar, "Everybody was really jacked up and couldn't wait to get out there and take the field. The Eagles had Wilbert Montgomery who was a great running back. They had Jaworski at quarterback and had a real good team. Everybody was excited knowing that if you put a couple of wins together, all of a sudden you're in the Super Bowl.

"We just came out real strong."

The players were not the only ones to come out strong. The more than 72,000 in attendance were in a state of near pandemonium when the teams took the field. If referee Fred Silva delayed the kickoff by even a few seconds, there was a chance that the fans enthusiasm could shake Tampa Stadium to its very foundation.

According to Selmon, the players on the field noticed and were even further energized by the fans bedlam. "The excitement generated by the fans, the electricity was like I had never seen before. The fans were just unbelievable. You walk out in that kind of atmosphere, it was a great atmosphere."

Times columnist Hubert Mizell had more perspective on the overall importance of the playoff game due to his career experiences, but he was also aware of how worked up the crowd at Tampa Stadium was. "As a reporter who covered Super Bowls, World Series, Olympics and a load of other major sports occurrences, the Bucs-Eagles game would not rank among the best of those, but for the Tampa Bay area, there was a unique twinge not unlike the ugliest chap in town suddenly gaining a date with the pettiest girl. It was easily the biggest sports happening in Tampa Bay history."

The cacophony of sound came to a crescendo as Tony Franklin, Philadelphia's barefoot kicker, booted the opening kickoff towards Isaac Hagins. Hagins took the ball near the goal line and returned the kickoff out to the twenty. The Tampa Stadium crowd was sophisticated enough to know not to be a distraction to their own offense, but as Doug Williams walked up to the line of scrimmage for the first play, an audible hum could be heard from every corner of the stadium.

Two running plays by Eckwood and Bell moved the Bucs to the 26. On third and four Williams dropped back to pass and was protected well by his offensive line. Williams delivered a rifle shot to Jimmie Giles at the Tampa Bay 45 to give the Bucs a first down. Two more Ricky Bell runs and a Doug Williams quarterback sneak on third and inches gave the Bucs a first down at the Philadelphia 44.

The Bucs ran into their first bit of adversity on the following play when Darryl Carlton, the University of Tampa graduate who had filled in so admirably for Charley Hannah at right tackle during the playoff push, was called for holding. The penalty moved the ball back to the Tampa Bay 46.

Doug Williams and the offense didn't shrink from the challenge of 1rst and 20; instead they offered evidence of how much they had grown. Williams shrugged off a strong pass rush and rocketed his second pass of the day to Jimmie Giles at the Philadelphia 38. Ricky Bell followed the pass with a hard run up the middle to the 31 for a first down.

The Bucs converted yet another third down on a Jerry Eckwood run to the 21. On the next play the Eagles discovered just how powerful a running back Ricky Bell was. After clearing the line, Bell cut to the left, lowered his head and carried three Eagle defenders to the 13-yard line before being stopped. The drive bogged down following a drop by Larry Mucker and McKay made his first gamble of the day.

Despite having seen his team fail on crucial short yardage situations during their late season slide, McKay believed his offensive line was the more physical unit on the field. They were cast-offs and rookies to the rest of the league, but to McKay they were the force that would carry the Bucs deeper into the playoffs. On fourth and one from the 11 Doug Williams took the snap and squeezed between the blocks of Steve Wilson and Greg Roberts for a first and goal from the 10.

Sensing that the Eagles line was becoming demoralized, McKay decided to use his former Trojan tailback as a blunt object to beat the Philly defense into submission. On first down Bell bludgeoned his way to the 8. On second down he ran over Philadelphia players to the 4. Finally on third down, Bell easily reached the end zone as his own personal bodyguards, Johnny Davis and Greg Roberts, cleared a path. Neil O'Donoghue's extra point capped one of the best opening offensive possessions in NFL playoff history.

The Bucs first drive down the field wasn't only impressive because of the yards consumed (80), the number of plays utilized (18) or the time of possession (9:25). It was impressive because the Bucs had shown that when things broke down or went wrong, they now had the maturity and fortitude to overcome. Four third down situations, one fourth down situation, a holding penalty, a dropped pass and a Philadelphia defense that was determined to stop Ricky Bell, all had been overcome by an offense that came into the playoffs as the least respected unit in the tournament.

The drive had done more than just boost the offense's confidence; it had actually made Tampa Stadium louder and more hostile for the Eagles. Additionally, while Tampa Bay was having its way with the Eagles defensive front, the Philadelphia offense was stuck cooling its heels on the sideline. The Philadelphia offense lost some of its sharpness while sitting idly by and the Tampa Bay defense made them pay for that.

Philadelphia's first drive generated only twenty yards, fifteen of which was provided by linebacker David Lewis. On Philadelphia's second play, Ron Jaworski completed a short pass to his fullback, Leroy Harris, at the 35. Lewis, not content with just defending the play, decided to send a message to the Eagles offense. Lewis delivered a jarring hit on the play and was called for unnecessary roughness. The penalty gave the Eagles a first down at midfield, but two plays later Lewis sacked Jaworski to end the drive. Lewis' hard hit and subsequent sack kept the noise showering down from the stands and sent a startled Eagles team back to the sideline. If Philadelphia had come to Tampa expecting an easy path to the NFC Championship they were sadly mistaken. The Eagles weren't up against a Buccaneer squad just happy to be in the playoffs and awed by the sight of a veteran playoff team. The Eagles were just now beginning to realize how wrong they and the rest of the National Football League were about Tampa Bay.

On Philadelphia's next possession the Eagles showed the jitters and lack of confidence that the Buccaneers were expected to show. After a bad punt by Tom Blanchard had given the Eagles possession at the Tampa Bay 48, Dick Vermiel saw the offensive drive stall at the 30 in the opening minutes of the second quarter. Vermiel sent in Tony Franklin to try a 47-yard field goal. After the snap, holder John Sciarra sprinted out of his stance with the ball and raced to the Tampa Bay 20 before being tackled. The fake field goal had successfully caught the Buccaneers off guard. Before Philadelphia could celebrate their cunning success, referee Fred Silva signaled that the Eagles had been charged with a delay of game penalty. The five-yard penalty for not getting the play off in thirty seconds wiped out the first down and moved the ball back to the 35. Franklin's 52-yard field goal fell short and the Eagles turned over the ball on downs.

Tampa Bay took possession and started another solid drive. If it weren't for a bad call by the officials Philadelphia would have been in a severe first-half hole. Repeating their successful initial possession, the Buccaneer offense overcame a holding penalty on Steve Wilson and a clipping call on Darrell Austin to drive to the Philadelphia 22. Included in the drive was another fourth down and inches conversion in which Ricky Bell plowed over the right side to gain four yards. It was the second fourth down conversion of the first half for Tampa Bay whose offensive line was manhandling the vaunted Philly line.

Facing a third and 14 from the 22 Williams dropped back and fired the ball to Jimmie Giles in the end zone. The tight end with receiver speed had beaten John Sciarra on the post route and hauled in the pass for an apparent touchdown. Fred Silva's officiating crew however ruled that Giles never had possession of the ball and ruled it incomplete. The sell-out crowd that had just erupted in cheers for Giles quickly shifted gears and showered the referees with a chorus of boos and worse. In fact the word bull***t was heard from all corners of the stadium. Tampa Stadium was not equipped with a video replay board at the time much to the luck of the officials. CBS replays showed Giles clearly in control of the pass with both feet well in bounds. Had the Tampa Stadium crowd seen this replay it is quite possible more profane words than male cow excrement would have made an appearance.

Rick Odioso, from his seat in the press box, did have the advantage of instant replay and to this day is convinced that Jimmie Giles was robbed. "I remember Giles caught a touchdown that could have sealed the game, but they didn't allow it. If they had the instant replay rule then, they would have overturned the call."

Neil O'Donoghue gave the enraged crowd something to cheer about as he connected on a 40-yard field goal to increase Tampa Bay's lead to 10-0 halfway through the second quarter. Three plays later Philadelphia's fortunes would get much worse with a little help from the number-one ranked defense in the National Football League.

After a clipping penalty on the ensuing kickoff pinned Philadelphia at their own 10, the Eagles attempted to get their leading rusher, Wilbert Montgomery, more involved. On first down Montgomery was met at the line of scrimmage by Lee Roy Selmon and driven into the ground for no gain. On second down Montgomery had barely taken the handoff from Jaworski when he was hit at the five by Randy Crowder. The defensive tackle that had risen from the depths of prison to resuscitate his NFL career jarred the ball loose and Wally Chambers alertly recovered the ball. Tampa Stadium continued to throb with excitement as the offense came back out onto the field with a first and goal from the five.

Two runs by Bell and an incompletion to Jimmie Giles left the Bucs with a fourth and goal from the one-yard line. For the third time in the game Coach McKay threw caution to the wind and ordered his team to go for it. The offensive line, emboldened by the confidence the coach was showing in them, created a gaping hole in the right side that Bell practically jogged through for his second rushing touchdown of the game. During the course of the first half the Tampa Stadium crowd had been sustaining a level of sound that seemed almost inhuman. As Neil O'Donoghue's extra point increased Tampa Bay's lead to 17-0 with 5:24 in the first half the crowd somehow managed to increase the intensity and the amplitude. With the crowd noise making it difficult for Jaworski's cadence to be heard, the Eagles next drive petered out quickly. Were it not for the only mistake of the game by Williams on the ensuing posses-sion, the noise would have continued unabated until the halftime break.

Trying to put the game away by halftime McKay opened up his offense. Williams saw Jerry Eckwood wide open at Tampa Bay's 45 and lofted a pass in his direction but the ball sailed too high and fell into the waiting arms of Philadelphia linebacker Jerry Robinson. The former UCLA standout returned the theft all the way to the 11 before being chased out of bounds. Two plays later Jaworski, unhurried for the first time on the day, saw Charles Smith beat Jeris White to the corner of the end zone and threw a tight spiral for the touchdown that cut the Bucs lead to 17-7 just before halftime.

The halftime statistics showed the breadth of the domination that the scoreboard did not. Time of possession was in Tampa Bay's favor 20:53 to 9:07 as were total yards (191-43). What's more Philadelphia's proud defense had not only given up yards and points but were being physically manhandled by the Buccaneer offensive line and Ricky Bell. The Eagles offensive stars were not just merely contained in the first half they were shut down. Wilbert Montgomery had only four yards on six carries while Harold Carmichael had yet to have a pass thrown his way by Ron Jawor-ski, who had spent most of the first half trying to avoid Lee Roy Selmon.

The Eagles were able to cut the lead to 17-10 five minutes into the second half as Jaworski led the Eagles on a rare sustained drive. The field goal may have improved Philadelphia's mood but Ricky Bell and Lee Roy Selmon snuffed out any hopes for the Eagles quickly getting back into the game.

Bell continued to run with abandon through the Eagle defense. Although the Bucs did not score any points in the third quarter, they managed to take a great deal of time off the clock with Bell gaining four to five yards a carry. When the Eagles did get the ball Tampa Bay's gentle giant quickly shut them down.

Selmon had spent most of the day in the Philadelphia backfield despite constant double and triple teaming. He had tackled Montgomery for no gain or for a loss on a few occasions already but had so far fallen maddeningly short of sacking the elusive Jaworski. On several plays Selmon had the Eagle quarterback dead in his sights only to take Jaworski down just as the pass had been released. With the Eagles in Buccaneer territory late in the third quarter Selmon finally got his man twice. On second and 10 from the Tampa Bay 38 Jaworski dropped back and was immediately pressured by Selmon. Jaworski was able to back-pedal away but only succeeded in losing more yards when Selmon finally caught him back at the Tampa Bay 47.

The result of the sack was a third and 19, an obvious passing situation. Selmon pinned back his ears and bull-rushed through his double team of blockers and chased down the beleaguered Jaworski at the Philadelphia 41. On back-to-back plays Selmon had single-handedly won the field position battle by sacking Jaworski twice for a combined loss of 21 yards.

Selmon's two sacks typified the way the defensive line was dominating the action. Looking back on that game, Bill Kollar felt it might have been one of the greatest performances of his career. "I had a pretty good game with seven pressures and hits on Jaworski, one of which should have been a sack but wasn't. I was up against Jerry Sizemore, a good tackle, but things just kind of rolled my way." Things were about to continue to roll the Bucs' way as well.

The Eagles meekly punted the ball away on fourth and 31 and watched helplessly as Ricky Bell brutally ushered in the fourth quarter in what was rapidly shaping up as a record day for the former scapegoat.

Inserting the double tight end formation, McKay contented himself with giving Ricky Bell the ball on the grandest stage the Tampa Bay franchise had ever played on and his former college pupil didn't disappoint. On third and one from the Philadelphia 49, Bell embarked on perhaps the most recognizable run of his career showcasing each of the elements that had caused McKay to choose him over Tony Dorsett two years before. From the snap of the ball Bell took the handoff and read the Eagles defense while following his blockers to the left. When he saw a hole being created in the line Bell shifted into a gear that was uncommon for a man his size and blew through to the other side, leaving a few diving Eagles defenders in his wake. When green shirts surrounded him, Bell downshifted into a more powerful gear and bulled for another five yards while carrying Herman Edwards on his back as though he were no more than a knapsack. When it was all over Bell had gained 26 yards on the play and put the Bucs in position to close the door on Philadelphia.

After sitting out a couple of plays to catch his breath, Bell re-entered the game to a standing ovation from a very appreciative Tampa Stadium crowd. Showing his team first attitude, Bell delivered the lead block for Doug Williams as the quarterback sprinted on a pass-run option for a first down at the Philadelphia 9. Two plays later Williams took advantage of the Eagles pre-occupation with Bell by dropping back and floating a perfectly thrown spiral into the waiting arms of Jimmie Giles in the right corner of the end zone. There wasn't any questioning of this completion and Tampa Bay was the proud owner of a two touchdown lead, 24-10, with 7:00 to go in the game. While the drive had been vintage McKay, power football setting up the big pass for a touchdown, it could be argued that it also was the quintessential Ricky Bell drive. Power running when needed, speed and shiftiness when required, devastating blocking when called upon all while showing an unselfish desire to keep his team rolling. It was possibly the greatest five and a half minutes of football Ricky Bell had ever known.

Sensing a trip to the NFC Championship Game was imminent, the Tampa Stadium crowd started to serenade the Buccaneers with a rousing rendition of Jeff Arthur's popular song. So involved in the hysteria of the moment, Buc fans could be forgiven for not really caring about Harold Carmichael's touchdown pass from Jaworski with 3:25 to go. When Tony Davis recovered the onside kick for Tampa Bay, the fans went back to singing about how it was a pirate's life for them. As they were working their way through the second stanza of "Hey, Hey Tampa Bay the Bucs Know How to Shine," the public address announcer interrupted the crowd with an important message.

While all of the celebrating had been going on in the stands, Ricky Bell had broken a record while helping to run out the clock. With just over two minutes to go in the game Bell had tied Lawrence McCutcheon's post-season record of 37 rushing attempts in a playoff game. On the next play Bell broke it as he carried for the 38th time. The fact that he had gained nothing on the play mattered not in the least to Tampa Bay fans, they all stood and gave Bell what seemed to be his hundredth ovation of the game and it was well-earned. The man who had once been considered a weak link had showed his true strength by running 38 times for 142 yards. The total was not only a testament to Bell but to his under-appreciated offensive line that had stood up to the challenge of the Philadelphia defense and had cowed the Eagles for the entire afternoon.

As Doug Williams took a knee on the final play of the game the National Football League was faced with a scene that they could have never imagined: the Tampa Bay Buccaneers and their fans were celebrating their status as the first member of 1979's final four and were one game away from appearing in Super Bowl XIV. The first team in the history of the NFL to win a playoff game this early in their existence, the achievement was made all the more remarkable because of how the Buccaneers had suffered their first two years.

In the locker room after the game the members of the Tampa Bay Buccaneers gladly let it be known that Pro Bowl berths and post-season honors could go pound sand, they were in the Final Four.

"Bring on Jimmy 'The Greek,'" demanded Wally Chambers, referring to the CBS prognosticator who, like most in the nation, had predicted a resounding Bucs loss. "We'll take him on now."

Chambers continued, "All year long people would say the Bucs never played anybody good. Well, Philadelphia is one of the best teams in pro football, and we beat them."

Center Steve Wilson claimed that he and his teammates played with a mission to win the game and win the game only. But he and his teammates couldn't help being a little proud of proving the naysayers wrong. "You hear all this stuff about how the Bucs shouldn't be in the playoffs because they played such an easy schedule. People can laugh if they want to, but give us credit for winning the division. We wanted to prove that teams from the NFC Central can play football and I think we did."

Chimed in linebacker Richard "Batman" Wood, "I think we convinced America."

"The country has seen the Bucs," proudly stated tight end Jimmie Giles. "We are not the 0-26 team they were thinking of. Everybody everywhere had to learn we're no flukes."

According to the players the cold-blooded precision with which they had dispatched the Eagles was testament to the work of their head coach.

"McKay should be coach of the year," said Doug Williams, who had engineered several long drives and completed an efficient 7 of 15 passes for 132 yards and a touchdown. "He has been tremendous, but only we (Bucs players) really know that. The week before the Kansas City game and the two weeks since then, our practices have been the best we've ever had here."

That practice had produced possibly the most complete game the Bucs had played on the largest stage in franchise history. In addition to Williams, the Bucs offense had been paced by Ricky Bell's record performance and Jimmie Giles' touchdown. Williams was only too happy to point out after the game that the Tampa Bay offense was no longer a weak link to the team.

"I had a better feeling all week," said Williams. "All our practices were good. We were relaxed. We played like there was no tomorrow and we played for today. Everybody played his heart out and that's the way you have to play. The offensive line did its job and when you hand off to Ricky Bell you know you are going to get 195 percent out of him."

As for Bell, he customarily ducked the compliments and instead focused on his teammates. The total victory was the result of "everybody is playing together." Bell did happily admit that the win was a welcome return to the style of football he had grown up playing and hoped it was a portent of things to come.

"I'm used to it," Bell said when asked about carrying the ball 38 times. "I did it at Southern Cal, and I have been doing it here lately."

Quipped McKay when asked if he was working his star back too hard, "The ball isn't that heavy."

While Bell's play was special, it was the performance turned in by the Tampa Bay defense that had truly taken the nation's breath away. Wilbert Montgomery was held to just 35 yards, Ron Jaworski was sacked and beaten several times and the fleet Eagles receiving corps featuring the towering Harold Carmichael had been rendered ineffective until the game was almost over.

What made the display all the more amazing was that the Bucs rarely went into an attack mode; instead they had followed McKay's instructions to sit back, let a play develop and then absolutely punish anyone who took possession of the ball. The Bucs seemed almost glee-ful afterward about how their coach had let them become assassins on the field.

"Coach John McKay told us to make them pay if they had the ball," recounted secondary coach Wayne Fontes. The strategy McKay wanted his team to use was to hit the ball carrier as hard as possible to make him think twice about running around end or over the middle. The plan worked to perfection as the Buccaneers noticed the Philadelphia skill players became increasingly skittish as the afternoon wore on.

"We intimidated them," rejoiced Dewey Selmon. "Anytime a receiver keeps dropping balls when he's five yards in the open, you know he's intimidated."

Dewey gave praise to the coach for the brutal strategy, "Their receiv-ers were coming across the line at eight yards and we were waiting for them at 10," said Dewey.

The quick linebacker also commended the offense for building a lead that forced the Eagles to play from behind and right into the defense's hands. "Today the offense probably played its best game ever. The key thing was that they gave us an early lead when they scored on the first drive of the game. It completely surprised them (the Eagles) and gave the defense confidence."

Dewey's little brother, the NFL Defensive Player of the Year, also gave kudos to the offense for building such a big lead. "That 17-0 lead we had was very important," commented Lee Roy. "It relieved a tremendous amount of pressure from the defense. We knew the pass was coming and we were ready to tee off."

Outspoken linebacker David Lewis stood up for his coach and asked the question that many in the NFL would be at a loss to answer. "A lot of people don't like Coach McKay, but how can anyone now say we aren't a pretty good ball club?"

As for McKay, he seemed content to quietly drag on his victory cigar and let his players bask in the glory.

No more needed to be said. McKay and his "motley" crew had won and the critics had lost. More importantly, the Tampa Bay Buccaneers were now just one victory away from the Super Bowl.

A Dream Deferred

S itting in his office at One Buccaneer Place many years after the defeat of the Philadelphia Eagles, Doug Williams put the victory into historical perspective. "In the history of my time with the Buccaneers there was no doubt that was the biggest game," surmised Williams.

"Besides the Super Bowl (against the Raiders in 2003), that game has to rank, the Philly game, as one of the greatest all-time victories in Tampa Bay history."

At the time it was the biggest win in team history and the local papers trumpeted the Buccaneers playoff victory with headlines so large and column space so generous that one would think they had landed on the moon after curing cancer and bringing peace to the Middle East.

"**1 Down, 2 To Go,**" blared the *St. Petersburg Times*, with a sub-head that declared **"Believe It!"**

The *Tampa Tribune*, not to be outdone, commented that the Bucs had **"Shown the Country!"**

One segment of the country that now believed in the Tampa Bay Buccaneers was the Philadelphia Eagles.

"This is not an expansion team," said an obviously impressed Dick Vermeil, the Eagles head coach. "It is a pro football team, a conference championship football team that won 10 games. They definitely were the better football team."

The Philadelphia boss continued, "The credit goes to John McKay and his staff and his players. There was no question about who was the best football team. The game wasn't as close as the final score."

After missing out on Coach of the Year honors McKay appreciated the kind words of Vermiel. As the week of the title game began he still felt it necessary to lead the charge in making sure his team was now thought of as something other than an oddity. "I can understand not being on television and such because we hadn't been winning until this year," the coach told the national press corps. "But I hope people realize that we really do have some good players. But we still must play with enthusiasm and intelligence to win. If the players aren't jumping up and down this Sunday, they'll be sitting down on January 20th (Super Bowl Sunday). But I think this is a confident team and a good team and Sunday we'll put on the old orange and white with a little bit of red in it and fight, fight, fight."

They had played so well that the Buccaneers were just one of four teams remaining in the battle for a Super Bowl championship and now they sat down to find out who they would "fight, fight, fight" against.

The Buccaneers "upset" of the Eagles wasn't the only surprise during the divisional round. The Los Angeles Rams, led by back-up quarterback Vince Ferragamo shocked the Dallas Cowboys 21-19 at Texas Stadium. The victory was monumental for the Rams but also for Tampa Bay. Had Dallas won, the Buccaneers would have traveled to the Lone Star state for the NFC Championship Game. The Rams upset meant that the Buccaneers would play for the right to go to Super Bowl XIV in Tampa Stadium. The September victory over the Rams had done more than show the Bucs were on equal footing with Los Angeles, it had given them home-field advantage.

Rick Odioso and other members of the front office had gone out on the town to celebrate after the playoff victory over Philadelphia thinking that their duties as playoff hosts had ended. They were pleasantly shocked to find out that they had one more week of overtime pay to look forward to. "The one thing I recall was that we were busy (the week leading up to the Eagle game). I remember going out to dinner after that game, really thrilled that we had won. We found out the next day that we were hosting (the NFC Championship). We thought we were done hosting for the year, and then we found out we had to host another one." No one affiliated with the Buccaneers were going to complain about that fact though.

Tampa Bay's 21-6 victory over the Rams earlier in the season sent many in the community into a state of Super Bowl fever. Travel agencies and ticket brokers throughout the area advertised special rates for a trip to Pasadena to see the Buccaneers play in the big game. John McKay knew that any similarities between the Rams team the Bucs had defeated and the Rams team that would be coming to Tampa this Sunday were purely coincidental and he let the community know it.

"The Rams are a tough football team and we must play well to defeat them," McKay said. "I don't think playing the Rams instead of the Cowboys in itself is any advantage. We were rooting for the Rams because that meant we would play at home which we would rather do quite naturally. But the only reason was the home field advantage.

"Their whole offensive line is playing real well now. They weren't intact when we played them before. This team is much better than the one we played. Their secondary is more intact now too. On offense the increased use of Billy Waddy, Ron Smith and Wendell Tyler gives them tremendous speed. I always thought Tyler was a super back at UCLA and deserved more national acclaim. He can break one at any time.

"If you believe that you can just line up and defeat a team a second time just because you beat them the first time, you will find that's not the case. The Rams will be as high as they possibly can and they will not take us lightly. This is the opportunity to go to the Super Bowl. We will need an effort at least equal to last week and probably even better to defeat them."

The entire team knew that they could not look past the Rams to a Super Bowl berth. Linebacker "Batman" Wood recalled that the whole week of practice was intense. In meeting after meeting the coaching staff drilled both units about the importance of playing a complete game. The defense in particular, according to Wood, was given a rather formidable goal: shut the Rams out of the end zone. "We knew it was going to be a tough game. Our goal was to not let them score a touchdown. If we don't give up a touchdown we're going to the Super Bowl."

McKay and Wood were offered a mid-week distraction from the pressure of the title game when their former team, the USC Trojans, played the Ohio State Buckeyes in the Rose Bowl. While the ex-Trojans were undoubtedly consumed with the Rams, they would have been heartened by the play of their alma mater. The Trojans pulled out a 17-16 victory when Charles White scored from one yard out with just 1:32 to go in the game.

The Rose Bowl was just one of three New Year's Day bowl games of interest to the Tampa Bay area. A team from the Sunshine State was culminating their own season of surprise this day. The Florida State Seminoles under head coach Bobby Bowden had enjoyed their first undefeated regular season in school history. The 11-0 'Noles were rewarded with an Orange Bowl match-up with the Oklahoma Sooners. Florida State showed their inexperience with big games in losing 24-7 as the Sooners rolled for 411 rushing yards. The bowl defeat didn't dampen expectations for the Seminoles as their fans and alumni eagerly anticipated life under Bowden.

As the Seminoles were being rudely introduced to big-time college football, most of the nation was watching the action from the Louisiana Superdome. In the Sugar Bowl the Alabama Crimson Tide clinched another national championship for their legendary coach, and close friend of John McKay, Paul "Bear" Bryant. Major Ogilve scored two touchdowns to pace the Tide's 24-9 victory over the Arkansas Razorbacks.

McKay hoped that his new team would play as well against the Rams as did his old team and that of his old friend and rival.

Many Tampa Bay fans missed the day of bowl games, choosing instead to spend the day and the evening camped out in the parking lot of Tampa Stadium. It was the second week in a row that fans had shown their commitment to the Buccaneers by camping out in the parking lot of Tampa Stadium for tickets. This week the revelers would be fighting off the effects of hangovers as they huddled around portable TV's to see the Seminoles fall short of a perfect season. In addition to the pounding headaches some of them were suffering from, they also had to contend with an unusual adversary, at least in the Bay Area's balmy climate: sub-freezing temperatures.

Fans of the Bucs' NFC Central counterparts in Chicago, Detroit, Green Bay and Minneapolis may have viewed camping in sub-freezing temperatures as quaint. For many Floridians it was a completely new experience. People were bundled up in sweaters, mittens and down jackets, many of which were brand new and emblazoned with the Buccaneer logo. Fans handed over anywhere from nine to fourteen dollars for the 28,000 tickets that hadn't already been spoken for by season-ticket holders. When the tickets finally ran dry late on that New Year's Day, some enterprising fans immediately flaunted Florida law and began scalping the seats. Some scalpers were charging up to five times face value to anyone willing to pay.

If anyone had doubted it before, the fans quest for ducats proved the following fact incontrovertibly: The Tampa Bay Buccaneers were the hottest ticket in town.

When the NFC Championship Game got under away it became quickly apparent that for the first time in 1979 the Buccaneers were not up to the challenge before them. Just as Florida State showed its inexperience in major bowls against a seasoned team, so to did Tampa Bay against Los Angeles.

The intensity and brutality of the game was markedly enhanced from a regular season contest and the Buccaneer offense in particular seemed unprepared. The first moments of the game made an impression on Doug Williams that things were not as they had been during the September victory over Los Angeles. "Either a different Ram team or not the same Buccaneer team showed up," Williams remembered.

After an exchange of punts the Rams started to move the ball on the ground behind their mammoth offensive line. The Los Angeles front wall paved open paths for Lawrence McCutcheon, Cullen Bryant and Wendell Tyler, and the trio of backs happily gained chunks of four to five yards a carry. The effect on the Tampa Stadium crowd was almost stupefying. None of the runs was artistically interesting, instead it was a steady, methodical bludgeon of a drive from the Rams' 31 to Tampa Bay's 17. With each gain against their defensive stalwarts, the partisan Buccaneer crowd grew quieter and quieter. As they would for the whole game, the Tampa Bay defense stiffened and managed to re-invigorate the crowd when Lee Roy Selmon stripped Tyler of the ball at the 15 where "Batman" Wood recovered it.

The excitement was short-lived as the Bucs offense failed to move the ball and quickly punted back to the Rams. Los Angeles simply picked

up where it had left off and efficiently moved the ball back deep into
Tampa Bay territory one small run at a time. Were it not for an illegal
formation penalty wiping out Bryant's four-yard touchdown run, the
Bucs would have been in a big psychological hole. Buoyed by the penalty the Bucs defense stiffened once more. This time the Rams were able
to generate some points out of their drive when Frank Corral booted a
19-yard field goal to give Los Angeles a 3-0 lead on the first play of the
second quarter.

During the first quarter of play the Rams had possessed the ball for
more than ten minutes. The fact that the Rams were employing a power
running game from the I formation was not lost on McKay. Sadly, McK-
ay's defense seemed unable to stop it. The Bucs defense had admirably
held the Rams out of the end zone but needed their offensive teammates
to initiate a sustained drive so that they could get some much-needed
rest. The offense, particularly Ricky Bell and Doug Williams, tried their
best but just couldn't find their way past the Rams' defense.

A Mark Cotney sack of Vince Ferragamo on a safety blitz stopped
the Rams next drive but not until Los Angeles had run the clock down to
eight minutes left in the half. The Rams were not only being efficient on
offense they were being brutal as well. The Bucs lost Wally Chambers for
the game on this drive when his arthritic knees finally wore down from
the strain. Bill Kollar quickly replaced Chambers, but without the ex-Bear
in the rotation the Bucs were in danger of becoming physically drained
on the defensive line before the first half ended. The offense would need
to put together a sustained drive to prevent this from happening.

Things looked bright when Bell blasted for nine yards out to the Buccaneer 29 to secure Tampa Bay their initial first down of the game. The
momentum of that play disappeared quickly when the next three plays
garnered only one yard. Ironically the one-yard came on Doug Williams'
first completion of the half, a short screen to Bell that was stopped almost
immediately by the Rams swarming defense.

It was an exhausted Tampa Bay defense that took the field and the
Rams were merciless in their attack. Los Angeles continued to pound
away with their trio of backs but now was able to exploit the Tampa Bay
secondary as well. Ferragamo, who until this point had hardly dropped
back to pass at all, completed four play-action passes for big gains. The
last of these passes, to tight end Charle Young at the Tampa Bay four,

wasn't enough for a first down but made Frank Corral's next field goal a chip shot. The 21-yard field goal doubled the Los Angeles lead to 6-0 with :47 to go before intermission.

With little time to go before the half, McKay decided against throwing deep and instead settled for some short passes to help calm down his young and erratic quarterback. McKay probably hoped to instill some confidence in his offense, which in generating only one first down in the entire game so far had looked particularly nervous on the biggest stage in the National Football Conference. When Williams hit Bell on another screen, this time for 11 yards, McKay's plan seemed to pay off as the team rushed to the line with their heads high for the first time and the crowd that had seemed asleep for the most part came back to life. All that was lost on the next play when Williams' pass was intercepted at midfield with :11 in the half. The Rams gladly ran out the clock and headed to the locker room with a 6-0 lead.

The halftime statistics painted a grim picture of the first thirty minutes of the game. The Rams had run 42 offensive plays to Tampa Bay's 24, out gaining the Bucs 219-43. The Rams also held a time of possession advantage of 20:44 to 9:16. It was this statistic that was especially painful. The Bucs defense was based on speed and reaction and they were now a tired team, down a man with the loss of Wally Chambers. If they had any hope of making a trip to Pasadena for the Super Bowl the offense would have to step up and make some plays

On the opening drive of the second half the Tampa Bay offense seemed to find a little rhythm with the running game as Bell ran for a couple of solid gains. The momentum was scuttled by a holding penalty on Jimmie Giles and once again the Bucs punted away after a three and out possession. Tom Blanchard's punt was a low line drive, a punt returner's dream, and Eddie Brown of the Rams caught it at the six and raced down the right sideline to LA's 43 before being knocked out of bounds by Rick Berns. Right away the Tampa Bay defense, tired and beat up, was back out on the field to face the Rams running onslaught. Two plays later things got even worse for Tampa Bay.

Wendell Tyler turned the corner on third and six and made it to the Tampa Bay 40 before being knocked out of bounds by Cedric Brown.

The officials ruled that Brown had actually hit Tyler while the Rams running back was out of bounds and flagged Tampa Bay an additional 15 yards. A livid crowd was jolted awake and profusely voiced their displeasure but the damage had already been done. Sadly, while the controversy surrounding the penalty on Brown swirled few noticed Lee Roy Selmon limping to the sideline. On the play Selmon's ankle had been pinned awkwardly while trying to fight off his blocker. Selmon limped back on the field two plays later, but could barely get out of his stance to rush Ferragamo and returned to the bench afterward. On the next play Mike Washington was able to keep Preston Dennard from maintaining control of Ferragamo's pass in the left corner of the end zone, forcing yet another Frank Corral field goal attempt. This time the kicker's 37-yard attempt was wide left and the Bucs still only trailed 6-0. The moral victory for the defense was severely dampened by the news that they would now be without the services of Lee Roy. Eugene Sanders would replace Lee Roy in the rotation and while the rookie had made some solid strides during 1979 he was hardly an adequate replacement for the franchise's rock and the NFL's Defensive Player of the Year.

With the best player on the team out of the game, it was incumbent on the Bucs offense to generate some points in a hurry. But as their luck would have it on this day the offense not only offered up yet another three and out, they also lost their field general as well. On third down Williams was chased out of the pocket by his old nemesis Fred Dryer. Williams got a pass off, but was hit upon release by defensive tackle Mike Fanning. It didn't appear to be a hard hit, but as Williams walked to the sideline his right arm hung limp at his side. The injury would prove devastating. "Mike Fanning came across my arm," Williams said. "I tore the bicep tendon." A few minutes later the Bucs medical staff walked Williams to the locker room for observation.

When the Bucs got the ball back a few moments later, following a courageous stand by the Bucs second unit defensive line, back-up quarterback Mike Rae took command of the huddle and immediately benefited from McKay's opening of the playbook.

On third and six from Tampa Bay's 24, Rae pitched the ball out to Jerry Eckwood who took it and ran parallel to the line of scrimmage. The Rams defense read this as McKay's trusted power sweep and ran towards Eckwood. The rookie tailback pulled up however, and threw the halfback option pass far down the right sideline to a wide-open Larry Mucker. Unfortunately the pass was short and Mucker had to wait on the ball, caught it at the Ram 34 and was tackled immediately by safety Dave Elmendorf. If Mucker had been hit with the pass in stride he would have easily scored, but as it was the Bucs finally made a big play. The pass went for 42 yards and in a blink of an eye the Buccaneers were in good position to take the lead in a game in which they had been completely outplayed.

As the crowd settled back into their seats to see if their team could wrest the lead away, the bad luck that had been plaguing Tampa Bay all day struck again. Two runs by Bell only picked up four yards and on third down Rae threw for Giles in the end zone. Giles and cornerback Eddie Brown collided in the end zone and the pass fell incomplete. Giles, Rae and over 72,000 fans screamed for a pass interference penalty but the ruling by Pat Haggerty and his officiating crew was that Brown had been going for the ball and therefore there was no pass interference. Had the officials ruled differently, the Bucs would have had the ball first and goal from the one-yard line. As it stood, they faced fourth and six. Rather than trying a long field goal, McKay opted to go for the conversion and watched as Rae's pass to Isaac Hagins was nearly intercepted by Eddie Brown.

With their best scoring chance of the game gone by the boards, the Buccaneers offense watched from the sideline as the Los Angeles running game once again powered through a tired and battered Tampa Bay front wall. As the third quarter turned into the fourth quarter the Rams ground their way to the Tampa Bay 24 where they were faced with a fourth and two.

Rams coach Ray Malavasi opted to go for the conversion, feeling that a touchdown drive at this point in the game would kill off any hopes for a Tampa Bay comeback. Once again the Buccaneer defense, reaching deep down into whatever physical reserve they could muster, prevented the Rams from putting the game away. As Wendell Tyler attempted to run around the left side on a power sweep, "Batman" Wood fought off his blocker and tackled the Ram back before he could turn the corner. The tackle gave the Buccaneers offense the ball again and brought cheers from the crowd.

The subsequent Bucs drive showed that if there were any hopes about lady luck shining on Tampa Bay at all this day, they were quickly erased.

After a rare completion to Isaac Hagins, only the fourth completed pass of the day for Tampa Bay, Mike Fanning sacked Rae. The Bucs punted the ball back and watched helplessly as Tom Blanchard got off his worst punt of the day, just ten yards, giving the Rams a first down at mid-field with just over ten minutes to play.

Two witnesses on the sideline to Blanchard's ill-timed gaffe were Doug Williams and Wally Chambers. The two had returned to the bench area, but in street clothes. Chambers' knees and Williams' biceps were too badly injured to allow them back into the game. While knowing that their leader on offense could not play would hurt their chances, the fact that he had still come out to rally his teammates kept the Bucs spirits high. The Rams drove into field goal range and Frank Corral connected on his third of the game to make the score 9-0. The Bucs, rather than falling apart, attempted to get back in the game and put a scare into the Rams while earning the respect of their opponents.

Shrugging off the past 50 minutes of ineptitude and heartache, the Bucs offense drove down the field with intensity as the fourth quarter waned. On a reverse from Ricky Bell, Larry Mucker ran through a surprised Rams defense that was already in celebratory-mode and raced to the Los Angeles 27 with just over three minutes left in the game. The Bucs knew that if they could get a touchdown here, they could either try an on-side kick or trust their defense to hold the Rams one more time before attempting a game winning drive. With a little bit of luck and skill, the Bucs just might make that flight to Pasadena to tangle with the Steel Curtain of Pittsburgh after all.

After an incompletion to Morris Owens, Rae dropped back and rolled to his right and unleashed a rainbow of a pass into the end zone where Jimmie Giles caught it between two Ram defenders. Tampa Stadium erupted, as the fans were jubilant over the fight shown by their Bucs. With a Neil O'Donoghue extra point the score would be 9-7 with over two and a half minutes to go, plenty of time for the Bucs to come back and win the game and secure a place in NFL history. As the fans dared to dream great dreams, the officials huddled around a yellow penalty flag and conferred. An uneasy silence fell over Tampa Stadium as the crowd realized what was going on down on the field. When the official's conference broke, a referee took the ball and placed it back at the 32-yard line and signaled offsides on Tampa Bay. Greg Roberts, the rookie who had made such great strides at guard throughout the year, was called for moving just a nanosecond before the snap, wiping out the touchdown. It was a tough but accurate call and it deflated the team. Nolan Cromwell easily knocked down two more passes by Rae and the Rams offense ran the remaining time off the clock. The dream of the Super Bowl was over.

Curiously, as the Rams were putting the finishing touches on their big victory, the Tampa Stadium crowd came to their feet and sent down a standing ovation. The applause wasn't for the visiting Rams, although they did deserve recognition for shutting out the Buccaneers. The applause was for the home team. Even though they had been denied a Super Bowl, the fans wanted to let their Bucs know that they were proud of them and were truly grateful for the unexpectedly wonderful ride they had been taken on in 1979. While the Bucs hadn't changed many opinions in the national press and were still the subject of jokes despite the playoff appearance, they had altered the perception of the team within the Tampa Bay community. They had played with skill, and character and with class and Tampa Bay fans were proud of them for it. As the final seconds ticked off the clock a message on the scoreboard read "Let's Hear it For the Bucs," and the crowd, which was just as large now as it had been before kickoff, gladly obliged.

The Buccaneers had also changed the perception of the team they had just played. Unlike the Eagles, who had come in expecting an easy victory, the Rams had paid the Buccaneers the highest compliment by bringing their best game of the season. Perhaps it was the 21-6 loss back in October, or it had been the films of the Bucs dominance of Philadelphia, but the Rams came to Tampa knowing that these were not the same old Buccaneers. The Rams players ran towards their locker room to celebrate their National Football Conference championship, but they ran with bodies that ached from one of the most physical match-ups in NFC Championship Game history.

The respect of your peers and your community may not be as much fun as a spot in the Super Bowl, but considering how far the Buccaneers had come in 1979 it may have proved to be the more valuable prize.

In the somber locker room afterward the players looked not so much at what might have been, but on what an incredible thrill they had experienced in 1979.

"We got to the NFC Championship Game and most teams don't get that far and we are an expansion team," said a down but not out Richard "Batman" Wood.

With his right arm in a sling, a grimacing Doug Williams refused to feel down over not making the Super Bowl or on his 2 for 13 passing day. After all there was still a lot of work to focus on and there was no time to look back in sorrow.

"Can't hang our heads about this," Williams said. "You got to keep your head up about this. If it were left up to everyone else, we would have won about five or six games this year. We wouldn't have even been here if it had been up to everyone else. We won a lot of football games, we got this far and only four teams did."

Rick Odioso was also disappointed about the loss. Perhaps even more so than the players, Odioso had a true perspective of just how close the Buccaneers had come to NFL immortality. "The NFL had all of the Super Bowl tickets locked up in the vault in our stadium that day. But they went back to Los Angeles with the Rams." The NFL had a policy that whoever won the NFC title would be given their allotment of Super Bowl tickets immediately to facilitate their distribution. Odioso did remember with some humor that not all the Super Bowl tickets made it back to the Golden State. "Dominic Frontiere, the boyfriend and future husband of Rams owner Georgia Rosenbloom, got in trouble for scalping Super Bowl tickets."

Richard "Batman" Wood freely admits to being devastated by the outcome of the NFC Championship Game, but also was thankful for the well wishes of the fans. "We knew the people in Tampa appreciated us. But it was also sad. I felt that I had reached a plateau. It's really hard to talk about it."

Looking back on the final game of the season for the Buccaneers, Lee Roy Selmon had only happy memories. Sure his ankle had been severely twisted and his team fell just ten points short of a Super Bowl, but he left the field knowing that he and his teammates had made football history. He had also discovered as he and his teammates were serenaded by a sell-out crowd as they limped to the dressing room that he and the Tampa Bay Buccaneers were truly at home.

The serenade meant a lot to the Buccaneer players, and even a quarter of a century later Lee Roy Selmon was still touched by the sentiment.

"It was great, our fans had always been so supportive of us from the first day we got here. They never wavered from their enthusiasm and support. Even though we were coming short of our goal, one game out of the Super Bowl, and we all wanted it so desperately; I thought it was very classy of our fans to cheer us on anyway. To let us know that they appreciated the season. I think they felt for us, because I think they knew as well as us our goal was the Super Bowl. That was an unexpected response, but when you think about it, it was not a surprise either. As disappointed as we were as players, that was kind of an uplifting moment."

John McKay's men may have come up short of the Super Bowl but they had done so much more. The successful 1979 season had vindicated their careers and the reputation of their coach on multiple levels.

The 3-4 defensive scheme that so many said would not work had been employed so well by Tampa Bay that the defense achieved the status of league leader in total defense.

The I formation running game that for years had been laughed at produced a 1,200-yard rusher behind a makeshift offensive line.

Cast-offs such as Wally Chambers, Randy Crowder, Mark Cotney, Richard "Batman" Wood and many others had proven their doubters wrong. Under John McKay's tutelage these men had become champions.

And perhaps most importantly the Buccaneers NFC Central Division championship proved that the man once derisively referred to as a "college" coach was the equal of the best the NFL had to offer. No one else had taken an expansion team this far so fast and it would be many years before anyone else would come close. The 0-26 streak of 1976 and 1977 had once been an albatross around the coaching legacy of John McKay. Thanks to the 1979 Tampa Bay Buccaneers, that streak would only make this accomplishment and his coaching career all the more lustrous.

From First Back to Worst

*T*hroughout the 1980 off-season many fans played the painful game of "what-if." What if the Bucs had played the Steelers in the Super Bowl that year instead of the Rams? The heavy underdogs from Los Angeles had carried a 19-17 lead into the fourth quarter only to lose 31-19. What if Tampa Bay's number one rated defense had been given a fourth quarter lead to protect and Ricky Bell was charged with running off as much time as he could? Could the Buccaneers have prevailed over the legendary Steel Curtain?

Lee Roy Selmon chuckled when asked that question 25 years later, but even he couldn't help but think about it. "I don't know. I know how we'd feel going into the game," he said while pausing to laugh and think a little bit. "I don't know how we'd feel coming out of it, but going in we'd think we're going to win it."

After the laughter ended, Selmon seriously contemplated a match-up with the Steelers. With a touch of melancholy Selmon stated unequivocally that the Bucs would have played their hearts out. "If we made it to the Super Bowl we'd have gone onto the field believing we were going to win it. We didn't have that opportunity, but that was all right.

"It was a great season."

Richard "Batman" Wood exuded confidence in the Bucs chances to rip through the Steel Curtain. "I think we would have won," Wood proclaimed proudly. "I really do. It would have been a great game, I can tell you that. I watched the Super Bowl, thinking the whole time we should have been there. I don't think they (the Steelers) would have run the ball on us. It would have been a great defensive game."

Doug Williams also felt the Buccaneers would have had a reasonable chance to dethrone the Steelers. "I would have to say we certainly would have had an opportunity. Just like against the Eagles we would have had nothing to lose. They (the Steelers) had a bunch of great football players and hopefully they would have taken us for granted. Man for man and pound for pound they would have been the better team but as we all know sometimes that ain't the case when it comes to winning."

Former PR assistant Rick Odioso recalled talking to Coach McKay the day following the loss to the Rams in the NFC Championship Game. Noticing that the normally effusive coach was a little down in the mouth, the young Odioso attempted to cheer him up. "I remember saying 'Cheer up Coach. We'll be back next year. We've got Lee Roy, Doug and Ricky. We'll be back.' And he said, 'You can't count on tomorrow, you only get so many chances.'" Sadly, McKay's words would prove to be prophetic.

The young Buccaneers did not handle the role of favorite very well in 1980. With opponents going all-out against the Bucs week in and week out, the Buccaneers struggled to a 5-10-1 record. Some solace from the season was gained when the Buccaneers defeated the Los Angeles Rams 10-9 at Tampa Stadium in the team's first ever appearance on prime time television.

In 1981 the Buccaneers rebounded to win the NFC Central Division title for the second time in three years. The 1981 playoffs weren't nearly as much fun as 1979. The Dallas Cowboys throttled Tampa Bay 38-0 at Texas Stadium.

The Buccaneers qualified for the playoffs a third time in 1982 during the strike-shortened season. For the second straight year they fell in Dallas, 30-17.

The loss to the Cowboys also marked the end of the height of the Buccaneers under Coach McKay. After making the playoffs in three of four years, the success stopped. Over the next three years, McKay would see the team he built crumble under the strain of economics, age and in one instance tragedy.

The largest impediment to the Tampa Bay Buccaneers continuing the success they had generated in the late seventies and early eighties was the miserly ways of their owner Hugh Culverhouse in his negotiations with Doug Williams.

In 1983 Williams' contract expired. The contract he signed as a rookie was quite low, even by the standards of the 1970's. Williams made $50,000 his first season, despite being a number-one draft choice who was thought by management to be the future of the franchise. In 1982, the last year of his contract, Williams made $120,000, which meant he was making less than some back-up quarterbacks in the league. Having led the Bucs to three playoff appearances in four seasons, showing improved decision-making skills and still possessing possibly the strongest right arm of any quarterback in the National Football League, Williams and his agent undoubtedly believed he would be richly rewarded for his work. Williams and his agent even had a price in mind, a multi-year deal worth $875,000 per season. They quickly discovered that Hugh Culverhouse had a much smaller figure in mind.

According to his autobiography *Quarterblack,* the first offer Williams received in February of 1983 was a three-year deal worth $400,00 per season. That was quite a raise over his previous salary, but compared to the other starting quarterbacks, it would have made the five-year veteran one of the lowest paid signal callers in the NFL. In addition, Williams believed that Culverhouse tied too many strings to the deal. Part of the deal was a $250,000 loan from Culverhouse to Williams so the quarterback could be a partner on a land development deal. Williams saw that as a Culverhouse ploy, trying to saddle him with debt so that he would be desperate to sign any contract that was offered. Williams declined and let everybody in the press know that he was hurt by the low offer and the strings attached to it.

Two months later a horrible tragedy put even more strain on the relationship between the Buccaneers and their field general. Williams' young wife Janice suddenly died of a brain tumor in April, leaving Williams alone to raise their daughter Ashley. When Janice Williams was buried in Louisiana, Hugh Culverhouse attended the services but to Doug it felt as though he came to garner good PR. According to Williams Culverhouse arrived right before the service began and left right after it ended without talking to the young widower. The rude act soured Williams on the owner of the franchise and hardened his stance in negotiations.

In June of 1983 a tense situation was worsened even more when the Buccaneers traded a first round draft choice to Cincinnati for quarterback Jack Thompson. Thompson, nicknamed the "Throwin' Samoan," was a career back-up who had yet to distinguish himself in the NFL. While the trade of a number one draft choice for a back-up quarterback outraged Bucs fans, Williams was even angrier at Hugh Culverhouse when he learned that Thompson would make $200,000 a year! William's agent Jimmy Walsh called the Buccaneers and said that if the Bucs would add that $200,000 to the $400,000 they had offered originally Williams would gladly re-sign. The Bucs declined saying they couldn't afford to pay Williams that amount and keep Thompson. The message to Williams and his agent was clear: the Bucs offer of $400,000 was final.

Williams, still coping with the loss of his wife, was in no mood to fight the Buccaneers any longer. He was hurt and angry that all of the effort he had put into making Tampa Bay a championship contender was not appreciated. With all of this negative emotion swirling through him, Williams felt he had little choice but to accept a contract with the rival United States Football League. In August of 1983 Doug Williams signed to play for the USFL's Oklahoma Outlaws. His contract with the Outlaws paid him what he felt we was worth, three million dollars over five years. Tampa Bay's commander was now gone.

Williams' tenure in the USFL wasn't a joyous time, but it kept him in the game and he continued to grow as a quarterback. When the league folded, Williams took a job as the back-up quarterback of the Washington Redskins. When injuries put him in the role of starter, Williams showed just how much he had grown. Williams guided the 1987 Redskins into the Super Bowl and made history in the process as the first African-American to start at quarterback in the title game.

Williams not only started the game, he absolutely finished the Denver Broncos in a second quarter that was as gratifying to Williams as it was shocking to the football establishment. Having endured the taunts coming out of Grambling that a black man could not succeed at quarterback, Williams enjoyed shredding the Broncos defense for 35 points in just fifteen minutes. Williams ended the day with 340 passing yards and four touchdown passes. Those statistics cemented his selection as the game's Most Valuable Player and erased forever the notion that a black man couldn't handle the pressure of leading an offense in the biggest game of the year.

While Doug Williams eventually overcame the heartache of his divorce from the Buccaneers, Tampa Bay did not and collapsed during the 1983 season. Jack Thompson tried gamely, but showed he was no substitute for Doug Williams as the Bucs went 2-14 on the season. Lost in the Williams-Culverhouse saga was the toll it took on head coach John McKay. McKay had grown closer to Williams than any other player on the roster, and losing him hurt the head coach a great deal. The coach spent years and a lot of energy looking for a replacement for Williams but to no avail.

Rick Odioso believed Williams leaving more than any other event led to the nosedive of Buccaneer fortunes. "The biggest downfall of the team was A: not re-signing Doug and B: the unsuccessful attempts to replace him. Using up draft choices, money and attention that could have gone to other areas of the team."

"It just wasn't the same team after Doug left. Doug's absence seemed to sap the defense more than the offense. The thought was that if the team wasn't going to pay Doug, they weren't going to pay me."

"For a long time, we were always short a draft pick while trying to replace Doug. Arguably, until Brad Johnson in 2001 we never had a quarterback to replace him."

In addition to the departure of Williams, advancing age and a serious injury deprived the Buccaneers of their greatest player. In 1983 and 1984 Lee Roy Selmon was among the team leaders in sacks and tackles and was named to his fifth and sixth Pro Bowl appearances. As 1984 wound down Selmon found himself the victim of back problems. The injury was serious enough to cause Selmon to miss the entire 1985 season, which saw the Buccaneers defense fall from being among the league's best to the league's worst. In 1985 the Buccaneers defense became something of a pushover, which Lee Roy's presence would have been able to lessen. The out-manned defense coupled with a struggling offense led to the second 2-14 season in three years. Worse still, Lee Roy's back didn't improve and he decided after the 1985 season to retire from professional football.

Selmon left as the Buccaneers all-time leader in sacks (78.5) and as an accomplished run stopper (742 career tackles). Selmon also left as possibly the most popular Buccaneer of all time, sometimes being referred to as Mr. Buccaneer. Perhaps Selmon was destined to leave football early, for over the next twenty years he would go on to become one of the most important men in the community, far surpassing his contributions as a football player. While his fame as a player had helped to make him a community leader, it was Selmon's work ethic that made him a successful businessman and civic father in his post-football career.

The Ronald McDonald House, the Children's Cancer Center, the Special Olympics, the NAACP and the United Negro College Fund all found a willing partner in helping to spread the word and raise funds for their noble causes. On top of all of this Selmon also helped the University of South Florida start a football program during his time as athletic director and opened a chain of popular eateries in the Tampa Bay area. By the time the late nineties rolled around some could be forgiven for forgetting that this civic dynamo had once earned his fame as a master of bringing down opposing quarterbacks.

In the late nineties the city of Tampa rewarded Selmon for all he had done for the community and university by naming the expressway that ran through downtown the Lee Roy Selmon expressway. It was fitting that the city pay tribute to the man who had given his heart to Tampa by naming the thoroughfare that ran through the heart of the city after him.

Given how much Selmon the entrepreneur came to mean to Tampa, the premature ending of his football career was not a tragedy. Sadly the same couldn't be said for the shocking end of Ricky Bell's career.

1979 proved to be the high point of Bell's professional career. After rushing for over 1,200 yards Bell's productivity fell by more than half in 1980. Limited by a variety of injuries, Bell managed only 599 yards on the season. The 1981 season would be even worse for the former Trojan star. Carrying the ball just a scant 30 times, Bell gained only 80 yards the entire season. There were disturbing reports that Bell was having a hard time bouncing back from his injuries. Confusion spread among the community with some fans and reporters feeling that perhaps Bell was dogging it, that he had lost his hunger after proving the critics wrong in 1979. Others feared that Bell's success in 1979 was a fluke and that he had fallen back to the form he had showed in 1977 and 1978. Not sure of the reason, Coach McKay only knew that Bell was not the back he had been and reluctantly traded away his former pupil to the San Diego Chargers before the 1982 season so the young man could be closer to his family.

Bell's stay in San Diego was very brief as he only appeared in two games during the strike-shortened season. He complained of acute pain in his knees and joints and the Chargers put Bell on injured reserve when it became apparent he simply could not handle the strain of football anymore. The Chargers sent Bell to see an arthritis specialist and it was then that he learned why he couldn't regain his strength.

Bell was diagnosed with dermatomyostis, an inflammation of the skin and muscles. It is a very rare disease and it was preventing Bell from building and retaining the muscle mass he had acquired during all his years of training for football. The disease was also slowly sapping away all of his strength as well.

After the 1982 season Bell decided that he would treat the disease as he had always treated opposing defenses: head on. He started a training regimen in the hopes of returning to the Chargers in 1983. The training regimen didn't produce the desired results. Bell's weight plummeted from 225 pounds to 196 pounds. Reluctantly, the proud Bell realized he would have to give up football so that he could tackle the disease. The now former football star engaged in a variety of treatments while also earning a real estate license. Buoyed by his wife Natalia and his daughter Noelle, Bell kept his optimism and would constantly tell anybody who asked him that he was doing fine and was going to beat the disease. Bell was so convincing that many people who didn't know of his disease couldn't even tell that Bell was a sick man.

As the year 1984 progressed Bell's condition worsened. Doctors informed him that the disease had spread to his heart and that he might have as little as six months left to live. Undaunted, Bell continued to meet with friends, help his wife with her work on a master's degree and look after his daughter. One of his visits in 1984 was back to Tampa to look in on some old teammates. Bill Kollar was a defensive assistant on the Buccaneers coaching staff that year and recalled being surprised by the physical change in Ricky. "He came back and had lost a bunch of weight, had that sickness." While Bell's physical stature may have changed, it was apparent that even five years removed from his best professional season, he still had great presence at One Buc Place. "He was a great guy," Kollar recalled. "Struggled initially, but then had a huge year. All the guys liked him, a heck of a guy and a heck of a teammate. He was well respected."

On a typically beautiful Southern California day in late autumn of 1984 Natalia kissed Ricky good-bye and headed out to class at Cal State Los Angeles. She recalled that Ricky was in a lot of pain but wasn't particularly down or depressed. During her class Natalia was informed that Ricky had been rushed to the hospital.

After Natalia had left home, Ricky Bell was felled by a heart attack triggered by his disease. The medical term for what struck Bell was cardiomyopathy, a muscular disease of the heart that was related to his dermatomyostis. Medical professionals were called to his home and raced him to a Los Angeles hospital but there was nothing more that could be done. At 11:06 on the morning of November 28, 1984 Ricky Bell's heart, which had powered him through turmoil to the greatest triumph of his professional life just five years before, gave out. Ricky Bell, who was considered the perfect teammate by his Buccaneer brethren, was dead at the age of 29.

John McKay and the rest of the Buccaneers received word of Bell's death later that day while practicing in Tampa. Linebacker Richard Wood told the *Los Angeles Times*, "One of the trainers came and told me. I didn't know what to do so I got down on my knees on the field and said a little prayer. I wish they could have waited until after practice before they told me. But, at the time, nothing else mattered. I still think of him once a week. I look at his picture and I think of the good times."

Recollecting Bell's fortunes as a professional athlete, Hubert Mizell of the *St. Petersbug Times* recalled the former Trojan as a hard worker whose demise baffled and stunned not just his teammates but the Tampa Bay area as well. "Ricky was a terrific guy," Mizell said. "After a slow start he did some excellent work. Seemed to be maturing into a solid NFL runner when the mysterious weakness appeared. Nobody would've guessed it was a ghastly disease that would eventually cost Bell his life."

What impressed Mizell most about Bell was that he never let himself be defeated by those who unfairly compared him to other backs. Instead the hard-running Bell worked himself ragged and became a fan favorite for other reasons. "Bell never made most critics feel he was a better idea than Tony (Dorsett) or Earl (Campbell) but his work ethic and attitude caused most Bucs followers to become reasonably stout supporters."

Before the 1984 campaign finished Coach McKay announced that he would resign as head coach following the season finale. Heartbroken over losing players that he had adored such as Williams and Bell, McKay just was not having as much fun coaching as he once did. There was also the fact that the use of illegal narcotics, which was a growing problem in the NFL, had invaded the Tampa Bay locker room as well. That brought a type of dynamic that could make any coach cringe. John McKay felt that at the age of 61 it was the right time to get out of football and spend more time with his family and on the golf course. Given McKay's love of being iconoclastic, he couldn't leave the field of play without a memorable exit line.

In the season finale at Tampa Stadium against the New York Jets the Bucs led 41-14 with less than two minutes to go in the game. Many in the stands were still somewhat disappointed because Buccaneer running back James Wilder was a mere 23 yards shy of the NFL record for most offensive yards in a season. Coach McKay was one of those who wanted to see Wilder set the record so he tried to do something about it. McKay ordered kicker Obed Ariri to attempt an onsides kick, which an angry Jets team recovered.

Having been denied possession of the ball, McKay ordered his defense to lay down on the field and let the Jets score so that the Bucs could get the ball back in time to allow Wilder another chance. A stunned Johnny Hector, the Jets running back, ran uncontested into the end zone to cut the Bucs lead to 41-21 with just under a minute remaining.

The Bucs took possession and fed Wilder the ball until time ran out, but it was to no avail as the back finished 16 yards short of the mark. As the teams left the field Jets coach Joe Walton and a cadre of New York players confronted McKay and engaged the departing coach in a heated shouting match. Pushing and shoving ensued as numerous Bucs players came to the defense of their coach. Calm was settled and the players all left the field without any further altercation.

Afterwards, Walton told the New York writers that McKay had perpetrated an embarrassment that had "set the NFL back 20 years." McKay on the words exchanged with the Jets at midfield admitted, with his tongue planted firmly in cheek, that he was "shocked, shocked to hear language like that on a football field."

McKay had come in with a reputation for being an imaginative coach with a wonderful sense of humor who wasn't in awe of the traditions of the National Football League, and for better or worse he left with the same perception.

Hubert Mizell for one came to miss McKay over the years but understood completely why he resigned. "As we would learn through the years, (Hugh) Culverhouse was not providing heavy assets with which to turn those winless beginners into seasoned winners. McKay overcame much to reach that NFC Championship Game."

"After the joy of 1979, things became bittersweet for the Trojan great. Give him applause for making it fun for a lot of us, and delivering that wonder season of '79, but it was a tired, fed up McKay who could go no further in the middle 1980s. Selmon had to quit due to ailments so John had no interest in going on without Lee Roy."

From 1985-1995, Tampa Bay would suffer eleven straight losing seasons. None of the coaches during that streak could match McKay's on-field success. Worse, none of them would have McKay's winning personality either making Buccaneer woes all the more unbearable.

In the summer of 1995 after more than a decade of losing, the Buccaneers enjoyed some positive national recognition. The occasion was Lee Roy Selmon's enshrinement into the Pro Football Hall of Fame in Canton, Ohio. Induction into the hall is a testament to a player's ability to play his sport at a level far exceeding those of your peers. In order to be voted in a player must be selected by a committee of national writers and Hall of Fame members. Needless to say only those who truly know great football when they see it can nominate a player for the Hall of Fame. Selmon's selection not only validated his career, but it also validated the franchise despite its long history of struggles.

Selmon spent several years on some bad Tampa Bay teams, but on his day of induction he chose to focus on the greatness of the 1979 season. Recalling the teammates who had helped him make it to within one game of the Super Bowl in 1979, a humbled Selmon thanked all of them for their sacrifice, singling out two in particular.

Selmon acknowledged that he wouldn't have made it as far in professional football as he had if the Buccaneers had not drafted his older brother. Dewey Selmon had come to the Bucs the same year as Lee Roy and had suffered both the highs and lows. While Dewey never achieved the same level of success as his baby brother, he had helped to build the Bucs defensive unit into a dominant force in 1979. Dewey continued to play an important role in Lee Roy's football career as he gave the introductory speech before Lee Roy took the podium at the induction ceremony.

"I knew I probably would have been lost if I came all the way to Tampa without him. That was the greatest move I think the Tampa Bay Buccaneers made in the draft that year," Lee Roy told the audience.

Selmon continued, "There's one other teammate I'd like to mention besides my brother Dewey and that's Ricky Bell."

"Ricky Bell fought a hard battle on the football field. He never quit and gave it his all each and every game and in practice. When Ricky became ill, he fought that way with his illness until the very day that he left us. I'll never forget that about Ricky."

Unfortunately, as the years went by many fans forgot about Ricky Bell and the 1979 season. Even the passing of the man who led Tampa Bay to the highest level of football couldn't bring those accomplishments to the forefront.

John McKay passed away in June of 2001 from kidney failure related to his diabetes at the age of 77. National stories focused on McKay's success at USC and the 26-game losing streak, but little was mentioned of the 1979 team and the three playoff appearances in four years that McKay had led the team to. With a record of 44-88-1 McKay was viewed as a college coach who struggled with the pro game.

This view of McKay seemed wholly unfair to those men that played for and covered the coach.

In the opinion of former *Times* columnist Hubert Mizell any historical assessment of McKay should include the 1979 season. "McKay should be remembered for enduring the roughest start in NFL history with the 0-26," the writer said in an interview many years later. "But then doing one of the more remarkable turnarounds by coming within one win of the Super Bowl just two seasons after the 26th of those defeats."

Added Bill Kollar, "I really enjoyed Coach McKay, felt he was a great coach. To take an expansion team like that and get to a championship game when we did was an outstanding deal for him. Most of the players loved him for how far we came so quickly. Back then the expansion rules were quite different than what they are now. When Jacksonville and Carolina came in the league the rules were easier. Things were a lot tougher back in '76. It's a great tribute to McKay on what he was able to do."

McKay's former quarterback agreed. "John McKay is always a winner," says Doug Williams. "Even though we weren't sophisticated, he always knew in his own dry wit way how to motivate. When it comes to the history of the Buccaneers John McKay should be up there."

Richard "Batman" Wood may have paid McKay the highest compliment of all by attempting to pattern his coaching style and philosophy in high school and NFL Europe after McKay's. In fact, Wood replicated McKay's success with a brand new team by coaching Wharton High School in Florida to the state championship game. "It was ironic, it was a brand new high school and five years later we're playing in the state championship. I thought about the Buccaneers the whole time. I let my coaches do the coaching (just as McKay had done). I think about what he said and did. I'm probably a little bit more intense. But he expected us to work hard and his expectations for us were very high.

"He was a good man," Wood continued. "He didn't curse at us, didn't swear at us. He carried himself with a lot of pride and happiness. And he was a fun-loving person, but when he meant business he meant business, like any father would."

From his vantage in the team offices, PR assistant Rick Odioso saw a man who didn't suffer fools well, but treated everybody with grace no matter their position with the club. "I liked him, he was always nice to me. I think he was successful in both college and the pros. He was a great coach. I always thought it was funny that a lot of people thought he would move back to California after he coached his last game. But he never left Tampa."

Lee Roy Selmon couldn't agree more about McKay's place in football lore. "A legendary coach," Selmon simply said. "Coach McKay's career at USC and to come here and do what he did was nothing short of legendary.

"An expansion team is a tough team to build and for a coach to come in and say I'm going to do it this way and withstand all the pressure, the criticism that goes with that. There were a lot of second-guessers in the media, but he stayed course and never wavered. That's leadership. I think that's what you need if you are going to be successful. He knew how he wanted to build the team and it worked. I think that speaks loudly for his talent, his skills, and his approach to the game. To me it speaks volumes and its unfortunate the focus of concentration is on that 0-26 period."

McKay's status in Tampa would be enhanced if the franchise he helped to build would commemorate the accomplishments of the 1979 team. When an ownership change occurred in the mid-nineties, most of the effort rightly went into building a team that eventually became a Super Bowl champion in 2002. With the championship accomplished, it could be time to look back at the ancestors of the 2002 team.

Former PR assistant Rick Odioso feels that the powers that be in the franchise may be warming up to the idea of remembering the early days of the franchise. "My impression is that when the Glazer's took over the team and changed the colors, they didn't have much interest in the history of the franchise. Now Jon Gruden, the new head coach, does. In 2002 Gruden had a reunion at Hooters where they traced down a bunch of former players."

Perhaps this will change even more in the years to come. An example of the team reaching out to its past was evident in the hiring of Doug Williams as a personnel executive in 2004. After his Super Bowl victory, Williams moved into the coaching ranks and became a success. In 1998 Williams took over for his legendary mentor, becoming the head coach at Grambling when Eddie Robinson retired after a career of over fifty years at the school. After posting a winning record at Grambling, Williams decided the time had come to prove his mettle as an NFL executive

The Buccaneers are also now commemorating the past. The 2005 football season saw the Buccaneers sporting a 30th anniversary patch on their uniforms. Current Head Coach John Gruden, whose father Jim was an assistant under McKay in the early 80's, has scheduled an annual reunion dinner and invites former Buccaneers to attend practices and speak with the team. The organization has shown that it has not forgotten those who came before, but the question remains will the new generation of Buccaneer fans know the story of the first group of players to catapult the franchise into the upper echelon of the NFL?

One can only hope they will.

CHAPTER
NOTES

*T*he source for most of my research material was found at the Pro Football Hall of Fame in Canton, Ohio. It was there that I read through the press releases and game programs of the 1979 season.

Repeated trips to the Hillsborough County Public Library and the Youngstown State University Maag Library provided me with back issues of the *Tampa Tribune, St. Petersburg Times* and *New York Times*. These provided me game stories, summaries and player/coach quotes from the locker room.

Personal interviews with Jack Harris, Bill Kollar, Hubert Mizell, Rick Odioso, Lee Roy Selmon, Doug Williams and Richard Wood provided me with behind the scenes insight that couldn't be found in old newspapers. I am eternally grateful for the time these gentlemen gave to me.

Sadly I could not interview John McKay or Ricky Bell. An interview with McKay would have been a thrill of a lifetime for me. The quotes interspersed throughout the book come from McKay's autobiography, Buccaneers press releases and game stories in the *Tampa Tribune* and *St. Petersburg Times*.

Paul Stewart's wonderful web site, Bucpower.com, is quite possibly the most comprehensive source of Buccaneer history on the internet. The site provided me many missing links that I couldn't have found elsewhere.

The following pages list how these sources were utilized in each chapter in the book.

Chapter One

Lee Roy Selmon, personal interview, 1 November 2004.
Doug Williams, personal interview, 25 July 2005.
Richard Wood, personal interview, 20 July 2005.

Chapter Two

Lost Treasures of NFL Films: The Birth of the Bucs, NFL Films, 2001.
Klein, Dave. "You're Wrong, McKay." *Pro Football Weekly,*
    24 October 1977: 6.
Jack Harris, personal interview, 19 January 2006.
Lee Roy Selmon, personal interview, 1 November 2004.
Doug Williams, personal interview, 25 July 2005.

Chapter Three

McKay, John and Jim Perry. *McKay: A Coach's Story*. New York:
    Atheneum, 1974.
Lee Roy Selmon, personal interview, 1 November 2004.
Doug Williams, personal interview, 25 July 2005.

Chapter Four

Rubin, Bob. "Thank God for My Years Behind Bars," *Pro Football Monthly.*
    November 1979: 24-27, 74.
Bill Kollar, personal interview, 9 March 2005.

Chapter Five

Lost Treasures of NFL Films: The Birth of the Bucs, NFL Films, 2001.
Harris, David. *The League: The Rise and Decline of the NFL*. New York:
    Bantam Books, 1986.
McKay, John and Jim Perry. *McKay: A Coach's Story*. New York:
    Atheneum, 1974.

Chapter Six

Boggs, Frank. "The Family That Plays Together Stays Together." *Pro!*
    31 July 1976: 9B-15B.
Greene, Jerry. "Brotherly Shoves." *Pro!* 25 August 1979: 3C- 12C.
Hand, Jack. "Lee Roy Selmon: Strong but Humble." *Pro!* 7 October 1979:
    13, 113.
Marshall, Joe. "Time for Good Times in Tampa Bay." *Sports Illustrated,*
    1 October 1979: 26-31.
Rick Odioso, personal interview, 7 March 2005.

Lee Roy Selmon, personal interview, 1 November 2004.

Richard Wood, personal interview, 20 July 2005.

Chapter Seven

Israel, David. "Tampa Bay Doesn't Really Deserve to Win." *Gridweek,* October 1979.

Williams, Doug and Bruce Hunter. *Quarterblack: Shattering the NFL Myth.* Chicago: Bonus Books, Inc., 1990.

Huber Mizell, personal interview, 17 November 2004.

Rick Odioso, personal interview, 7 March 2005.

Doug Williams, personal interview, 25 July 2005.

Chapter Eight

Bellow, Paul. "How Ricky Got His Bell Rung." *Sport,* July 1978: 57.

Hendrickson, Joe. "Ricky Bell." *1977 Pro Football Annual:* 33-41.

Hubert Mizell, personal interview, 17 November 2004.

Doug Williams, personal interview, 25 July 2005.

Richard Wood, personal interview, 20 July 2005.

Chapter Nine

Rick Odioso, personal interview, 7 March 2005.

Lee Roy Selmon, personal interview, 1 November 2004.

Richard Wood, personal interview, 20 July 2005.

Chapter Ten

Oates, Bob. "How Tampa Bay Became a Winner." *Football Digest,* January 1980.

Lee Roy Selmon, personal interview, 1 November 2004.

Doug Williams, personal interview, 25 July 2005.

Richard Wood, personal interview, 20 July 2005.

Chapter Eleven

Rick Odioso, personal interview, 7 March 2005.

Doug Williams, personal interview, 25 July 2005.

Chapter Twelve

Bill Kollar, personal interview, 9 March 2005.

Huber Mizell, personal interview, 17 November 2004.

Rick Odioso, personal interview, 7 March 2005.

Lee Roy Selmon, personal interview, 1 November 2004.

Doug Williams, personal interview, 25 July 2005.
Richard Wood, personal interview, 20 July 2005.

Chapter Thirteen

Hubert Mizell, personal interview, 17 November 2004.
Lee Roy Selmon, personal interview, 1 November 2004.
Doug Williams, personal interview, 25 July 2005.
Richard Wood, personal interview, 20 July 2005.

Chapter Fourteen

Bill Kollar, personal interview, 9 March 2005.
Hubert Mizell, personal interview, 17 November 2004.
Rick Odioso, personal interview, 7 March 2005.
Lee Roy Selmon, personal interview, 1 November 2004.
Doug Williams, personal interview, 25 July 2005.
Richard Wood, personal interview, 20 July 2005.

Chapter Fifteen

Rick Odioso, personal interview, 7 March 2005.
Lee Roy Selmon, personal interview, 1 November 2004.
Doug Williams, personal interview, 25 July 2005.
Richard Wood, personal interview, 20 July 2005.

Chapter Sixteen

Dufresne, Chris. "The Last Days of Ricky Bell." *Los Angeles Times,*
    4 March 1985: 1, 14-15.
Gruden, Jon and Vic Carucci. *Do You Love Football?!* New York: Perennial,
    2004.
Underwood, John. "Gone With the Wins." *Football Digest,* October 1983:
    41-49.
Williams, Doug and Bruce Hunter. *Quarterblack: Shattering the NFL Myth.*
    Chicago: Bonus Books, Inc., 1990.

Bill Kollar, personal interview, 9 March 2005.
Hubert Mizell, personal interview, 17 November 2004.
Rick Odioso, personal interview, 7 March 2005.
Lee Roy Selmon, personal interview, 1 November 2004.
Doug Williams, personal interview, 25 July 2005.
Richard Wood, personal interview, 20 July 2005.